War Essays

War Essays

Zainab Bahrani

UCLPRESS

First published in 2025 by
UCL Press
University College London
Gower Street
London WC1E 6BT

Available to download free: www.uclpress.co.uk

A CIP catalogue record for this book is available from The British Library.

ISBN: 978-1-80008-752-1 (Hbk)
ISBN: 978-1-80008-754-5 (Pbk)
ISBN: 978-1-80008-753-8 (PDF)
ISBN: 978-1-80008-760-6 (epub)
DOI: https://doi.org/10.14324/111.9781800087538

I dedicate this book to the people of Iraq, who have endured decades of war and sanctions, and who continue to live with the devastating after-effects today, and in solidarity with the people of Gaza and Palestine with whom our pasts and our futures are intertwined.

Contents

Part IV: ISIS/Daesh

List of figures

Acknowledgements

The writing and publication of this book was made possible by an Andrew Carnegie Fellowship, awarded in 2019, for which I offer thanks. Through the past twenty-one years people have spoken for Iraqis or instead of Iraqis; rarely have Iraqis been permitted to speak about or write about the war or occupation of their country. My sincere thanks to my editor, Pat Gordon-Smith, who understood the need for this book as a form of historical documentation and narrative from a perspective such as my own, and whose editorial remarks and observations helped me to shape the book's aim of inscribing the texts into an analytical frame of interpretation meant to disrupt the standard approaches to the history of this war, and the history of archaeology in Iraq. I would also like to offer my heartfelt thanks to Matthew Peebles. Without his editorial skills and constant work to bring it into shape, there would be no book. I am very grateful to the team at UCL Press, and to the three anonymous reviewers whose remarks were not only helpful but provided the reinforcement I needed to pursue this unusual project of chronicling the war and its aftermath through the lens of archaeology and cultural heritage destruction, and the debates around them.

I would like to thank colleagues and friends in Iraq with whom I worked in 2003–4, who have not lived to see this volume published but whose memory remained with me throughout the writing process: Selma al Radhi, Lamia al Gailani, Donny George Youkhanna, Burhan Shakir Sulaiman, and the unforgettable Hajji Abid Attiya. In Iraq I would also like to thank Haider Almamori, Maryam Omran Moussa, Nawala al Mutawalli, Saad Eskander, Muzahim Mahmoud Hussain, Yasmine Abdul Karim, and Sahar Basil al Qaisi. At Columbia University I am indebted to Eric Foner, Gayatri Spivak, Ipek Cem Taha, Safwan Masri, the late Hilary Ballon, and David Rosand. I am also grateful to Alice Stevenson, David Wengrow, Kim Benzel, Mark Al Tawil, Nada Shabout, Helen Malko, Gabriel Rodriguez, Tim Trombley, and Faith Batidzirai for their help.

I am grateful to the following institutions for first publishing the texts in this volume, and for allowing their republication here; I have left these works unaltered other than the addition of a few minor notes: *The Nation*; Columbia University, Department of Art History and Archaeology; *The Wall Street Journal*; *The Guardian*; the British

Council; Getty Conservation Institute; Boydell Press; *October*; Pluto Press; *Document Journal*; *Future Anterior: Journal of Historic Preservation* (University of Minnesota Press); the Museum of Modern Art (New York); the Institut du monde arabe; and Hazan.

Permission to publish photographs was generously granted by Dominique Collon, Steven George, Roger Lemoyne, Hanaa Malallah, Stefan Maul, the Brooklyn Museum, and Pluto Press.

New York City, April 2024

Cover illustration: artist's note

My Country Map. 2008. Layers of burnt canvas and oil on canvas, 200 × 200 cm.

Deliberately inaccurate, this borderless map explores my feeling of being trapped by the consequences of the Iraq wars. Cities are positioned randomly with names burned into canvas, reflecting the destruction and fragmentation caused by the wars. After the 2003 invasion, designated safe Green Zones and unsafe Red Zones were established. A red cloth copy of a Baghdad city bus map is used to symbolise cities in the west of Iraq which have seen extreme violence. A fragment of green appears, inspired by the colour worn by pilgrims seeking protection.

Hanaa Malallah, 2008

Introduction

Twenty years after Operation Iraqi Freedom

المقدمة. عشرون عاماً على عملية الحرية للعراق

Synopsis

Two decades after the 2003 Iraq War (called Operation Iraqi Freedom), its legal justification based on false evidence and its systematic destruction of Iraq's infrastructure, which resulted in massive suffering, are now well known. The war and occupation also overturned the discipline of Mesopotamian archaeology and had consequences that impacted the trade in antiquities and museum practices across the globe. This introductory chapter sets out the reasons for the compilation of this series of essays and lectures into a book: I see the book as a historical record – an eyewitness account of an Iraqi archaeologist who lived through these events both in Iraq and in the United States – and the collected essays as a record of interventions and commentaries that span twenty years, from the start of the 2003 war until 2023.[1] The introduction considers discussions around archaeology and heritage from the lead-up to the war and its attempted justification in late 2002, the invasion of Iraq in March 2003, headed by the US and UK and joined by an international coalition, and the following occupation of the country. From there, I consider the damage and loss of monuments and cultural heritage in Iraq over the past 20 years, surveying the forms of destruction that have taken place as a direct consequence of both warfare and targeting, as well as the subsequent damage that has resulted from infrastructural development and archaeology in the service of the state, and from the involvement of the global market in the illicit trade of antiquities. At the same time, I take this series of essays as a point of departure for reflecting upon the autobiographical voice in the scholarly narrative. I see the repositioning of the essays, framed by a personal narrative, as fitting within new forms and genres of archaeological writing on the coloniality and history of the field. The introduction sets up the framework of this metanarrative and also begins to open up theoretical reflections on destruction and preservation as dual aspects of war, a theme that will unfold throughout the following pages. The book thus redeploys the essays into a contribution to an emerging form of self-reflexive and decolonial archaeological writing.

المستخلص

عَقْدان قد مَرّا على حرب العراق عام 2003 (والتي عُرِفَت بعملية الحرية للعراق)، تلك الحرب التي بُنِيَت مُسَوِّغاتُها القانونية على أدِلَّةٍ كاذبة والتي أسفرَت عن تدمير مُمَنهَج لبُنى العراق التحتية، كانت حَصيلَتَهُ تِلكَ المعاناةِ الهائلة التي غَدَت اليومَ جَلّيةً ذائِعةَ الصيت. لقد قَلَبَت الحربُ والاحتلال دقّةَ الأمور كذلك فيما يخصُّ مجالَ علم آثارِ وادي الرافدَين فعادَت بعواقِبَ أثَّرَت في تجارة الآثار والمُمارَسات المتحفية حول العالَم. يُحَدِّدُ فصلُ المقدِّمة الأسبابَ التي دَعَت إلى تجميع هذه السِلسِلة من المقالات والمحاضرات ليَضُمَّها كتابٌ واحد: ذلكَ لأنّي أرى هذا الكتابَ سِجِلّاً تاريخياً – فهو رِوايَةُ شَهادةِ عَيانٍ لعالمةِ آثارِ عراقيّة تَسَنّى لها مُعايشةُ أحداثِ هذه الحِقبة في كُلٍّ من العراق والولايات المتحدة – كما أرى المقالاتِ المجموعةِ هنا توثيقاً لمُداخَلاتٍ وتعليقاتٍ امتدَّت لعشرين سنة، منذُ نشوب الحربِ عام 2003 حتى عام 2023. لقد عُنِيَت المُقدِّمةُ بما يَدورُ من نِقاشاتٍ حولَ مجال الآثار والتراث منذ الفترة التي مَهَّدَت الطريق إلى الحرب ومحاولاتِ تَبريرِها في أواخِرِ عام 2002، وما تَلاها من غَزوِ العراق في آذار 2003، بقيادةِ كُلٍّ من الولاياتِ المتحدة والمملكةِ المتحدة وما انضمَّ إلَيهِما من تحالُفٍ دوَلي، وما أعْقَبَ ذلكَ من احتلالٍ للبَلَد. من هنا، فأنا أعُدُّ أيَّ ضَرَرٍ أو فُقدانٍ قَد أَلَمَّ بآثار العراق وإرْثِهِ الحضاري عَبرَ العشرين سَنَةٍ الماضية، مُحصِيَةً بذلِكَ أشكالَ الدَمار التي وَقَعَت، كتَبِعاتٍ مباشِرة لكُلٍّ من الحَربِ واستغلال قَطّاعَي تطويرِ البُنى التحتية والآثار لأغراضٍ سياسية، فضلاً عمّا لَحِقَها من ضَرَرٍ جراءَ ذلك، ومن جَراء ضلوع السوق العالمية في تجارةٍ غير مشروعةٍ للآثار. في الوقت ذاته، فإنني أتَّخِذُ من سِلسِلة المقالات هذه نقطةَ انطلاقٍ لانعكاس صوت وموقف الذات في السَرد العلمي. فأنا أرى أن إعادةَ ترتيبِ المقالاتِ، وتأطيرِها بقالبٍ سَرديٍّ شخصي، يتلاءَم مع الصِياغات والأنواع الجديدة للكتابة في مجال علم الآثار فيما يخص الكولونيالية وتاريخ هذا المجال. تضع هذه المقدمة إطاراً لهذا السرد الما ورائي، كما تبدأ كذلك بفسح المجال لانعكاساتٍ نظرية عن الدَمار والحِفاظ كثنائيةٍ من مظاهر الحرب، وهو الموضوع الذي ستُفصِحُ عنه الصفحات الآتية. لذا يُعيد الكتاب توزيعَ المقالات ويُحيلُها إلى مُساهمةٍ في ذلك التيار الناشئ الذي يدعم انعكاس الذات في الكتابة في مجال علم الآثار والديكولونيالية.

War

War changes everything. It changes territories and demographics; it transforms the conditions of existence in the 'theatre of war', as it is so called, and it shifts the coordinates of the world so that the boundaries of this theatre of war are extended to those who live their lives at a great distance from the field of battle. Such was the case with the Iraq War. The shock and awe campaign of 2003 and the occupation that followed changed both Iraq and the United States, albeit in very different ways. Iraq, which by all accounts was transformed almost beyond recognition, was devastated – physically, materially and demographically – while in the US, democracy began to be eroded in the service of the war on terror, in which Iraq was a main battleground. These changes on both sides of the theatre of war had a direct impact on the academic arena in which I work. In tangible, material and quantifiable terms, numerous antiquities and works of modern art were looted in the spring of 2003 while Iraq was under US military rule. What was not plundered was then heavily damaged throughout the following years of war and occupation, and by the dismantling of the state and the institution of new neoliberal systems of economic development and resource extraction. The discipline of Mesopotamian archaeology, in particular, whose primary focus is on the ancient sites of what is now Iraq was transformed. In many ways the transformation was not to an entirely new form of archaeology, however. It is perhaps better phrased as a return to an early twentieth-century version of itself, as it became once again an archaeology in the service of empire, similar in many respects to the era of the British Mandate. But it went beyond that imperialist model. To some extent the war changed the larger field of archaeology in general, its field practices and definitions of ethics, its areas of focus and paths of enquiry. It also propelled new discussions around collecting antiquities and museum practices. And finally, it led to the foregrounding of preservation and conservation as disciplinary concerns, where previously they had been silent partners to archaeology's reputation of digging in exotic lands along with its sensationalist claims of discovery. In the background of this transformation ran the dominant, revitalised discourse of the benighted Orient, and of the benefits of Operation Iraqi Freedom, a civilising mission at the start of the new millennium.[2]

This book is a historical account of the Iraq War, seen through the writings of an Iraqi archaeologist. In it, I bring together a collection of academic papers, lectures and shorter pieces written for the press during the 20-year period 2003–23. Some of these relate my first-hand experience of the war and occupation in Iraq itself, others were written at a distance, in the US. Because they are presented as documents of the time in which they were written, they have not been altered or updated (depending on the place of original publication they therefore present a variety of spelling, punctuation and referencing styles).[3] Rather, as I present them again, I reposition them retrospectively into a form of biographical narrative. They become a point of departure for another text, a text that is not at ease in any particular genre and is perhaps aligned more with the catachresis of postcolonial criticism and decolonial writings than with archaeological historiographies or compendia of collected essays.[4]

The book is also a personal account which shifts back and forth between academic writing, op-eds, and the track of the autobiographical path upon which these writings move. I write primarily from the standpoint of a scholar of antiquity, an Iraqi archaeologist and art historian educated in Europe and America, now living and teaching in New York. I see this intersection of both subject position and genres as a way forward in archaeological writing, that is, of writing in a colonial field with which I have wrestled for many years. Although some important moves have been made towards what theoretically inclined archaeologists call an 'undisciplining' of archaeology, the coloniality of the field endures in the museum, at the dig site and in the academic arena.[5] Along with these discussions, my own stance remains firmly within my earliest work and my early academic positionality in postcolonial studies and decolonisation. Several years before the 2003 war, I had already argued that coloniality and the imperialist foundations of the discipline of Mesopotamian archaeology had to be confronted, as they continued to influence the readings and interpretations that are deemed acceptable to the discipline, as well as museum displays and histories of collecting.[6] At the same time, the present volume's movement between genres of writing, between the personal and the public, between my interventions into a hegemonic discourse and participation within that discourse itself, might be viewed through the lens of the more recent directions of undisciplining and decolonisation in archaeological writing.

It all began with an interest in the power of the act of naming and representation. I had been reading a great deal of the philosophical writings of Jacques Derrida, alongside Babylonian literature, where, in the Babylonian creation myth, a thing does not exist until it is named. Representation, both visual and textual, is a powerful thing, as the ancient Mesopotamians so clearly recognised.[7] In a 1998 article, I argued that the use of the name Mesopotamia, which became widely accepted as the proper name (in place of the Arabic or Turkish) at the height of British and French interests in the region, served to reconfigure the terrain and to cut off the present population from the past – a past which was deemed to belong to the West, just as the craze for digging and collecting Assyrian and Babylonian antiquities spread across Europe and

North America. Then, in *The Graven Image*, I addressed the long-term relationship between antiquity, racial theory, and the claims of empire, stressing that the role of the ethnographer in cultural translation must be heeded in art history and in archaeology as well.[8] The title of that book referred to the ancient Assyrian and Babylonian ontology of the image, but at the same time it was meant to reference the image of the Orient in Western academic discourse. It was a book that took on the epistemological frameworks and limits of the field of ancient Oriental studies (a term that is still current as I write this chapter). These themes reappear here once again in the context of war, and alongside more direct forms of wartime censorship. Throughout, I wrestled with my own discomfort in being an Iraqi scholar working in a colonial field, one that came into formation at the height of French and British imperialism and their mandates over the region. Decoloniality and epistemology are therefore two main concerns that emerged in my early work – concerns with which I continue to grapple, as epistemic violence remains firmly ensconced at the core of the discourse of archaeology.[9]

Through the first-person account that threads through the prefaces of each section, pulling the earlier texts together, I describe the context in which they were written. As a result of my own subject position, moving back and forth between the US and Iraq, the pronoun 'we' at times refers to we Americans and at times to we Iraqis. I have therefore deliberately left the inconsistency of that changing positionality in the text. As the war and occupation unfolded, I found myself having to take on questions around ethics and law, as well as the meaning of archaeology, heritage and the writing of history. Underneath it all there was also the reality of grief, anger, shock, of facing the war's devastation in Iraq while carrying on with this work. These are some of the issues that arise, and are carried through the prefaces of each section.

They also serve to contextualise and historicise the earlier texts. In this way, these essays are redeployed as a contribution to a form of self-reflexive and decolonial archaeological writing. The essays also aim to open up discussions on the link between destruction and preservation as aspects of war, a theme that unfolds through the rest of the volume. At the same time, in constructing this book out of the earlier pieces of writing, I also wanted to bring to light alternative narratives of this war. Accounts of what happened at the Iraq Museum, at Babylon, and with the archives removed from Iraq, were restricted at the time. Journals and publishers were uninterested in the Iraqi side of the story; it was seen to lack the neutrality that was so easily accorded to military archaeologists and the public relations office of the occupation authority. In this book,

I provide alternative accounts from my own first-hand experience in Iraq, as well as from close colleagues in Iraq who witnessed these episodes – colleagues whose versions of events and crucial work to secure and preserve Iraq's heritage were written out of history. As I recount some of these, I continue to hope that the other silenced narratives of this war and occupation will be unearthed in the future.

The civilising mission

Operation Iraqi Freedom was described as the gift of liberation for the people of Iraq.[10] But as we have learned from Aimé Cesaire, regardless of its self-professed noble aims, colonisation corrupts the coloniser; rather than conducting its civilising mission, it decivilises the colonial.[11] Thus, in Iraq itself, among local communities and in several neighbourhoods, perhaps it should have come as no surprise when we began to hear more and more about the US and multinational forces holding prisoners without charge or trial, in a similar way to the practices of administrative detention in earlier colonial occupations. And we began to see troops brutalising civilians in their day-to-day activities. I saw and experienced this behaviour on several occasions in Iraq when, outside the American context, I was seen only in my Iraqi identity as one among a population of lesser people. And while I was in Iraq, Frantz Fanon's words from 1959 seemed to echo into 2003: 'Colonialism is not satisfied with merely holding a people in its grip and emptying the native's brain of all form and content. By a kind of perverted logic, it turns to the past of the oppressed people, and distorts, disfigures, and destroys it'.[12]

Heritage became a pawn in this war and occupation in several ways: the targeting and occupation of heritages sites, museums, archives and religious shrines; the looting and international marketing of things of historical or cultural significance; and finally, the policing of the narrative of these events by means of the systematic denial of space in academic publications and the press to Iraqis and other scholars or writers who attempted to present alternative reports to the officially authorised ones. The latter often took the form of heroic accounts of rescue, protection and restoration, when the catastrophic reality was quite the opposite. The texts within this volume are therefore concerned with these fields of heritage, but they inevitably involve the larger frame of war, and the laws of war and occupation. What are the forms of damage, targeted and not targeted? What forms of heritage destruction and appropriation of historical or cultural materials by an occupying power are deemed acceptable or not by the international archaeological community or by international law? What is the stance of international humanitarian law with regard to these events and acts, and were the conventions on the protections of cultural property, established at the end of the two world wars, followed in this war?

The best-known and the most widely reported event in the cultural sphere was the looting of the Iraq Museum in Baghdad in April of 2003, but what really happened at the museum is still not clear.[13] According to members of the staff who I knew well, and whose side of the story was of little interest at the time, they had considered and prepared for the possibility of damage to the museum in the lead-up to the invasion. Because of the experience of 1991, when nine regional museums were looted during the postwar uprisings against the regime, they knew that they must. The uprisings were then brutally put down by Saddam Hussein, and the lost artefacts later appeared for sale in the West and were trafficked in the global market in antiquities. But in the case of the 2003 museum looting, baseless allegations soon appeared in the Western press and televised media accusing the curators of secreting antiquities for their own personal profit or on behalf of the regime, ruining reputations and endangering lives. A few years later, an official investigation conducted in Iraq found that the curatorial staff had conducted themselves in an exemplary manner, following the protocols of museum disaster preparedness and emergency planning, according to international guidelines. Furthermore, one of the curators who was targeted with slanderous accusations was not even in Baghdad on the days in question. At the time, most publications seemed more concerned with the exact number of missing objects, and the conflicting tallies provided. However, as no proper inventory could be conducted, all these counts were meaningless, and I attempted to make clear that an inventory of what remained in the storage room and what was missing would probably require several years. The numbers debate aside, what I wanted to point out was that the relationship of history, monuments and one's sense of place in the world, and how this comes to be disrupted in war, results in forms of grief that are not limited to the violence of civilian deaths or the exact number of missing items. This grief of war also has to do with the loss of one's context and environment, when all that is known and familiar is ravaged by war, and all that remains is the bombarded and shattered shell of that past world. In the late spring of 2003, when I returned to Iraq to help with the salvage work at the museum, it was already clear that the results of the Bush administration's shock and awe campaign were urbicide and the devastation of the natural environment, the contamination of water sources, and finally, the destruction of history. This theme was to become an area of research and fieldwork for me in the following years.

In the midst of this disaster, the Bush administration was casually dismissive of its own responsibilities according to international law. In a televised press briefing in April 2003, US Secretary of Defense Donald Rumsfeld ridiculed the attention given to the looting and destruction of museums and archives:

> The images you are seeing on television you are seeing over and over and over. It's the same picture of some person walking out of some building with a vase and you see it twenty times. And you think, my goodness, were there that many vases? ... Is it possible that there were that many vases in the whole country?[14]

This remark may be dismissed as a sign of ignorance or ineptitude, but that would be a mistake. The Pentagon clearly had prior notice of the potential for looting. Several leading archaeologists in the US and UK had spoken to their governments in the lead-up to the war and provided lists of museums, archives and heritage sites along with their geospatial coordinates. Their governments chose to ignore these lists, which had, in fact, been provided by the archaeologists at the request of officials of these same governments.[15] As Human Rights Watch stated at the time, under the laws of war, specifically the Convention for the Protection of Cultural Property in the Event of Armed Conflict of 1954, known as the Hague Convention, the US was required by international laws of war and occupation to protect museums and cultural property.[16] The events of April were not a matter of ignorance or incompetence. The laws and conventions of war and occupation were knowingly disregarded, just as they were in the occupation of heritage sites as military bases – a topic that is also taken up in this volume.

In the cultural sphere, the benefits of the antiquities trade and its wide dispersal of artefacts for the good of global cultural heritage was an idea that was widely repeated; it was one of the immediate responses to the results of the ground war in the arena of the arts and archaeology. The *Art of the First Cities* exhibition at the Metropolitan Museum of Art in New York opened in the spring of 2003 to rave reviews, including in the *New York Times*. However, the *Times* also used the exhibition to make the case for the advantages of collecting looted antiquities in the foremost museums of the West. The exhibition, the reviewer wrote:

> is, not incidentally, also an implicit justification of universal institutions like the Louvre, the Hermitage, the British Museum and the Met. They are, at their best, more than keepers of other culture's booty. They are open, democratic palaces of the people and global town squares, in which a civilized world decides what matters most about the past and what's worth transmitting to the future.[17]

Today, 20 years after Operation Iraqi Freedom, the same troubling issues of heritage remain, as does the divide of 'civilised' and 'uncivilised' in descriptions of humanity. The justification of market-oriented dispersal of antiquities and other works of art, manuscripts and objects, as being in the interest of civilised safekeeping, is a debate that continues. And the idea of safekeeping was already deployed in the nineteenth century when removing antiquities to Europe, as the 'primitive natives' were said to be incapable of appreciating antiquities. In more recent years, the recognition of both earlier colonial forms of appropriation and the illicit trade has been developed in the direction of provenance research, bringing strength to the repatriation movements that are growing, especially in former colonised lands.[18] Yet while research and critical accounts of nineteenth-century exploitation became academically acceptable, the narrative of the 2003 war and occupation was severely curtailed by the politics of publication and other forms of academic restrictions and exclusions. Additionally, postwar reconstruction policies and restoration projects remain a vague and muddled morass of top-down and external decision-making that has little to do with the people of Iraq, whose lives, communities and environments were affected by war, and more to do with which heritage sites are deemed to be of global significance. As a concern of this volume is the way in which the events of this war were represented, both in archaeological and heritage discourse as well as in the press and news media, it also addresses some larger themes within academic discourse and the politics of archaeology.

The politics of archaeology and heritage discourse

Archaeology is not limited to the study of the past. As many archaeologists and historians have shown, its forms of knowledge production are always interwoven with the present. This is the case well beyond Iraq. Especially (though not only) in colonial or formerly colonial contexts, the relationship of the present to the past then becomes a point of contention between forms of discourse and practices relating to that past. Within the discipline itself, the politics of archaeology is a topic that has been interrogated quite rigorously for several decades. Heritage studies has also taken up similar questions. Scholars in the latter field have pointed out that heritage – a recently constructed notion – is not limited to monuments of the past. It has to do with engagement and making meaning through it.[19] It can encompass such things as traditions of fishing, or areas of craft-making like weaving or carpentry. It involves the uses of space for such activities, and it includes the intangible and the transient, among other things. Yet while heritage discourse rightly accepts crafts and activities as heritage practices, it does not as readily recognise archaeological sites, tells (Arabic term for archaeological mounds or hills) or ruins as areas of meaning-making for the populations who have lived with them, next to them and within them. These arenas of ruins and monuments are relegated to the scientific and elite discourse of archaeology instead. Inadvertently, therefore, a divide is created which both disavows and misunderstands the relationship to ruins, tells, rock reliefs or historical structures in lands such as Iraq. Heritage discourse thus runs the risk of denying the materiality and tangibility of local sites and practices, and of local and historical forms of engaging with these ruins by people who live among them; people who have not (nor will they ever) read either authorised heritage discourse or the critique of it. Their world is unrelated to the regime of heritage and academic debates that circulate around it.

The management of heritage sites that fall under 'global heritage', according to international organisations such as UNESCO, is thus often approached as the top-down business of outside interests in contradistinction to these other areas of local meaning-making, which may be recognised when they include crafts but less so if they are activities related to archaeological sites that the West sees either as its own history, as global heritage, or as a part of nationalist state interests. This division of theoretical categories means that the relationship of people, especially of rural farming communities and herders, tribal groups, nomadic shepherds or sedentary agricultural labourers, with the ruins and tells in the environment of their day-to-day lives and experiences, is not normally recognised or taken into account. Iraqi archaeologists have been working to document such activities in the south of Iraq at tells and ruins, where people's lives and stories are entwined with the ancient remains that surround them. Everywhere in the country, from the south to Kurdistan, ancient tells and ruins of historical architecture become sacred sites. They have long been the places of sacred Yazidi and Shiite shrines.

Other ancient ruins are associated with Sufi or Christian saints, or with Jewish prophets. People continue to pray and make vows at these sites and to participate in unofficial religious practices such as tying ribbons and large pieces of cloth at shrines or upon trees in their ancient precincts. In southern Iraq people use tells as sacred and propitious burial grounds for their own family members, in the same way that in official Shiism, the dead are taken to historical cemeteries next to the shrines of saints. The stories about tells and monumental ruins among the people of Iraq who live near them are numerous, and some were already recorded by Arab and Persian historians and geographers in the Medieval period.

Histories of archaeology tend to focus on empire or the nation-state, disregarding these sorts of relationships and meaning-making around ruins and antiquities. Yet nationalist uses of the past on the one hand and the imperialist claims to it on the other are but two sides of the same coin. One of them recruits antiquity for its own – often ethnonationalist – agendas, related to the formation of particular power interests. The other channels it into the imperialist narrative of the civilisational high ground in the West, a narrative that has been criticised from several sides but remains firmly in place, nevertheless. Along with an imperialist narrative comes the colonial and postwar discourse of heritage management, or cultural-resource management. This a discourse that has drawn both scholarly attention and indigenous resistance elsewhere in the world. In the case of Iraq, there has been a blind spot to the fact of such local resistance. It is not that such resistance to top-down approaches does not exist, but more the case that it has been actively stifled both by heritage discourse in the West, and by powerful state actors and economic interests within Iraq and Iraqi Kurdistan – a topic that is taken up again in the final section of the volume.

Aside from critique, the field of landscape archaeology provides potential directions that may allow moving towards a better understanding of the local interactions with ruins and archaeological sites in lands such as Iraq, that are so densely filled with ancient sites. In this method, the body and embodied engagement allow a sensory and interactive participation that provides forms of knowledge not possible with deskbound analysis. Taking a material and phenomenological approach to encountering landscape and things within it can thus become a way to redirect and reinvigorate the study of archaeological or heritages sites, just as it has been for the study of an anthropology of landscape. It may allow a way forward beyond the binary divide of top-down international organisations and NGOs focused on high-profile world heritage sites, and the allocation of craft-work and intangible heritage to bottom-up approaches, with the unstated assumption that local people and communities had no history of relating to the landscape of ruins, tells and rock reliefs in the mountains before the arrival of Europeans onto the scene. These subaltern forms of interaction with, and understanding of, historical remains have neither been adequately acknowledged nor properly studied. Conversely – and at the risk of perhaps stating the obvious – in a place like Iraq and adjacent lands, weaving, carpetmaking, metalsmithing, calligraphy and other crafts have a history that is more akin to Western notions of high art.

To remedy some of these problems of earlier approaches, some archaeological field projects now include more local colleagues on their teams. However, another less admirable practice can also be noted in post-2003 Iraq. Foreign teams lay claim to sites their countrymen dug in the nineteenth or early twentieth centuries, as if they were ancestral lands. They reproduce the assumptions and conditions of colonial archaeology and its mode of production of knowledge. The disciplinary framework then remains in place, despite the talk about ethics in archaeology.[20] The context of the war, and the civilising mission of Operation Iraqi Freedom, also permitted the expansion and dissemination of American neoliberal values, including in the arena of archaeology, heritage and museums. These are some of the unstated assumptions and themes in archaeology and regimes of heritage management that are brought up and challenged in this book.

In material culture studies, the theoretical argument that persons and things are mutually constitutive has had a great deal of influence in the last two decades.[21] This is a useful methodology to consider in a study of people's relationship to ancient sites and monuments in Iraq, as people's lives are entwined with the remains of the past around them. In anthropology, the method of participant observation is understood to entail a place of self-reflection also, and I have kept this in mind as I write. The role of the individual in the interpretation must be recognised and acknowledged.[22] But it is also discourse and habitus that set the parameters within which individuals make their observations, and in the discipline of archaeology this discourse is colonial. Another current debate that comes into these discussions of the coloniality of archaeology and the museum has to do with repatriation and restitution. While calls for returning things taken during the era of empire have become more widespread, many works looted from Iraq 20 years ago remain in private hands today. These include not only antiquities and historical manuscripts but also works of Modern and contemporary art, as well as archival evidence of the oppression and atrocities of the Baathist regime and of ISIS.

As I reframe these earlier writings, I consider my own place in the observation of events as they unfolded. My time was divided between Iraq and the US. Immersed in both worlds, in both languages and ways of life, I experienced this movement between occupied land and the land of the occupier as an existential rupture. Writing about these events and experiences of war, especially within a disciplinary context, was not always possible. At first, I took up public writing in the press and wrote a number of opinion pieces. I then took up a sort of free-form academic writing in collaboration with the Iraqi artist Hanaa Malallah, who was displaced by this war; in an effort to question academic structures and hegemonic narratives, together, we began to produce pieces of academic writing as elements within art installations.[23] For myself, this writing within the work of art allowed a creative intervention into the controlled disciplinary framework that others have already described as a matrix of knowledge production that is fundamentally colonial.[24] In many ways I see this book as yet another form of undisciplined writing. I offer it as a historical record, a chronicle of sorts, of events in Iraq, and a personal reflection on the incomprehensible experience of war.

Notes

1 Articles first published in the United States appear here in US English.
2 In George W. Bush's presidential address of 13 April 2004, right after the defeat of Baghdad, Bush described the war as a gift of freedom to the people of Iraq; see https://georgewbush-whitehouse.archives.gov/news/releases/2004/04/20040413-20.html.
3 Some illustrations have been substituted or omitted.
4 I use 'catachresis' in the sense of a deliberate rhetorical misuse or transformation of words or genres of writing by the colonised, which acts to unsettle a normative discourse. See B. Ashcroft, G. Griffiths and H. Tiffin (eds), *Key Concepts in Post-Colonial Studies*, London: Routledge, 1998.
5 For the arguments about the need to undiscipline archaeology, see Alejandro Haber and Nick Shepherd, 'After ethics: Ancestral voices and post-disciplinary worlds in archaeology – an introduction', in *After Ethics: Ancestral voices and post-disciplinary worlds in archaeology*, edited by Alejandro Haber and Nick Shepherd, 1–10 (New York: Springer, 2015).
6 Zainab Bahrani, 'Assault and abduction', *Art History* 18 (1995): 363–83; 'Conjuring Mesopotamia: Imaginative geography and a world past', in *Archaeology Under Fire*, edited by Lynn Meskell, 159–74 (London: Routledge, 1998); *The Graven Image* (Philadelphia: University of Pennsylvania Press, 2003).
7 On this point, see Zainab Bahrani, 'Assault and abduction', *Art History* 18 (1995): 363–83.
8 Zainab Bahrani, *The Graven Image* (Philadelphia: University of Pennsylvania Press, 2003), Chapters 1–3.
9 Gayatri Chakravorty Spivak, 'Can the subaltern speak?', in *Marxism and the Interpretation of Culture*, edited by Cary Nelson and Larry Grossberg, 271–313 (Urbana: University of Illinois Press, 1988); Alejandro Haber, 'Archaeology after archaeology', in *After Ethics: Ancestral voices and post-disciplinary worlds in archaeology*, edited by Alejandro Haber and Nick Shepherd, 127–37 (New York: Springer, 2015).
10 George W. Bush, presidential address, 13 April 2004. See n. 2, above.
11 Aimé Cesaire, *Discourse on Colonialism* (New York: Monthly Review Press, 1950).

12 From an address 'On National Culture', presented to the Second Congress of Black Writers and Artists, Rome 1959; in *The Wretched of the Earth* (New York: Grove Press, 1963), 210.

13 The official name of this institution is 'The Iraq Museum', in both Arabic and English. This was the name used in Iraq and inscribed on the wall of the current building when it was erected in 1966. Since 2003, many archaeologists and journalists have erroneously identified its official name as 'The National Museum of Iraq'.

14 Donald Rumsfeld, Defense Department televised briefing, 11 April 2003: https://www.c-span.org/video/?176134-1/defense-department-briefing. Also quoted in Brian Whitaker, 'Free to do bad things', *The Guardian*, 12 April 2003, www.theguardian.com/world/2003/apr/12/iraqbriefing.iraq.

15 See Part I in this volume, as well as McGuire Gibson, 'The theft of Iraq's antiquities', *London Review of Books* 31, no. 1, 1 January 2009, https://www.lrb.co.uk/the-paper/v31/n01/mcguire-gibson/diary. See also Gibson's preface to the English-language edition of Muzahim Hussein, *Nimrud: The Queens' Tombs*, translated by Mark Altaweel and edited by McGuire Gibson (Baghdad: Iraq State Board of Antiquities and Heritage; Chicago: Oriental Institute of the University of Chicago, 2016).

16 Human Rights Watch report, 'Liberation and looting in Iraq', 13 April 2003, https://www.hrw.org/news/2003/04/13/liberation-and-looting-iraq-0.

17 Michael Kimmelman, 'Way, way back, to the dawn of the beginning', *New York Times*, 9 May 2003, https://www.nytimes.com/2003/05/09/arts/art-review-way-way-back-to-the-dawn-of-the-beginning.html.

18 See Dan Hicks, *The Brutish Museums* (London: Pluto Press, 2020). The work of the Department of Ancient West Asian Art at the Metropolitan Museum of Art in provenance research has led to the repatriation of antiquities to Yemen, at the initiative of the curators rather than requests by the state.

19 Laurajane Smith, *Uses of Heritage* (London: Routledge, 2006); Rodney Harrison, *Understanding the Politics of Heritage* (Manchester: Manchester University Press, 2010).

20 Sarah Tarlow, 'Decoding ethics', *Public Archaeology* 1 (2001): 245–59; Lynn Meskell and Peter Pels, eds, *Embedding Ethics* (Oxford: Berg, 2005); Yannis Hamilakis and Philip Duke, eds, *Archaeology and Capitalism: From ethics to politics* (London: Routledge, 2007); Alejandro Haber and Nick Shepherd, eds, *After Ethics: Ancestral voices and post-disciplinary worlds in archaeology* (New York: Springer, 2015).

21 *Journal of Material Culture* 11, no. 1/2 (2006), special issue: *Landscape, Heritage, and Identity*, edited by Christopher Tilley; Tim Ingold, *Making: Anthropology, archaeology, art and architecture* (London: Routledge, 2013); Ian Hodder, *Entangled: An archaeology of the relationships between humans and things* (Malden, MA: Wiley Blackwell, 2012); Bruno Latour, 'How to talk about the body? The normative dimension of science studies', *Body and Society* 10 (2004): 205–29.

22 Claude Lévi-Strauss, *Structural Anthropology* (New York: Basic Books, 1963).

23 See https://www.3rrr.site/research-archives; https://www.hanaa-malallah.com/post/no-map-but-trenches.

24 Alejandro Haber, 'Archaeology after archaeology', in *After Ethics: Ancestral voices and post-disciplinary worlds in archaeology*, edited by Alejandro Haber and Nick Shepherd, 127–37 (New York: Springer, 2015).

Part I
War in Iraq

القِسم الأول: حَربٌ في العراق

Preface

تمهيد

Synopsis

The years 2003–4 are set apart in this book as the period of the invasion and establishment of the Coalition Provisional Authority (CPA) by the US Department of Defense, with Paul Bremer appointed at its head as the Provisional Coalition Administrator of Iraq, where he ruled by decree. Most notably, the Bremer de-Baathification decree had both an immediate and a long-term detrimental impact on the historical heritage of Iraq. Museums, universities and libraries were stripped of their staff. Archaeological and historical sites and monuments were left unguarded. While the ground war in March and April of 2003 targeted Iraq's infrastructure, the subsequent months saw the stripping down of most of the qualified professional staff from educational institutions and museums. Iraq was under the authority of the US Department of Defense, and an occupying army ruled the land, the movement of people and all decision-making regarding public spaces and institutions. In July of 2004, sovereignty was officially handed over to the interim Iraqi government set in place by the CPA. The international community of archaeologists began to recognize unprecedented levels of looting and selling of Mesopotamian antiquities from archaeological sites as well as some that were clearly from the looted museum collections. During the first two years of the war and occupation, my time was divided between Iraq, the country of my birth, and the United States, the country where I lived and worked. The preface also provides a personal account of this movement back and forth – especially in the wake of the ground war in the spring of 2003, when I first saw the ruination of Baghdad after the 'shock and awe' campaign.

المستخلص

في هذا الكتاب تم وضع عامَي 2003–2004 بمعزَلٍ، كونها تمثِّل فترة الغزو وتأسيس سلطة التحالف المؤقتة (CPA) من قِبَل وزارة الدفاع الأمريكية وتعيين بول بريمر لرئاستها كمسؤولٍ عن سُلطة التحالف في العراق، حيث حَكَمَ بمرسوم. من الملاحظ جداً، إن مرسوم بريمر لاجتثاث البعث كان له أثر سلبي آنياً وكذلك على المدى الطويل في الإرث التاريخي للعراق: لقد جُرِّدَت المتاحف، والجامعات من كادرِها، كما تُرِكَت المواقع الأثرية والتاريخية بدون حِراسة؛ ففي حين استهدفت الحرب البرية في آذار ونيسان من عام 2003 البُنى التحتية للعراق، شَهِدَت الأشهر التي تَلَتهُما تجريدَ المؤسّسات الثقافية والمتاحف من كوادِرها المحترفة والمُتمكّنة علمياً. لقد كان العراق تحت سلطة وزارة الدفاع الأمريكية، وقد كان هناك جَيشٌ مُحتَلٌّ يحكمُ أرضَه، وحركة الناس وجميع ما يتعلّق باتخاذ القرار فيه من فضاءاتٍ عامة ومؤسّسات. في تموز عام 2004، سُلِّمَت السِيادة رسمياً إلى حكومة العراق المؤقّتة التي تم تعيينُها في هذا المكان من قِبَل سلطة التحالف المؤقتة. لقد بدأ المجتمع الدوَلي للآثاريين بالتعرُّف على مستوياتٍ غير مسبوقة من عمليات النهب والبيع لآثار وادي الرافِدَين التي تعرَّضَت لها المواقع الأثرية وكذلك المجموعات المتحفية. خلال العامَين الأوَّلَين من الحرب والاحتلال، كان وَقتي مُقَسَّماً بين العراق، البلد الذي وُلِدْتُ فيه، والولايات المتحدّة، البلد الذي عِشتُ وعَملتُ فيه. يروي التمهيد كذلك عن حركتي تلك ذهاباً وإياباً بين البَلَدَين – لا سِيَّما في أعقاب الحرب البريّة في ربيع عام 2003، عندما رأيتُ للمرة الأولى تدميرَ بغداد بعد حملة "الصدمة والرعب".

'The American Empire: Get Used to It'. These were the words on the cover of the *New York Times Magazine* of 5 January 2003, as the United States and its allies geared up for the Iraq War. The main article in that issue argued in favour of embracing an American imperial expansion that was to bring freedom and democracy to the world. The American Empire, the author wrote:

> is not like empires of times past, built on colonies, conquest and the white man's burden ... The 21st century imperium is a new invention in the annals of political science, an empire lite, a global hegemony whose grace notes are free markets, human rights and democracy, enforced by the most awesome military power the world has ever known.[1]

Both shocking and exhilarating for its readers, it touched upon a sentiment that was not uncommon in the North American winter of 2002–3. The leading papers and television media were calling for war – a war that they argued was just and justified, a war of revenge simultaneously packaged as a benevolent gift of freedom to the people of Iraq. These contradictions did not seem to matter, as one sensed the terrible excitement in the air of a lead-up to war. Yet there was also a massive antiwar movement rising across the world, including in the US. On 15 February of 2003, hundreds of thousands of people walked out into the streets of New York City protesting the American federal government's push for war. In a coordinated international protest, six to ten million people in over 600 cities also made their voices known. The largest turnout of protestors that day was in the countries that were to form the coalition for the war.[2] We were among them, my family and I, as well as the majority of colleagues from the Faculty of Arts and Sciences at Columbia University – where, just a few months earlier, I had been appointed to my dream job, a teaching position in the Department of Art History and Archaeology, a department ranked foremost in its field. We oriented ourselves towards the aim of halting the march to war, but the city's crackdown on the protestors that day was swift and hard. The NYPD barricaded and attacked protestors with horses and pepper spray. Hundreds of people were arrested for minor offences.[3] There was a great deal of distress. Yet there was also a real sense of solidarity, with the rally near the United Nations including speakers such as the brilliant South African civil rights leader, Archbishop Desmond Tutu. The frigid temperatures that February day were record-breaking, but the protestors persevered. The rulers of these democracies, a form of government that American and allied policymakers hoped to export to the benighted world of the Global South, ignored the voices of their own people. The course of the invasion of Iraq had begun, and no amount of evidence or reasoning seemed sufficient to prevent it.

In the lead-up to the shock and awe air campaign that winter, the US military air-dropped leaflets on the Iraqi people. Alongside images of monuments and archaeological sites, their bilingual texts read: 'Coalition forces do not wish to harm the noble people of Iraq ... the coalition does not wish to destroy landmarks. The coalition will destroy any viable military targets'. Given that Iraq had long been identified in Western scholarship as ancient Mesopotamia, the Land of the Two Rivers, and described in that scholarship as the cradle of civilization, archaeological sites and the museums that held collections of antiquities from these sites were an issue right from the start. Archaeology was a main topic in the months prior to the invasion, inside both the US and UK governments – the two that spearheaded the war – as well as in the press, as Iraq was understood to hold important world-historical landmarks, especially those of the Judeo-Christian tradition.[4] As I had been trained in the history of art and visual theory, as well as in archaeology, I noted the imagery that was used in making the case for war, and then the imagery of the war itself, transmitted back, in real time, for viewers in the US. Our television screens and newspapers were saturated with American flags and rising pride in the new technologies of armed conflict. That compelling imagery and direct streaming persuaded citizens to feel a participatory commitment to the war effort. It was entirely successful.

Media coverage of the shock and awe campaign that began on 20 March 2003 consisted primarily of a type of image that was shot from above, with a tilted perspective looking upon the city of Baghdad by night, its wide and magnificent Tigris river vanishing into the depth of pictorial space, the smoke clouds above, all looked similar to the apocalyptic paintings of the fall of Babylon and Nineveh by the early nineteenth-century British painter John Martin. With an art historian's eye, all I could see was the Orientalist fantasy of these televised scenes. And like a video-game spectacle, from a bird's eye view, buildings exploded, as if no people, no life forms were there beyond the bomb clouds and demolished structures. In clean and sanitized scenes of pinpoint demolition, the cityscape was targeted, as if to say, as they do at the end of the credits in films: 'This is an ethical production; no people or animals were hurt in the production process'.

As the air assault was followed by the ground invasion in April, news emerged of the extensive damage to basic infrastructure (electricity, water, communications) across Iraq, and of massive cultural damage in the looting of museums, libraries, archives and archaeological sites.[5] The archaeological community of the world was incredulous, as several archaeologists who had previously excavated in Iraq had provided detailed information and locations of cultural sites and institutions to the Pentagon and to the British Ministry of Defence that winter. Yet members of the military inside Iraq said that they had no knowledge of the locations of museums or libraries. At a UNESCO meeting in Paris on 17 April 2003 where I was present, it emerged that no guards had yet been posted at the Iraq Museum in Baghdad, although the international press had reported on the museum looting by 13–14 April. During the meeting, an American colleague who was able to reach the military command in Baghdad through satellite phone was requested to send GPS coordinates for the Iraq Museum. A great deal was said at that Paris meeting about the necessity of international efforts, but with little result. It was then that I began to plan going back to Baghdad myself.

The first piece included in this volume was written in the wake of this looting of the Iraq Museum. I would soon return to Iraq to help with salvaging what remained at that museum, to begin conducting an inventory in the storage rooms, and to work towards finding and returning some of the missing antiquities. The contributions in this part cover this period of the war, the time of shock and awe, followed by the rule of the CPA and the new American administration of Iraq, headed by Bremer. Most of the essays in this section were written in haste, sketched out quickly in the immediate aftermath of very specific events that were yet unfolding. In many ways the writing process was the opposite of my academic research, which is slow and methodical. Like Surrealist automatic writing, I now think, though at the time I didn't consider the process. I'm reminded of André Breton's remarks in *Le message automatique*, where he says that he recorded a series of words, his own words, spoken as if from an actor offstage.[6] Disconnected from and disoriented by the overwhelming surge of American prowar patriotism and propaganda in public discourse, I continued to write as a means of coping with the grief that the war brought into my life, shattering my world. Several details were edited out later, but most of the essays in Part I were written without hesitation. Somewhere in the background of this period of writing lay an unstated conviction. For me, writing these public-facing works about archaeology and heritage destruction in war was not a form of scholarly analysis; it was a way to document the depredation and erasure of history for future generations. It was also a coping mechanism in the midst of real despair. The first article in this part, published in *The Nation*, was written in the days immediately following the ground war and the looting and destruction of the museums and libraries of Iraq. It marks the start of a new direction in my work.

In the lead-up to war, the essential structure of my relationship to my field of study, as well as to my teaching and my research, changed. Both my career and my personal life were derailed. I felt removed from my context. It was several years before I was to be granted tenure at Columbia, but public speaking, writing and volunteer work began to take up much of my time. I saw myself placed into a position in which I had to explain the importance of historical architecture, of monuments, archaeological sites and museum collections, but also repeatedly to reassert that the euphemism of 'collateral damage' referred to human beings. The second essay in this section, 'The scholar as activist', addresses this change in my work's direction. It was not a paper written for publication; it was meant for a university audience of students and faculty at Columbia. As I explain in the synopsis, the title of this lecture, delivered in the autumn of 2003, was suggested by a senior colleague at Columbia, Gayatri Chakravorty Spivak. Despair set in, but so did a stubborn determination to do the work of salvaging what was left, to write and to speak in order to bear witness to these events.

It was a strange and contradictory time for my new direction. In March of 2003, two days before the bombing of Iraq began, I was awarded a Guggenheim Fellowship, a prestigious academic award not usually given to young or untenured scholars, as I was, at that point in my career. Considering the timing, I was unable to feel any happiness or to celebrate this accolade. Nevertheless, the Guggenheim allowed me to take some time away from teaching so that I could write my next academic book, *Rituals of War*, which, though focused on antiquity, was certainly tied to the atmosphere of that tumultuous period. The fellowship also gave me time to write shorter essays and articles about the current war. Most of the other pieces in Part I, written over the course of the next year, address looting and the illicit trade in antiquities, which increased exponentially from April of 2003, and which is still a major problem afflicting Iraq and the neighbouring countries.[7] The one significant exception is Chapter 5, 'Days of plunder', which was written at the end of August 2004, on the same night that I returned from a second trip to Iraq. That op-ed, in which I first reported the use of Babylon as a US and coalition military base, was published in the British newspaper, *The Guardian*, but only after it was at first turned down by the leading papers in the US. It was a first-hand account of what I had seen that spring and summer, as Senior Advisor to Iraq's Minister of Culture, Mufeed al-Jaza'iri, a position that I had accepted only after being assured that rule of the country was to be transferred to Iraq within two or three months; the CPA was then to depart. Given my vociferous opposition to the war, it was clearly naive to believe that promise of self-rule for my country. I returned to New York at the end of that summer with a new understanding. Any suggestion that sovereignty was to be handed to Iraq in July of 2004 was only a charade. Authority clearly remained in the hands of the ruling coalition headed by the US, including all decisions having to do with historical or archaeological sites, museums and archives. The latter included the notorious decision to airlift out the Baathist archives – including the secret-police surveillance files kept on the citizens of Iraq – to the Hoover Institution in Stanford, California.

By the summer of this second year of occupation, the idea of Iraqi rule and self-determination was more clearly revealed to be a fiction. The CPA had already dismantled state and civil institutions, and promoted a sectarianised division of people, enshrining it into law, even though most Iraqis, including some in the newly imposed government, were opposed to these new laws foisted upon the country.[8] Paul Bremer's 'Hundred Orders' were decrees made in 2003 and 2004, which, according to the CPA, were 'binding instructions or directives to the Iraqi people that create penal consequences or have direct bearing on the way Iraqis are regulated'.[9] The first of these was 'the De-Baathification of Iraqi Society', the second was 'the Dissolution of Entities', and the ninth had to do with the new management and use of public property. Bremer became in effect the US Viceroy in Iraq.[10] In order to impose unrestricted neoliberalism that would permit expansive resource extraction, he promulgated orders that included 'the full privatization of public enterprise, full ownership rights by foreign firms of Iraqi businesses'.[11] The hundred decrees also had a devastating impact on the cultural heritage, museums, libraries and archives of this land, as the essays in this volume reveal. From this time, I began to interrogate the occupation of heritage sites as military bases from the perspective of archaeological and critical theory. At first writing about these events for the historical record and to bring them to the attention of the general public in the West, I soon began to study them as aspects of the history and rituals of war.

Notes

1 Michael Ignatieff, 'The American Empire: The burden', *New York Times Magazine*, 5 January 2003. https://www.nytimes.com/2003/01/05/magazine/the-american-empire-the-burden.html. Ignatieff was the Director of the Carr Center for Human Rights Policy at the Harvard Kennedy School.

2 'Millions join anti-war protests', *BBC News*, 17 February 2003. https://news.bbc.co.uk/1/hi/world/europe/2765215.stm. Phillis Bennis writes that it was the largest and most international protest to date. See Bennis, 'The global war on terror: What it is, what it's done to the world', in *War with No End*, 11–32 (London: Verso, 2007).

3 New York was the only city that did not permit protestors to walk peacefully through their own streets. See the report by the executive director of the New York Civil Liberties Union, Donna Lieberman, 'NYC policies and the anti-war protests', https://www.nyclu.org/en/publications/nypd-policies-and-2003-anti-war-protests.

4 See Deborah Solomon, 'Iraq's cultural capital', *New York Times Magazine*, 5 January 2003. https://www.nytimes.com/2003/01/05/magazine/the-way-we-live-now-01-05-03-primer-iraq-s-cultural-capital.html. Solomon provides a historical summary and reports that several monuments were damaged already in the US bombings of the First Gulf War of 1991. The Arch of Ctesiphon and the walls of the Assyrian palace at Nimrud were damaged, while the minaret of the al-Askari mosque in Samarra took a direct hit by allied bombers. The temple precinct and ziggurat at the archaeological site of Ur was also left with craters and bullet holes.

5 Tim Friend, 'Dirty water may become Iraq's biggest killer', *USA Today*, 1 April 2003; International Committee of the Red Cross, Daily Bulletin, 2 April 2003. https://www.icrc.org/en/doc/resources/documents/update/5l8jaa.htm; D. B. Berry 'UN: Condition critical in Basra – water, electricity cut off to much of Iraq city; relief demanded', *Newsday*, 25 March 2003; Jonathan Steele, 'Museum's treasures left to the mercy of looters', *The Guardian*, 14 April 2003. https://www.theguardian.com/world/2003/apr/14/internationaleducationnews.arts; Human Rights Watch, 'Liberation and looting in Iraq', 13 April 2003. https://www.hrw.org/news/2003/04/13/liberation-and-looting-iraq-0.

6 André Breton, 'Le Message automatique', *Minotaur* 3–4 (1933): 54–65.

7 The first scholarly book to be published on the looting and destruction of Iraq's heritage was Khaled Nashef's *Tadmir al-turath al-hadari al-Iraqi Fusul al-Karitha* (Beirut: Dar al-Hamra, 2004 [in Arabic]). Nashef was a renowned Palestinian archaeologist who specialized in ancient Mesopotamian and Syrian archaeology. To date, his book remains the most thorough documentation of the event.

8 See Haifa Zangana, 'Songs of Iraqi resistance', in *War With No End*, 61–75, n. 5 (London: Verso, 2007), where the author quotes a survey conducted as a collaborative project between the University of Michigan Institute for Social Research and Eastern Michigan University, June 2006. See also Thomas Crampton, 'Iraqi official urges caution on imposing free market', *New York Times*, 14 October 2003. https://www.nytimes.com/2003/10/14/business/iraqi-official-urges-caution-on-imposing-free-market.html. The official is named in the article as Ali Abdul Amir Allawi.

9 Web archived at https://web.archive.org/web/20100206084411/http://www.cpa-iraq.org/regulations/; also publicly available via the FDLP Electronic Collection Archive.

10 See James P. Pfiffner, 'US blunders in Iraq: De-Baathification and disbanding the army', *Intelligence and National Security* 25 (2010): 76–85. Pfiffner relates that these decisions were made and implemented against the advice of senior military officers and US intelligence officials.

11 Antonia Juhasz, 'Ambitions of empire: The Bush administration economic plan for Iraq (and beyond)', *Left Turn Magazine* 12 (February/March 2004); also quoted in David Harvey, *Spaces of Global Capitalism*, 10 (London: Verso, 2005).

1

Looting and conquest

The Nation, 14 May 2003[1]

'النَهْب والفَتْح' الأُمّة، 14 آيار، 2003

Synopsis

This short essay was written a few days after Baghdad fell to US troops, an event that was also marked by the looting of the city's Iraq Museum, which was widely covered in the Western media. I was in New York at the time. Seeing my distress, my colleague, the American historian Professor Eric Foner, suggested that I write something and try to place it in the leading progressive American journal, *The Nation* (a journal which took an antiwar position from the start). The resulting article focuses mostly on the looting of the museum and the complicity of the antiquities trade in a global market trafficking heritage objects in the midst of war. It argues that although the looting of the Iraq Museum was presented as the result of ignorance or poor planning on the part of the US military, it was in fact to be expected. For several months before the war, scholars and archaeologists had spoken to various arms of the US government, warning them about such a possibility. Individual archaeologists and representatives of the Archaeological Institute of America met with members of the State Department, the Department of Defense and the Pentagon, providing comprehensive lists of museums that were endangered. The military's decision to disregard these warnings about museums and archaeological sites had disastrous consequences. The essay contends that the fate of the Iraq Museum was not an unfortunate accident of war. The Iraq National Library and Archives, the Museum of Modern Art, and various other cultural institutions, museums and art galleries suffered extensive damage and looting. At the archaeological site of Babylon, US Bradley tanks rolled across the ancient processional way in an act that had no military rationale but the declaration of conquest. The essay, written as it was in the first weeks of the ground invasion, points out how the war in Iraq links archaeology and heritage to strategies of war, as well as to the global market in antiquities.

المستخلص

لَقَد كُتِبَت هذه المقالة القصيرة بعدَ أيّامٍ قليلة من سقوط بغداد بيد القوات الأمريكية، ذلك الحَدَث الذي كان من أبرَز وقائِعه نَهْبُ المتحَف العراقي في المدينة، والذي حَصَلَ على تغطية واسعة من قِبَل وَسائط الإعلام الغَربيّة. لَقَد كُنتُ حينَها في نيويورك. وقد اقتَرَحَ عليَّ زميلي المؤرِّخ الأمريكي البروفسور إيريك فونَر، وهو يرى معاناتي، بأن أكتُبَ شَيئاً وأن أُحاولَ نَشرَهُ في المجلة الأمريكية التقدُّميّة الرائدة، *الأُمّة* (وهي مجَلّةٌ اتَّخذَت منذ البداية موقِفاً مُناهِضاً للحرب). تُركِّز المقالة التي كُتِبَت إثرَ ذلك جُلَّ اهتمامِها في أعمالِ النَهْب التي تَعرَّض لها المتحف فضلاً عن تواطؤ تجارة الآثار في السوق العالمية لتهريب قِطَع الآثار إبان الحَرب. جادَلَت المقالة بأنَّهُ على الرُغم منَ أنَّ ما قَد تَعَرَّض له المَتحَف العراقي من أعمالِ نَهبٍ قَد نُسِبَ إلى الجَهل أو سوء التخطيط من قِبَل الجَيش الأمريكي، إلّا أن ذلك في الواقِع كان مُتَوقَّعاً. على مَدى عِدّة أشهُرٍ قَبل الحَرب، قامَ الباحثون والآثاريون بمخاطَبة مُخْتَلَف أذرُع الحكومة، مُحذِّرين إياهم من هكذا احتمالية. لَقَد التقى علماءُ آثارٍ يُمَثِّلون أنفُسَهم فضلاً عن آخرين يُمَثِّلون معهد آثار أمريكا بأعضاءٍ من وزارة الخارجيةً، ووزارة الدفاع، والبَنتاغون، مُقَدِّمين لهم قوائمَ شاملة عن المتاحف التي كانت في خَطَر. إنّ قَرارَ الجَيش بالتَغاضي عن تِلك التحذيرات بخصوص المتاحف والمواقع الأثرية كانت له عواقِبٌ كارثيّة. تؤكِّد المقالة إنَّ هذا المصير للمتحف العراقي لم يكُن حادِثاً عَرَضياً مؤسِفاً للحَرب. فقَد عانَت دار الكُتُب والوثائق الوطنية في بغداد، ومتحف الفن الحديث، فضلاً عن مُختَلَف المؤسّسات الثقافية الأخرى، والمتاحف والمعارض من أضرارٍ جَسيمة وأعمالِ نَهْبٍ على نطاقٍ واسِع. في موقع بابل الأثري، كانت دبّابات برادلي الأمريكية تتدحرَج عبر طريق الموكب القديم في عملٍ لم يكن له أي مُبرِّرٍ عسكري سِوى إعلان الفَتح. إن المقالة التي كُتِبَت هنا كما كانت تَظهر في الأسابيع الأولى من الغزو البَري، تُشير إلى الكيفية التي ربَطَت بها الحربُ في العراق ما بَين علم الآثار والتراث وما بين استراتيجيات الحرب، كما ربطَتها كذلك بالسوق العالمية فيما يخص تجارة الآثار.

The looting of Baghdad's museums has generally been represented as an accident of ignorance or poor planning. Not enough attention has been paid to the fact that for several months before the start of the Iraq War, scholars of the ancient history of Iraq repeatedly spoke to various arms of the US government about this risk. Individual archeologists as well as representatives of the Archaeological Institute of America met with members of the State Department, the Defense Department and the Pentagon. We provided comprehensive lists of archeological sites and museums throughout Iraq, including their map coordinates. We put up a website providing this same information. All of us said the top priority was the immediate placement of security guards at all museums and archeological sites. US government officials claimed that they were gravely concerned about the protection of cultural heritage, yet they chose not to follow our advice.

The Iraq Museum in Baghdad was one of the three or four most important archeological museums in the world, a treasure house of objects included in every standard art history textbook, housing the earliest narrative reliefs and the oldest written works in world history. As has now been well documented, by 12 April the entire museum had been looted. The looters used professional glass-cutting tools, cranes and trucks over a period of 48 hours, as a US tank stood idly outside. At one point a few soldiers strolled into the museum, watched for a while and then left.

The looting of this unparalleled museum was not an isolated incident or a casualty of the chaos of war. Before this raid, a group of looters emptied museums in Basra and Mosul while coalition troops looked on. Even after the museum lootings had sparked an international outcry, Iraq's libraries and galleries were allowed to be plundered and burnt.

US troops not only neglected to protect historical sites and cultural property; they abused such sites themselves. US forces bombed Baghdad's thirteenth-century university building, one of the oldest universities in the world. US troops transformed the ancient site of Ur into a military base, even digging trenches into the ground. US tanks rolled through the ancient streets of Babylon, an act that had no military value but to declare conquest.

The destruction of cultural heritage during war can fall into the category of collateral damage, but looting that takes place under the supervision of an occupying force is another matter. The 1954 Hague Convention establishes that it is the responsibility of the occupying power to protect the cultural patrimony of the occupied land. While the United States never ratified that convention, the Defense Department promised to abide by the Hague Convention in several responses to the scholarly community. An 18 March letter to this effect to the Society for American Archaeology is posted at www.saa.org. In any case, the United States is a signatory to the Geneva Convention, which makes clear that the protection of museums, as of hospitals, is the responsibility of the occupying force. The United States clearly violated this convention. While the Oil Ministry was, and remains, well guarded, at the time of an emergency meeting about the looting, on 17 April at UNESCO in Paris, no military guard had yet been posted at the museum. The museum's director of research, Donny George, who had been asked to attend the UNESCO meeting, declined the invitation, explaining that he had to stay in Baghdad to guard what was left of the collections.

Blame must be placed with the Bush Administration for a catastrophic destruction of culture unparalleled in modern history. Thousands of cuneiform tablets and ancient Christian, Muslim and Jewish manuscripts are gone. Most of the country's works of art have disappeared. Much of the nation's cultural heritage has been lost. US Defense Secretary Donald Rumsfeld's response to this devastation? 'Freedom's untidy. And free people are free to make mistakes and commit crimes.'[2]

And who stands to benefit from this plunder? The illicit trade in antiquities, which funnels works from countries such as Egypt, Greece and Italy to collectors based in New York, London and Geneva. Collector William Pearlstein, of the American Council for Cultural Policy (ACCP), an organization that met with the White House and the Pentagon right before the war and right after the looting, is appealing for the cultural theft to continue by other means, calling Iraq's antiquities-preservation laws 'retentionist', and saying he 'hoped that Iraq would grant more excavation permits and consider export permits for redundant objects'. Everyone, from professional organizations to religious fanatics, is now laying claim to Iraq's past, some pretending to speak for the Iraq Museum or the Department of Antiquities. This opportunism opens the door to more cultural and historical plunder, a base scramble much like the parceling off of sites and antiquities that occurred in the nineteenth century.

At this point, the US authority in Iraq has yet to allow an international team of experts to assess damage to archeological sites, monuments and museums. By the time help can go in, some structures – such as the 2,000-year-old Great Arch of Ctesiphon, which has suffered for years due to the banning of monument-preservation materials under the embargo – may very well collapse (Figure 1). Perhaps private interests such as the ACCP will be allowed in first. All of these decisions have been designated a US project. US archeologists, art historians and historians must take a stance against this. They must insist on the international cooperation of world academics, with involvement based on expertise. Decisions about excavation permits and the organization of cultural property should not depend upon the whims of the occupying force. Ultimately, such decisions must be left to the Iraqi Department of Antiquities and Heritage, as only Iraqis can have the right to decide how to proceed.

Even in antiquity, and by the Babylonians and Assyrians themselves, the destruction of cultural property was understood as an act of psychological warfare. Historical annals from ancient Mesopotamia describe how the identity and power of a people is directly linked to its cultural monuments. Recent empires – the Habsburgs, the British and the French – all appropriated the cultural heritage of colonized lands, but at least they safeguarded it in museums and promoted its study. The destruction that the US military has allowed to occur in Iraq has no parallel.

Notes

1 https://www.thenation.com/article/archive/looting-and-conquest.
2 https://www.upi.com/Defense-News/2003/04/11/Rumsfeld-Looting-is-transition-to-freedom/63821050097983.

2
The scholar as activist

Columbia University, Center for Comparative Literature and Society, 25 November 2003

’الباحِث كناشِط‘ جامعة كولومبيا، مَركَز الأدَب المُقارن
والمجتمع، 25 تشرين الثاني، 2003

Synopsis

In the spring of 2003, I went to Iraq to work on the salvage of the Iraq Museum after the April looting. As I had previous experience working as a curator at the Metropolitan Museum of Art in New York, I thought that I could volunteer my time and knowledge to my colleagues in Baghdad. This paper chronicles my first return to the city of my birth in the aftermath of war. No air travel was permitted by the coalition occupation forces at that time, other than military flights, so all civilian movement was limited. After travelling to Amman, Jordan, by air, and there purchasing supplies for the museum, I made the long 12-hour road journey to Baghdad by car and crossed the border at Trebil. When I returned to New York, my colleague, Professor Gayatri Spivak, encouraged me to reflect upon the question of what it means for a scholar to be an activist, and how such activism can take the form of hands-on conservation work – a type of close-up work that can be conducted in addition to public-facing scholarship. The essay here is the text that I wrote soon after returning from Iraq, later in 2003, which I delivered at Columbia's Center of Comparative Literature and Society in November of that year.

In the lecture, I presented a description of the conditions in Iraq, from the deserted checkpoint of the border crossing to the conditions at the museum. The museum was a disaster zone, and the process of working there to collect the pieces of broken artefacts was akin to excavating and recording fragments and their exact locations at an archaeological site. Yet when the military took over the museum, much of this meticulous work either stopped or was severely hampered by new rules. In the end, no proper survey of the kind that we initiated at that time could be completed because of the forced eviction of the staff and the control of the Coalition Provisional Authority (CPA). The lecture thus took up some larger academic themes such as the relationship between war, colonialism and the politics of antiquities. But it also addressed the experience of war, loss and grief, and questions of law, ethics and commitment. I had not contemplated the term 'activist' in relation to myself until asked to do so by my colleague, but in the context of this lecture I began to consider this aspect of a scholar's work. In addition to public speaking and writing, I argued, it had to include the silent and unacknowledged labour of such things as post-disaster museum salvage in times of war, hands-on conservation efforts, and field surveys in conflict zones. It also had to consider the scholarly texts that form the basis of our intellectual work as theoretical archaeologists and historians.

المستخلص

في ربيعِ عام 2003، ذَهَبتُ إلى العراق للعمل على إنقاذِ المتحفِ العراقي بعد أعمال النَّهْب التي حَدَثَت في نيسان. بما أنّ لَديَّ خِبرةً سابِقةً كأمينة متحف في متحف الميتروبوليتانِ للفن في نيويورك، فكَّرْتُ أنَّ بإمكاني التطوُّع بوقتي ومعرفتي لزملائي في بغداد. تُوَثِّق هذه الورقة البحثية عَودَتي الأولى إلى مَسقَط رأسي في أعقاب الحَرب. حينَها، لم تكُن قوات الاحتلال التابعة للتحالف لتسمَح بأيّ رِحلاتٍ جَويّة، بخِلاف الرحلات العَسكريّة، لذا كانت التحرُّكات المَدَنيّة بمُجمَلِها محدودة. بعد سَفَري إلى عَمّان في الأردن جَوّاً، وشَرائي للمُستَلزمات التي يحتاجُها المتحف من هناك، قُمتُ برحلةٍ بَريّة استغرقَتني اثنتَي عشرة ساعة للوصول الى بغداد بالسيّارة عابِرَةً الحدود في طريبيل. عِندَما عُدتُ الى نيويورك، شَجَّعَني زميلي البروفيسور غاياتري سبيفاك على أن أُعطي تصوُّري حولَ مسألَة ما يَعنيه للباحِث أن يُصبِحَ ناشِطاً، وكيف يُمكِن لهكذا نشاط أن يَتَّخِذ صيغةَ تدريبٍ عَملي على أعمال الصَون – كنوعٍ من العمل المُفَصَّل عن قُرب الذي يُمكِن إجراؤه فضلاً عن المِنَح الدِراسيّة المُوجَّهةً للعامّة. إن هذه المقالة هنا هي النَصُّ ذاتُه الذي كَتَبتُهُ بعد فترة وَجيزة من رجوعي من العراق لاحِقاً في عام 2003، والذي سَلَّمتُهُ إلى مَركَز الأدَب المُقارن والمجتمع في جامعة كولومبيا في تشرين الثاني من العام ذاتِه.

قَدَّمتُ في هذه المحاضرة وصفاً للأوضاع في العراق؛ ابتداءاً من نقطة تفتيشٍ مهجورة عَبْرَ الحدود إلى الأوضاع في المَتحَف. لقد كان المتحف منطقةً منكوبة، وكانت عملية جَمع القِطَع المكسورة لِلُّقى شَبيهَةٌ لما يحدُث عند تنقيب وتسجيل الأجزاء المتناثرة ومواقِعَها بدِقّة في مَوقعٍ أثَري، لكن حين خَضَع المتحَف لسَيطَرة الجَيش، تم إيقاف معظم ذلك العمل الدقيق أو عَرقَلتُهُ بشِدّة من خلال القوانين الجديدة. في النهاية، لم يكُن من الممكن إجراء مَسْحٍ صَحيح بمستوى دِقّة المَسْح الذي بدَأنا به حينَها بسبَب

الإخلاء القَسري للكادِر وسيطرة سلطة التحالف المؤقتة. لِذا تناولَت المحاضرة عِدَّة مواضيعِ أكاديمية أكبر كالعلاقة بين الحرب، والكولونيالية وسياسة التعامل مع الآثار. لكنَّها تَطَرَّقَت أيضاً الى تجربة الحَرب، والفَقْد، والأسى، ومسائِل القانون، والأخلاق، والالتزام. لم أُفكِّر يومَها بعِلاقَتي شَخصيّاً بمُصطَلَح "ناشِط" حتّى دَعاني لذلك زَميلي، لكنّني ضمن سِياق هذه المحاضرة، بدَأتُ بأخذ هذا الجانب من عمل الباحِث بالحُسبان. إلى جانِبِ الحَديث والكتابة للعامّة، فقَد جادَلْتُ، بأنَّ هذا يجب أن يتضمّن العمل الصامت وغير المُدْرَك لهكذا أشياء كالعمل على إنقاذ المتحف بعد النَكْبة في وقت الحرب، وجهود التَدريب العملي، والمسوحات المَيدانية في مناطق النِزاع. يجب أن يأخذ في الحُسبان أيضاً النصوص البحثية التي تُشَكِّل القاعدة للعمل الفكري كمُنظِّرين آثاريين ومؤرِّخين.

When I was first invited to speak on the subject of the scholar as activist at the Center for Comparative Literature and Society I was somewhat taken by surprise. My research and writing are on art and archaeology, and on the preservation of historical architecture and artefacts and curatorial work in museums. Although I actively and publicly opposed the war this past year, at a time when opposing the war here in the US has been heavily criticised by both those on the Right and those on the Left, I had not thought of myself as an activist. Monuments and museums, after all, are the worlds of cultural refinement, elite institutions and aesthetic distance, separated from the lives of people or human rights. But the First Gulf War of 1991, known as Operation Desert Storm, had already created a sense of estrangement or cognitive dissonance. Surveillance images and military maps sorted out cities, such as the historical one in which I was born, as legitimate targets, as well as ancient sites that needed to be protected for the sake of what they classified as 'global cultural heritage'. How, then, could I or we find this term anything but callous? How could I continue to attend to curatorial work or research without an emergent activist streak that already then, in 1991, troubled my supervisors and senior colleagues?

At the same time, since the drumbeats for this war began, it has been clear to me that the loss and destruction of what has come to be called 'cultural heritage', monuments, or historical architecture, cannot be ignored. Such destruction can, and does, have a devastating effect on people and communities. Knowing through my work on antiquity that ancient peoples deliberately targeted historical monuments and memorials as a means of asserting power and erasing memory, I have not been able to set aside this aspect of the war as accidental collateral damage, as many colleagues in my field have done. Imperialism dominates others as subjects, but it also dominates the ways in which the other can be defined, understood, described, remembered or narrated into historical accounts. We are seeing this in Iraq today so clearly, and as scholars we must call attention to it. A sense of helplessness sets in when the media disseminates an incredible amount of misinformation, and the public believes it to be factual and correct. As an archaeologist, an art historian and a curator, I've turned my work to a critical interrogation of the place and aims of cultural destruction and historical erasure in war. And I've also turned it to the hands-on labour of picking up the pieces and fragments left by the shock and awe campaign. Activism for a scholar like me, then, involves theoretical reflection and writing on the one hand and public speaking on the other – truth to power. But it also involves direct action, the labour of working in a disaster or post-disaster zone, such as that of the Iraq Museum in Baghdad. I see working on the salvage of the museum, archives and libraries of Iraq as inseparable from the fate of human beings, and as such, it is an antiwar, anti-imperial act, when it is our own work, not imposed by colonial archaeology and occupation powers. Surveying and recording these aspects of cultural destruction is also a form of bearing witness so that future generations may know. If the aim is to erase and rewrite histories, then these are also acts of resistance.

Throughout history monument destruction has been calculated into the strategies of war, and in the Modern era it has been discussed quite openly as an aspect of military strategy known as psyops (psychological operations). Imperial and colonial powers have often made use of such strategies. As Frantz Fanon already stated in 1959, far from being concerned merely with the present or with overt political or economic issues, colonialism 'turns to the past of the oppressed people, and distorts, disfigures, and destroys it'.[1]

Although in the past months I have thought about little other than the destruction of museums, libraries, archives and historical sites in Iraq, it was never my intention to turn to the direction of becoming either a public intellectual or an activist. This was not a career path or direction that I chose, but one into which I have been catapulted by the events of war.

I went to Iraq soon after the shock and awe campaign, to help with the aftermath of the destruction that took place in the spring. It was a decision taken out of personal pain and sorrow, not a scholarly choice. When I heard or read the news of this war in March and April, I felt compelled to act. Not having any skills other than those of an archaeologist and curator, I went to Baghdad with those in hand.

I had not stopped to think of the details of how I was going, what I should take with me, or to weigh the pros and cons of entering a war zone under military occupation. After returning to New York at the end of August I reflected on this decision. Would it have been better not to enter my city while it was under military occupation? Perhaps. And what would I define as my Act of Activism now? Speaking and writing in public in New York City? Going to Baghdad, the city of my birth, during a war that I opposed and vociferously protested?

As Edward Said once said, activism involves taking action without regard for one's position.[2] What I think might be hard to accept is that being an intellectual or scholar activist means doing and saying things that are uncomfortable, and even threatening, to one's academic or professional standing, including saying things that may have a negative impact on tenure reviews and job security. Many senior colleagues in my own field of ancient Near Eastern archaeology are in favour of this war and occupation. It is not difficult to stand up for a cause if you have an entire community behind you. It becomes more difficult when it is an unpopular position, as my insistence on opposing the war and the invasion has been among many in the US where I now live, including expat Iraqis who, in their great enthusiasm to change the regime, support the invasion without regard for their fellow human beings at home. They, too, are collateral damage in the service of the democratic future these expats envision for Iraq. Here in the US, the push for war was strong and effective, and the media was full of pride in American military prowess, an attitude picked up by the general public. *The Washington Post* reported that an air and ground assault involving force never before seen in the history of warfare was before us.[3] In the feverish push for war, anything or anyone could be sacrificed.

I will now turn to what might be called a version of activism that I have been involved with in the past few months. It has been primarily hands-on work, rather than theoretical reflection or the public speaking of the winter and early spring.

By 12 April, the news of the looting of the Iraq Museum emerged. The astonishment and anger of the archaeological scholarly community (some of which was very much pro-war) was increased by the fact that many had warned that it would happen. Several colleagues had specifically asked arms of both the US and British governments to ensure that guards would be placed at museums. Long before the war, archaeologists had given the Pentagon and the British Ministry of Defence lists of archaeological sites, including the map coordinates in spreadsheets. In addition to archaeological sites, they identified museums and their locations in every city. I personally felt very conflicted about the wisdom of providing such lists. I was terrified by the announcement of a forthcoming shock and awe campaign, and all I could think of was the potential bombing of the population, including of my own friends and family; we had experienced this already in the 1990s. But there were colleagues who felt that raising this issue in public was important to do. Several of us had spoken to the press about it on quite literally a daily basis in order to raise some interest among the general public, but I fear that we failed in gaining any public sympathy. Americans were eager for war. They saw it as an act of vengeance or divine retribution. Even some friends here in New York City were enthusiastic. The air war began on 20 March; it soon turned into a ground war, and Baghdad fell to US troops on the 9th of April. The museums and libraries of Baghdad were looted between the 10th and the 12th. On the 12th, the news from the museum reached us here in New York. It took two days because the communications towers had been bombed. Iraq was cut off, and there was no form of communication with the outside world other than the satellite phones that the military and the foreign press had brought into Iraq.

US troops finally secured the Iraq Museum on 17 April (see Figure 2). During those four days between the 12th and the 16th, when we knew that the looting was ongoing and that nothing had yet been done to stop it, a small group of archaeologists and historians in Britain and the US spent 24 hours a day making hundreds of telephone calls and sending countless emails to the military, the British government, and US government vehemently insisting that troops be sent to secure the museum. We also spoke to the press. I believe that if we had not done so, no troops would have been sent for several weeks after.

In terms of the purported rescue efforts that are now being lauded in the press, some initial steps were taken immediately after news of the looting emerged. UNESCO called an emergency meeting in Paris, several days before the Iraq Museum had even been secured by US troops. Soon after, Neil MacGregor, the Director of the British Museum, convened a second emergency meeting in London, in conjunction with UNESCO, in order to organise plans for inventories, emergency conservation of objects, and the provision of equipment and supplies to the department of antiquities. I was called to both meetings to discuss practical plans and strategies. At the time I hoped that real steps for assistance would be taken, following the list of urgent requirements that our small international group of specialists had drawn up there. But there were to be both diplomatic and military obstacles to all these proposals. Nothing that we had outlined at UNESCO in Paris or in London could proceed as planned. Very soon after these meetings, I became frustrated with the lack of action from institutions and resolved to make my own way to Iraq, independently of any academic, cultural institution, government or NGO. I had no clear idea what exactly I would do once I got there, but I knew that I had to go. It is true that there were real risks involved that kept other scholars from acting, or the CPA from granting permission for in-country clearances, but there was a dearth of movement by NGOs and other institutions.[4]

When I arrived in Baghdad after travelling by car from Amman, Jordan, a trip that takes about 12 hours, I went directly to the Iraq Museum and was greeted warmly by its staff, many of whom were old friends, including the Director, Dr Donny George Youkhanna, whom I had known long before the war (Figure 3). It was obvious that the building that houses the State Board of Antiquities and Heritage (SBAH) as well as the museum had been ransacked, looted and damaged. Everywhere doors had huge, gaping holes in them. Of the office furniture, only a handful of chairs remained. Most of the office files and cabinets had been ransacked. The electricity was not functioning, and there was certainly no telephone or email communication. In Baghdad I began to work on the inventory of missing objects with some of the curatorial staff. A US military investigation team had by then been installed in the museum, and our curatorial work had to proceed with the presence of tanks and troops. Alongside the staff of the museum, I worked to compile an inventory of what was left in the storerooms and to assess the condition of the objects that remained. This was slow and methodical hands-on work. I was given permission by the staff to go through all the storage rooms in order to help determine the exact locations from which objects were taken, and types of objects that were missing. We had to pick up the shattered fragments from the ground, and record them carefully and systematically with exact findspots, as if on an archaeological dig. I also compiled information on specific missing pieces from the remaining registers and catalogues, from the museum's photograph archive, and from the archive of field notebooks.

While the military has by now submitted a final report of its own investigation to the Pentagon, it should be pointed out that, as far as I and the curatorial staff are concerned, the process of inventory-taking is only in its preliminary stage, and no final accounting can be made at this time. Despite many reports to the contrary, the registers and card catalogue do still exist, but due to the chaos of the looting and destruction of the offices, these records are not in a condition to allow a quick assessment of the losses.

I had travelled to Iraq along with two colleagues, Elizabeth Stone and Paul Zimansky, after raising some funds from the Mellon Foundation for the purchase of material and equipment for the museum.

The computers, digital cameras and office furniture that we bought in Amman and took with us remain, as far as I am aware, at this point the only tangible donation that they have received in the department of antiquities. We also provided the museum staff with two satellite phones (Thuraya phones), in order to permit communication with the outside world, one of their biggest obstacles to any reasonable working conditions.

Forty works were originally stolen from the museum's galleries (see Figure 4), although 13 of these were soon recovered or returned voluntarily. Most of the losses were from the storage magazines. Some of the gallery cases were smashed (Figure 5), and the staircase leading to the upper galleries was destroyed when looters apparently dragged a large copper sculpture down the stairs. This is one of the most important objects looted, and it was recovered only on November 3. It is an Akkadian seated male nude that bears an inscription of the Akkadian king Naram-Sin (2254–2218 BC). Many archaeologists had given up on this piece, assuming that it had been melted down by looters. The fact that it had not, and was hidden intact, indicates that the looters who took this object knew of its potential value on the antiquities market. Other well-known works that are still missing include the diorite portrait of the Sumerian ruler Enmetena, dating to 2450 BC, inscribed with a text on the right shoulder, a portrait of the high priest and scribe Dudu of the same date,[5] a number of ivories from Nimrud of the early first millennium BC, and some rare and important Hellenistic and Parthian sculptures, such as a now-decapitated sculpture of Nike, the goddess of victory.

A marble statue of Apollo from the ancient city of Hatra had been smashed to pieces; the head was missing (Figure 6). The fragments of shattered works had to be carefully collected and recorded exactly next to where they were found, so that they might be restored at some point in the future. The museum became an archaeological site, where every fragment and its location had to be noted carefully, and the meticulous sifting through of sherds became the foremost task. One might assume that the smashing of these statues was an act of iconoclasm, but these sculptures – which look Greek in their style of carving – were decapitated, their heads taken away by the looters to be sold in the antiquities market, while their bodies were left in pieces on the ground. This was a calculated theft of classical heads that, surely not incidentally, sell very well on the international antiquities market. It thus seems clear that the looting involved at least a faction of professional antiquities thieves who knew exactly what sorts of objects to take, and what types would fetch the best prices in the antiquities market. Among the many challenges that lie ahead is simply to convince museums and collectors here in the US to stop buying antiquities looted in Iraq, or any other country, for that matter.

Like the galleries, the condition of the storerooms is nothing short of disastrous. The museum has two main areas of storage, known as the 'old' and the 'new' storerooms, in two different locations in the building. Both of these were ransacked and looted. Things that were not taken were strewn about all over the floors, and numerous shelves, along with the many objects they held, were smashed or damaged in the process (Figure 7). The inventory of objects remaining in the storage rooms is still under way; the remains have to be analysed and recorded, carefully and systematically, fragment by fragment and layer by layer, as in the methods used in an archaeological excavation or the salvage of disaster sites. Somehow this seems clear after earthquakes or other natural disasters, but this procedure must also be followed in the aftermath of war. In my estimate, it will take at least 10 years to conduct an inventory and condition report according to anything resembling international museum standards. Until that time, we cannot possibly have a final statement on the extent of damage suffered by this museum. But there has, as yet, been no effort from international agencies to assist in such a careful survey or record of what in fact happened, and it is becoming increasingly difficult for the museum, especially after the recent forced removal of most of the senior curators from the premises by the Coalition Provisional Authority (CPA), leaving few with any institutional memory or experience to continue the work.

A large number of the objects missing from the storage rooms are cylinder seals, very popular among collectors. These are small cylindrical objects carved out of precious stones, which were used to authenticate documents; they were also worn as personal amulets and ornaments by the ancient Mesopotamians. They are only about an inch or two in length, and so are very easy to smuggle. A number of these have been found in the possession of people who were stopped at JFK customs here in New York City – including some that still have an Iraq Museum accession number written on them.

The fate of the museums is one small aspect of the destruction of history in Iraq. And it is not only archaeological material that is lost. The Museum of Modern Art in Baghdad was also looted; its contents will be more difficult to track down, as collectors of modern art are not scrutinised in the same way as those who buy antiquities. Many decades may pass before Iraq might reclaim these remarkable works of twentieth-century Modernists. Libraries and museums, galleries and collections were all extensively damaged or destroyed.

Another pressing problem right now is the ongoing looting and plunder at archaeological sites themselves. There are more than 10,000 listed archaeological sites in Iraq, and many more that have not yet been registered officially. A great deal of damage occurs during illicit digging for the market. Our colleagues in Iraq inform us that two or three ancient cities have been devastated by postwar looting already. Although it is against international laws, there is a market for such looting among private collectors of antiquities, along with some museums in the West and beyond. Obviously, since there is little border security in Iraq, it is easy to smuggle objects out and sell them from the neighbouring countries, relabelled as antiquities from elsewhere in the region.

Of course, the buyers are not in Iraq. The primary market is in the US, Western Europe, Israel and Japan. This illicit antiquities trade is a well-known form of organised crime, and it is said to be the third largest illegal trade after drugs and arms. A UN resolution banning the trade in Iraqi antiquities has been passed, but here in New York and elsewhere, museums and collectors continue to purchase antiquities.[6]

Another urgent concern at this time involves the potential destruction of archaeological sites and historical urban centres as a result of plans for large-scale construction and development. There is also the question of who now has the right to make decisions in a country under military occupation. The most recent reports from colleagues in Baghdad inform us that the CPA and National Geographic Television are planning to organise a travelling exhibition of the famous Nimrud gold, that is destined for the US. While some might argue that such an exhibition will have a beneficial result in raising awareness among the American general public of the significance of Mesopotamian arts and culture, it nevertheless raises important questions about decision-making around cultural institutions in an occupied land suffering from the ravages of war; if the CPA feels free to make decisions about exhibitions (as they have already done in July), or the granting of excavation permits without consulting the professional curators and archaeologists of Iraq (many of whom have been ousted from their jobs), the results will likely be damaging to the ancient objects. More importantly, it raises questions about the rights to cultural property in occupied lands. On the conservational level, travelling exhibitions, if they are not organised according to international museum and conservational standards around the handling and packing of objects, can result in irreversible damage to the artefacts. An exhibition commissioned and run by the CPA is not an acceptable plan. Likewise, decisions about where excavations are allowed to be undertaken and what types of proposals for excavations are scientifically and academically valid need to be made by the Department of Antiquities and Heritage rather than by politicians and military men. What is striking is the extent to which these problems simply perpetuate attitudes about archaeology that were set in place during the British Mandate occupation at the end of the First World War. And the sense of superiority to the people of Iraq, clear in the works of nineteenth-century writers who collected antiquities for the British Museum and in the military archaeologists working for the British Mandate, continues today. There is no question, they seem to say in the midst of this war, that Iraqi people are a lesser form of human being. These issues of cultural heritage and the politics of antiquities are therefore also issues of social and racial justice.

Arguments such as those suggesting that both art and an awareness of history are particularly Western concerns unknown to other peoples of the world, and claiming that ancient Mesopotamian artefacts are more valued and better protected here in the West than they are by the people of Iraq, are the same ones that have been used in the service of empire and the antiquities market since the early nineteenth century – a market that is the direct cause of the continuing looting at Iraq's archaeological sites, and that was at least one of the driving forces behind the looting of the museums in April. Another argument that is made is that the cultural heritage of places like Egypt and Iraq cannot be stolen because it was never really theirs, since (according to this view) these nation-states are modern formations and the populations today have nothing to do with those of the past. This argument was used in a recent court case in which looted antiquities appeared in the possession of a New York dealer. They argued in his defence that it is global cultural heritage.

The concept of global cultural heritage is therefore a two-edged sword. It can be a powerful means of calling for the protection of monuments and artefacts under international laws, but at the same time what is lost in the process of nominating certain things as global heritage is the awareness of local relations and interactions between people, places and cultural artefacts.

The destruction of cultural property, that is, monuments and artefacts, during war is nothing new. It has been a grave concern to human beings since the very earliest written accounts known to us. If as archaeologist-activists we have an ethical obligation to protect cultural heritage during armed conflict, it is because these objects are directly linked to the survival of human beings, as the ancient Mesopotamians understood very well, and as they recorded in numerous texts.

They understood historical artefacts and monuments as the agents of memory, entangled with people's daily lives. I would repeat once more, because of the preoccupation with the exact numbers of things lost, a point of continuous contention and heated debate – that the loss to Iraq is not something that can be calculated in numbers or in market values, which seem to be the primary concern in many press reports today.

For the Babylonians and the Assyrians, one of the greatest causes of anxiety in times of war was the potential for removal and destruction of monuments. There were even times when entire wars were waged in order to rescue works of sculpture that had been stolen in a previous battle. These concerns had to do with the agency and power of monuments and historical sites, and little to do with the value of precious materials. Rather, the Mesopotamians considered these monuments to be an integral part of the identities of their cities, pleasing to the gods, and part of the landscape of their collective memory.

It is interesting to note that the loss of objects from Iraq's museums and archaeological sites would have been understood by the ancients as a sign of the destruction of identity. That is why Assyrian and Babylonian kings of the first millennium BC such as Ashurbanipal and Nabonidus collected ancient texts and sculptures, objects that were by then already thousands of years old. That is the reason they protected and repaired ancient public monuments, excavated ancient temples and restored their foundation stones, and wrote about these acts of preservation. The survival of these monuments was considered to be directly linked to the survival of the people and also of the land.

Conversely, as we know from archaeological theoretical scholarship, it is true that antiquity can be, and has been manipulated for nationalist agendas such as those of Saddam Hussein, and likewise in the service of ethnocentric claims and ethnic cleansing. And ancients (in both East and West) attacked other people's monuments and took them into captivity in times of war.

Cultural property has never been detached from war and segregated into its own purely humanist realm. It becomes an instrument of war and occupation, of the rewriting of history and justifications of empire. It would seem clear then, that the international protection of heritage and humanitarian laws should not be suspended in times of war (as we are seeing today). In peacetime, United Nations or UNESCO ideals are easy to uphold. Indeed, it is precisely when it becomes difficult, in times of war, political chaos or upheaval, that we must consider it our obligation to do so. Alongside scholarly critical reflection and theory, or op-ed commentary, the decisions we make and actions that we take as scholars and intellectuals during such times have an impact – and this kind of direct action is, to me, what it means to be a scholar-activist.

Notes

1 Frantz Fanon, *The Wretched of the Earth*, translated by Constance Farrow (New York: Grove Press, 1963), 210.
2 See Edward W. Said, *Representations of the Intellectual* (New York: Pantheon Books, 1994).
3 Rajiv Chandrasekaran and Peter Baker, 'Troops advance halfway to Baghdad', *Washington Post*, 23 March 2003. https://www.washingtonpost.com/archive/politics/2003/03/23/troops-advance-halfway-to-baghdad/03a4cda6-b147-4d58-8b2b-04de648c673d/.
4 'In-country clearance' refers to the term used by US forces at the time for the official permission to travel inside the country.
5 Fortunately, both of these statues were recovered after the date of this lecture.
6 UN Security Council Resolution 1483 (22 May 2003), paragraph 7; see https://digitallibrary.un.org/record/495555?ln=en.

3
The Iraq War

Zainab Bahrani, W. Luttwak and D. Rieff, *Cultural Heritage in War: Moral and military choices*. New York: Columbia University Department of Art History and Archaeology, 2004

حَرْب' العراق'زينب البحراني، و و. لوتواك و د. ريف،
الموروث الحضاري والحرب: الخَيارات الأخلاقية والعسكرية،
نيويورك: جامعة كولومبيا، قسم تاريخ الفَن والآثار، 2004.

Synopsis

This paper was written for a presentation I was invited to give at the New York Historical Society on 21 November 2003; the following year it was published in the short volume *Cultural Heritage and War*. Of the three participants invited to speak that evening, I was the only one who was opposed to the war and occupation. One of my fellow speakers condoned the invasion on humanitarian grounds, and thus represented the views of many of the US Democrats, while the other speaker supported it as necessary for the protection of US interests and the security of the West, adhering to the perspective of the Bush administration. The paper and discussion addressed questions of destruction of cultural heritage and the varied forms that this destruction takes in wars. The paper describes the condition of the museum as I found it upon my return in the spring of 2003. Large marble sculptures and tiny glass vessels were smashed into fragments that were scattered across the floor and storage magazines had been the site of a rampage, where easily marketable antiquities had been taken while other artefacts were left behind. The essay then outlines the forms that wartime destruction can take, from inadvertent damage to deliberate targeting. It also raises concerns regarding postwar development plans and the construction of two airport projects at ancient sites. From these details of the Iraqi context, the essay goes on to question the usefulness of the concept of 'global cultural heritage', arguing that the case of the Iraq War revealed it to be a two-edged sword; such ideas were being employed in the service of the antiquities market – a market that is also the direct cause of the continuing looting of archaeological sites, which in turn directly impacts the country that is being plundered.

المستخلص

كُتِبَت هذه الورقة البحثية لعَرضٍ تقديمي كُنتُ قد دُعيتُ لإلقائِهِ في جمعيّة نيويورك التاريخية بتاريخ 21 تشرين الثانّي 2003، وفي العام الذي تلاه نُشِرَت في المُجلَّد القصير *الموروث الحضاري والحرب*. من بين المُشاركين الثلاثة المَدعوّين للحديث في تلك الأُمسية، كنتُ الوَحيدة التي عارَضَت الحرب والاحتلال. لقد تغاضى أحد زملائي المُتَحدِّثين عن الغزو لأسبابٍ إنسانية، وبذلك كان يمثِّل وجهة نظر العديد من الديموقراطيين الأمريكان، بينما دَعَمَ المُتحدِّث الآخر الغزوَ وعَدَّهُ ضَرورةً لحماية المصالح الأمريكية وأمن الغَرب، التِزاماً بمنظور إدارة بوش. استَهْدَفَت هذه الورقة البحثية والمناقشة مَسْألَتَي تدمير الموروث الحضاري والصِيَغ المُتعَدِّدة التي يَتَّخِذُها هذا التَدمير في الحروب. تَصِف هذه الورقة البحثية حالةَ المتحف كما وجدْتُها عِندَ عَودَتي في ربيع عام 2003. لقد تَحَطَّمَت مَنحوتاتٌ رُخاميّة كبيرة وأوعِيةٌ زُجاجيّة صَغيرة وأضْحَت شَظايا متناثِرة على الأرض بينما أصبحت مخازن المتحف موقِعاً مُجتاحاً، حيثُ تؤخَذ الآثار سهلَةُ التسويق في حين تُترَك اللُقى الأخرى. حَدَّدَت المقالة بعدها الصِيَغ التي يتَّخذُها الدَمار في زمن الحرب، من ضَرَرٍ غَيرِ مَقصود إلى استهدافٍ مُتعمَّد. كما أنَّها كذلك أثارَت دَواعي القلق بخصوص خُطَط التنمية لما بعد الحَرب ومشاريع إنشاء مَطارَين في مواقعَ أثَريّة. من تفاصيل السياق العراقي هذه، تَسترسِل المقالة مُسائِلةً عن فائدة فكرة ' التُراث الحضاري العالمي '، فهي تُجادل بأنَّ قضيّة حَرب العراق قد كَشَفَت بأنَّها سِلاحٌ ذو حَدَّين؛ إن هكذا أفكار تم توظيفُها في سوق الآثار—السوق التي كانت أيضاً السبب المُباشر لاستمرار أعمال نَهْب المواقع الأثريّة، والتي بدَورِها تؤثِّر في البِلاد التي نُهِبَت.

I too have a report from the field, but I think you'll find it's different from what we've heard up to now. In the first days after the fall of Baghdad to US troops on 9 April 2003, the Iraqi National Museum in Baghdad was looted. The place was ransacked, and thousands of objects were stolen. But that is not all. In the days before and after, many more museums and libraries in the country were also looted and destroyed. For thinking people all over the world, this was a great tragedy. Ancient Iraq is Mesopotamia, the land between the rivers, the so-called cradle of civilization, where Nineveh, Babylon and Ur flourished, where writing was invented and the first cities arose, where concepts such as history, monuments and war were contemplated and recorded for the first time by human beings. At the time of the looting there was a great outcry that the antiquities of Mesopotamia are global cultural heritage, a heritage that has suffered an appalling fate.

Here in the United States, news of the looting quickly transformed into a heated debate circling around, above all else, the exact number of objects that were stolen. In the first days after the looting, press accounts stated that 170,000 objects were lost from the Iraqi National Museum alone. By 29 April, Dr Donny George, the director of the Iraqi National Museum, informed a press conference in London that that number was incorrect: 170,000 was the number of catalogued objects in the collection. Within weeks the pendulum had swung in the other direction, and the media began to report widely and gleefully that only about 30 objects were stolen. But those reports were unfortunately also incorrect: 30 was the number of objects still missing from those that had remained installed in the galleries during the war.

The focus on numbers continues today, but both the US military investigators as well as the Iraq museum staff currently estimate the number of objects still missing from the Iraqi National Museum at between ten- and fourteen-thousand.

In terms of the rescue effort, some initial steps were taken immediately after news of the looting emerged. UNESCO called an emergency meeting in Paris several days before the Iraq museum even had been secured by US troops. Soon after, Neil MacGregor, the director of the British Museum, convened a second emergency meeting in conjunction with UNESCO in London in order to organize plans for inventories, emergency conservation of objects, and the provision of equipment and supplies to the department of antiquities.

I was called to both meetings in order to discuss practical plans and strategies. At the time I was optimistic and hoped that real steps for assistance would be taken following the list of urgent requirements that we, a small international group of experts, had drawn up there. But clearly there were to be both diplomatic and military obstacles to all these plans.

Very soon after the meetings I became frustrated with the lack of institutionalized action and resolved to make my own way to Iraq, independently of any academic institution or NGO. I had no clear idea of what exactly I would do once I got there, but I knew that I had to go. It is true that there were real risks involved that kept scholars or institutions from acting and the Coalition Provisional Authority from granting permission for in-country clearances. But at the time it did not occur to me to think of the security risks; and even if I had, those risks meant nothing in the face of the disaster with which I was confronted as both an Iraqi and a Mesopotamian archaeologist.

I hope that you will indulge me when I dwell upon my own personal response here. There is a point to it that has to do with the topic of this seminar, on the moral and military choices affecting cultural heritage and war. Because the immediate decisions that we as scholars and intellectuals must make at such times, can and do have an effect on the situation. But first I will give you an account of the conditions of the Iraqi National Museum, the Iraqi State Organization of Antiquities and Heritage, and the extent of losses and damage I found there in the summer of 2003.

The building that houses the State Organization of Antiquities and Heritage, as well as the National Museum, had been ransacked, looted and damaged. Everywhere doors had huge gaping holes in them. Of the office furniture, only a handful of chairs remained. All the files and cabinets had been ransacked. There was only sporadic electricity and there was certainly no telephone or email communication.

From the museum's galleries, forty works were originally stolen. Some of the gallery's cases were smashed, and the staircase leading to the upper gallery was destroyed when looters dragged a large copper sculpture down the stairs. One of the most important looted objects was recovered on 3 November. It is an Akkadian seated male nude, dating to 2300 BC, that bears an inscription of the Akkadian King, Naram-Sin. Many archaeologists had given up on this piece, assuming that it had been melted down by looters. The fact that it had not been melted and was hidden intact indicates that the looters knew of its potential value on the antiquities market.

A list of the 'Top 40' missing objects was compiled by the military investigators and sent to international law enforcement authorities. Thanks to their tremendous efforts, 13 of these objects have now been recovered. Other major objects that are still missing are a diorite portrait of the Sumerian ruler Enmetena, dating to 2450 BC; a portrait of a high priest of the same date; and a number of ivories from Nimrud of the first millennium BC, and some rare and important post-Hellenistic sculptures.

Rare Greek-style sculptures were decapitated, their heads almost certainly taken by looters to be sold in the antiquities market. This was not a case of iconoclasm, but deliberate and well thought-out thefts of classical heads that sell very well in the West. There is no question that the looting involved a faction of professional antiquities thieves, who knew exactly what sorts of objects to take, where to find them within the museum galleries and storage rooms, and what types of objects would fetch the best prices in the antiquities market. Among the main challenges that lie ahead are simply to convince museums and collectors here in the United States to stop buying antiquities looted in Iraq, or any other country for that matter.

The inventory of objects remaining in the storage rooms after the looting is still to be undertaken. Because of the horrendous mess that the looters left behind, the remains in the storage room must be analyzed and recorded, carefully and systematically, fragment by fragment and layer by layer, as in the methods used in an archaeological excavation. In my estimate it will take at least five years to do a thorough inventory and condition report according to international museum standards.

A large number of the missing objects from the storage rooms are cylinder seals, very popular among collectors of antiquities. These are very small cylindrical objects carved out of precious stones that were used to authenticate documents and were worn as personal amulets and ornaments by the Mesopotamians. They are only about an inch or two in length and so are very easy to smuggle.

A more pressing problem right now is the ongoing looting and plunder at archaeological sites. There are about 10,000 listed archaeological sites in Iraq and many more that have not yet been listed. These sites need to be guarded from looters because the damage that occurs during illicit digging can never be mended. Entire histories are lost forever in this way. Our colleagues in Baghdad inform us that two or three ancient cities have been totally destroyed by postwar looting already. Entire armies of looters dug up the ancient city of Isin. The mounds at the site of Larsa were created by looters; the site actually would be rather flat. At the site of Nimrud a relief of a winged sun disk was hacked out of the Assyrian palace wall, of the ninth century BC. This is not a case of random looting. This is a carefully selected segment of a palace wall, commissioned no doubt by a specific buyer.

Again, the market for objects obtained through such looting is made up of collectors and some museums in the West. Obviously, there is little border security in Iraq. It is easy to smuggle antiquities across and sell them in the neighboring countries, labeled as Jordanian or Syrian antiquities. I have personally seen several cases in which obviously Iraqi-type antiquities are sold as Jordanian.

Another urgent concern is the potential destruction of archaeological sites as a result of large-scale construction and development. Two postwar airport projects have already damaged two important sites, Ur and Nineveh. Before a contract for construction is given to any company, that site must be surveyed by archeologists in order to make sure that minimum destruction occurs through the development. Such requirements were part of the existing antiquities law of Iraq, established in the 1930s at the time of independence from British rule, and they should not now be ignored by the Coalition Provisional Authority. The CPA must also protect the archaeological sites by providing paid guards and an antiquities police. I understand that plans are now underway for the provision of about two thousand such guards. This and the protection of sites from development is standard in countries that are rich in antiquities, such as Greece, Egypt and Italy, and the same care and protection should be given to Iraq's antiquities by any ruling authorities. While progress in the recovery of lost works has been encouraging, and the work of the US military investigation can only be described as herculean, much work remains to be done before we can say that proper steps have been taken to ensure the protection of the cultural heritage of Iraq.

On the positive side, we have amazing stories of some almost miraculous recoveries. I have already mentioned the Akkadian statue found on 3 November. Among the best-known works that were stolen from the Iraqi National Museum were the marble head from Uruk and the Uruk vase (Figure 8), both dating to 3300 BC. This vase appears in every survey textbook on world art history and is one of the earliest narrative works of art ever to be made. It was rescued in June, thanks to the great efforts of Captain John Durkin from New York. The vase was returned in pieces, but these were old breaks that can now be repaired (Figure 9). The Uruk head, probably a very early representation of the great Sumerian goddess Inanna, was returned in September 2003. Both objects were originally excavated in the sacred precinct of the goddess in southern Iraq. Both objects are 'firsts' from the perspective of art history: the first narrative sculpture, the first identifiable ritual scene, the first encapsulation of an ideology, the first cult statue of an identifiable deity. So when the museum was looted and objects such as these were lost, they were lamented as a tragedy for world cultural heritage.

As an art historian speaking to the press, I too resorted to the concept of global cultural heritage. But what I want to stress here is that for the people of Iraq it was more than that. It was the looting and the destruction of our own history, a history that forms the basis of the identity of the people of this very ancient land. For myself, hearing of the loss on April 12 was devastating. The Iraqi National Museum was the first museum I ever saw. And Mesopotamian antiquities are the first works of art that I ever encountered. It was through works such as the

Uruk head and vase that I first came to be fascinated by art, that I first encountered sculpture. Mesopotamian artefacts, therefore, formed my very first associations with the notions of history and of art. To those scholars of culture who claim that the concept of cultural heritage is a modern Western development that ought not to be imposed universally, I would like to issue a word of caution. It is easy to move from this multi-culturalist argument to the belief that such refinements as aesthetic appreciation or an awareness of history are by rights the realm of the West. And from there it is easy to claim that ancient Mesopotamian artefacts are more valued and better protected here than they are by the people of Iraq. These are the same arguments that have been used in the service of the illicit antiquities market, a market that is the direct cause of the continuing looting of Iraq's archaeological sites.

It is true that the destruction of cultural heritage in war is a loss for all the people of the world. But what is important to remember is the fact that cultural destruction has very specific and singular local effects, and these effects are devastating. The concept of global cultural heritage is therefore a two-edged sword. It can be a powerful means of calling for the protection of monuments and artefacts, but at the same time what is lost in the process of nominating certain things as global cultural heritage is the awareness of local relations between people and cultural artefacts. As an art historian and archaeologist, I am able to demonstrate methodically through vast amounts of empirical data and historical documentation that a people's sense of identity and history are formed in relation to monuments and to historical objects. This is precisely why international laws on the protection of cultural heritage during armed conflict exist. The destruction of cultural property, of monuments and public art, during war has been a grave concern to human beings since the very earliest written accounts known to us. If we have an ethical obligation to protect cultural heritage, it is because these objects are directly linked to the survival of human beings.

Historical artefacts, works of art and monuments are the agents of memory, and even of a sense of self. Their loss is psychologically devastating, well beyond the loss that is calculated at numbers of missing objects or the market value of antiquities. I would like to draw a parallel that many here will be able to relate to. New Yorkers can understand this sense of loss, since many of us still mourn the missing World Trade Center structures themselves. While their destruction was certainly an event of world significance, and people everywhere saw it as a tragedy, New Yorkers felt it in a different way, not only because we lost friends and fellow citizens, but because the towers themselves were part of the horizon of our daily lives, part of the identity of our city. It was precisely this power of monuments and their relationship to a sense of local identity that the Mesopotamians seem to have understood very well.

In my own research and writing I have always been interested in the concept of an historical consciousness, a consciousness that I consider to be distinctive of Mesopotamian culture. The majority of Mesopotamian works of art were made with an acute awareness of the future, with an awareness of notions of historical time and its relation to monuments. It is remarkable that the loss of objects from Iraq's museums and archaeological sites in the past months would have been understood by the ancients as a sign of the destruction of local identity. In their own cultural and historical context, the artefacts would have been considered social agents of cultural memory. This is why Assyrian and Babylonian kings of the first millennium BC, such as Ashurbanipal and Nabonidus, protected ancient texts and sculptures, objects that were already by then thousands of years old. This is the reason that they protected and restored ancient public monuments, excavated temples and restored their foundation stones. The survival of these monuments was considered to be directly linked to the survival of the people and the land.

On the other hand, it is true that antiquity can be, and has been, used for extreme nationalist agendas and likewise in ethnic cleansing. Cultural property cannot be and has never been detached from war and segregated into its own untainted humanist realm. It would seem even more important, then, that the international protection of heritage should not be suspended in times of war. In peacetime, admirable humanist ideals like global cultural heritage are easier to uphold. Indeed, it is precisely when it becomes difficult to protect cultural heritage, in times of war, political chaos or upheaval, that we must consider it our moral obligation to do so.

4

In the fray: British and Swiss get tough about smuggling

Wall Street Journal, 18 February 2004

في‘ المَعمَعة: البريطانيون والسويسريون أصبحوا مُتَشَدِّدين تجاه التهريب’ *وول ستريت جورنال*، 18 شباط، 2004.

Synopsis

In this short article written for *The Wall Street Journal*, I point out the marketing of the materials looted from the museums, archives and libraries of Iraq, as well as from numerous archaeological sites. Because the many looted cultural works were destined for a lucrative global market in cultural goods, one with its most important centres in the US and Western Europe, the choice to publish it in the *Wall Street Journal* was deliberate for this particular aspect of cultural loss and destruction.

المستخلص

في هذه المقالة القصيرة التي كُتِبَت لصحيفة *الوول* ستريت، أَشَرْتُ إلى تسويق المواد المسروقة من المتاحِف، والأرشيف، والمكتبات في العراق، فضلاً عن عدد كبير من المواقع الأثريّة. لأنّ الكثير من الأعمال الثقافية المسروقة يَؤولُ مَصيرُها الى سوقٍ عالميةٍ مُربِحة خاصة بالسِلَع الثقافيّة، والتي تُعدُّ الولايات المتّحِدة وأوروبا الغَربيّة من أبرَز مراكزها، لذا جاء خَيارُ النَّشرِ في صحيفة *الوول* ستريت عَمْداً للتوعية في هذا الجانِب تحديداً من الخَسارة الثقافية والدمار.

British and Swiss get tough about smuggling

International laws covering art and antiquities have gone through major changes in the past year, largely as a result of the war in Iraq. Not since the

1970 UNESCO Convention on the Means of Prohibiting and Preventing the Illicit Import, Export and Transfer of Ownership of Cultural Property have they attracted so much international attention.

Earlier this month saw Not For Sale, a two-day Swiss–British conference, held in Geneva, on the traffic in artefacts from Iraq, Afghanistan and elsewhere. Bringing together an unusual group of antiquities dealers, collectors, academics, museum professionals, politicians, diplomats and law-enforcement officials from around the world, it was organized to discuss the implementation of new laws passed by Britain and Switzerland, and to consider strategies for better policing and tracking down of illegally excavated as well as stolen antiquities.

Both countries were known for being clearinghouses for stolen antiquities. To rectify that, they are now acceding to the Convention. In addition, last December Britain passed the Dealing in Cultural Objects (Offences) Act, which makes it illegal to knowingly deal in stolen artefacts. Both countries have also decided to adhere to UN Resolution 1483, passed last May, that calls for an international ban on the trade in Iraqi cultural property. To give the force of law to this resolve, the UK last year passed The Iraq Order 2003, which makes it a criminal offense to possess or deal in Iraqi cultural property removed from Iraq after 1990. The aim of these steps is to stifle illicit trafficking by introducing greater transparency to the antiquities market.

In addition, the two countries have agreed on the need for more cooperation among art professionals, academics and law-enforcement agencies; to set up expert task forces to work with law enforcement; and to create databases to track stolen artefacts.

The market in illicit antiquities is global. Along with trafficking in drugs and arms, it is one of the most widespread crimes. Iraq has lately become the crux of the problem of the global black market in antiquities because of the increased amount of theft. The Coalition Provisional Authority has only just been able to begin organizing and training an archaeological protection service, and once looted, antiquities can be moved easily across borders because of the general lack of security.

The looting of the Iraq Museum last April and the subsequent recovery of a number of its major objects – thanks to the US military investigation and military police – have received a lot of publicity. However, a continuing problem is the raiding of archaeological sites and the smuggling of a large number of antiquities out of the country. This has received much less attention from the media.

The extent of illicit excavation in Iraq today is unprecedented. Iraqi archaeologists and the CPA ministry of culture report that in the past 10 months the destruction at archaeological sites has reached a previously unimagined level. Local looters dig up antiquities, which are then taken out of the country to be sold on the black market. These objects range in size from three-inch-tall cylinder seals carved out of semiprecious stones, which can be easily concealed in a jacket pocket, to large-scale sculptures removed from the palace walls of the Assyrian kings (such as Ashurnasirpal's palace at Nimrud, 883–859 BC; see Figure 10). These antiquities have surfaced in the US, Switzerland, Italy and the UK.

While some objects can be recovered and have been, there is no reversing the damage inflicted on the ancient sites by the plunderers. Archaeology is a slow, painstaking process, in which scholars and their assistants excavate a site with the utmost care to avoid accidentally damaging or destroying still-buried objects, tombs, palaces and other historical evidence. Yet the looters' indiscriminate, illicit digging inevitably results in the destruction of the scientific and historical context. Since last April, entire ancient Mesopotamian cities such as Isin, Larsa and Mashkan-shapir – all of them major Babylonian metropolises – have been destroyed in this way in Iraq. It is no exaggeration to say that we are witnessing a large-scale destruction of Mesopotamian history – a history that, once gone, can never be retrieved.

Without the guards at ancient sites and police at border points in the country, Iraqi cultural heritage will continue to be plundered. Fortunately, however, the new laws passed by Switzerland and the UK will make it harder to bring those looted objects to market. It is a first step, but an important one, in stopping the worldwide traffic in stolen antiquities.

5

Days of plunder

The Guardian, 31 August 2004[1]

أيّامُ' النَّهْب' *الغارديان* 31 آب، 2004.

Synopsis

I wrote this article on the same night that I returned to New York from Baghdad. It was the end of August 2004, and I had spent the spring and summer of 2004 as the Senior Advisor to Iraq's Minister of Culture. The article is a first-hand account that exposes the US and coalition military destruction of heritage sites, especially the occupation of the military base at Babylon – a site where I worked for most of that summer, conducting a survey of war damage with Iraqi archaeologists there. My experience at Babylon would become the topic of a number of more extensive scholarly articles that I was to write over the next few years.

المستخلص

لَقَد كَتَبتُ هذه المقالة في اللَّيلة ذاتِها التي وَصَلتُ فيها إلى نيويورك عائِدةً من بغداد. كان ذلك في أواخِرِ شَهر آب من عام 2004، وكُنتُ قد قَضَيتُ رَبيَع وصيفَ عام 2004 كمستشارٍ أوّل لوزارة الثَّقافة العراقيّة. إنّ هذه المقالة تُمَثِّل رِوايةً مُباشِرة تَفضَح الدَمار الذي تَسَبَّبَ به الجَيش الأمريكي وقُوّات التَحالُف للمواقع التراثية، خاصةً ما يتعلَّق باحتلال القاعِدة العسكرية في بابل – حَيثُ الموقع الذي عَمَلتُ فيه مُعظَم ذلك الصَيف، وأجْرَيتُ فيه، برِفقةِ آثاريين عراقيين، مَسْحاً للأضرار التي خَلَّفَتْها الحَرْب هناك. ستُصبحُ تجربتي هذه في بابل موضوعاً لعَدَدٍ من المقالات العلميّة التي تناوَلَتها باستفاضةٍ أكثر والتي قُمتُ بكتابَتِها لاحِقاً عبرَ السنواتِ القادِمة.

Coalition forces are doing little to prevent the widespread looting and destruction of Iraq's world-famous historical sites

The destruction of the Bamiyan Buddhas by the Taliban was met with an outcry in the United States, Britain and the countries that form the coalition in Iraq. Yet the coalition forces can now claim, among other things, the destruction of the legendary city of Babylon.

Ironically, the bombing campaign of 2003 had not damaged archaeological sites. It was only in the aftermath, during the occupation, that the most extensive cultural destruction took place. At first there was the looting of the museums, under the watch of coalition troops, but that was to be followed by more extensive and active destruction.

Active damage of the historical record is ongoing at several archaeological sites occupied as military camps. At Babylon, I have seen the continuing construction projects, the removal of and digging into the ancient mounds over the past three months, despite a coalition press release early in June stating that work would halt, and the camp would be removed.

A helicopter landing zone, built in the heart of the ancient city, removed layers of archaeological earth from the site. The daily flights of the helicopters rattle the ancient walls and the winds created by their rotors blast sand against the fragile bricks (see Figure 11). When my colleague at the site, Maryam Moussa, and I asked military personnel in charge that the helipad be shut down, the response was that it had to remain open for security reasons, for the safety of the troops.

Between May and August, the wall of the Temple of Nabu and the roof of the Temple of Ninmah, both sixth century BC, collapsed as a result of the movement of helicopters. Nearby, heavy machines and vehicles stand parked on the remains of a Greek theatre from the era of Alexander of Macedon. The minister of culture has asked for the removal of military bases from all archaeological sites, but none has yet been relocated.

Iraq is ancient Mesopotamia, otherwise called the 'cradle of civilisation'. It has more than 10,000 listed archaeological sites, as well as hundreds of medieval and Ottoman Muslim, Christian and Jewish monuments. The coalition did not establish a means of guarding the sites, though they would be protected in any other country rich in antiquities. As a result, archaeological sites are being looted to an extent previously unimagined.

The looting supplies the appetites of an international illicit trade in antiquities, and many objects end up in places like Geneva, London, Tokyo and New York. The lack of border controls has only added to the ease with which the illegal trade in Mesopotamian artefacts functions. The looting leaves the sites bulldozed and pitted with robber holes. Ancient walls, artefacts, scientific data are all destroyed in the process.

But it is not only the stolen artefacts that are lost. The loss of this data is the loss of the ancient history of this land. Many important Sumerian and Babylonian cities have been irreversibly damaged in this way already. Passive destruction of this kind has been widespread under the occupation, but antiquity is not the only area of concern.

In Baghdad, the National Library and State Archives building is a burned-out shell in which the employees work in the most horrendous conditions. The Ottoman archive that records the history of the country, spanning the sixteenth to the early twentieth centuries, is in the gravest danger. Having been soaked by flooding last year, the archive began to mould. Upon the advice of conservators, the entire archive was removed to freezers to stop the mould.

Because of the lack of electricity and equipment, the only place that could be found with large freezers, and where power could be maintained, was an abandoned and bombed building that had previously been a Baathist officers' club. In Iraq, where it is not unusual for temperatures to soar up to 60C (140F) in summer, and where the Coalition Provisional Authority never managed to restore the electrical power to the country, this was no small feat.

The power in Baghdad (outside the US-occupied presidential palace and embassy buildings) is available, sporadically, about nine hours a day. If the archives should thaw, the documents will be destroyed. The conservation process needs to be done in a time- and climate-controlled manner if the archive is to be saved. But the Coalition Provisional Authority reassigned ownership of this building to the ministry of justice. There is now still no place to move this archive to, the loss of which would be the loss of the modern historical records of Iraq, much of which has not been studied or published.

In the midst of the disasters of Iraq under occupation, the condition of its cultural heritage may seem a trivial matter. But, as a historian of antiquity, I am painfully aware that there is no parallel for the amount of historical destruction that has taken place over the past 15 months in Iraq. The Geneva and Hague conventions make the protection of heritage the responsibility of the foreign powers during occupation.

Instead, what we have seen under the occupation is a general policy of neglect and even an active destruction of the historical and archaeological record of the land.

Note

1 https://www.guardian.co.uk/comment/story/0,,1293931,00.html.

6

Iraq's cultural heritage: monuments, history and loss

Metropolitan Museum of Art, 8 May 2003

المَوروث‘ الحضاري للعراق: الآثار، والتاريخ والخَسارة‘ متحَف الميتروبوليتان للفن، 8 آيار، 2003.

Synopsis

This paper was presented as a public lecture at the Metropolitan Museum of Art in New York, in the context of a symposium that the museum held in connection with the exhibition *Art of the First Cities: The Third Millennium BC from the Mediterranean to the Indus*; it was published in *Art Journal* the following year. In both the lecture and the article, I presented a personal account of my experience as a girl in Baghdad, learning about art, sculpture and monuments from the collection in the Iraq Museum. The initial presentation at the Metropolitan Museum was only days after the news of the looting and destruction of Iraq's museums and libraries was first reported. For the *Art Journal* article that followed, the text was updated with a discussion of what was known about the antiquities looted from the Iraq Museum at the time of publication. The paper provides a description of some of the major pieces that were lost, explaining them as archaeological and art-historical works in the sociohistorical context of the ancient Mesopotamian world in which they were produced. Thematically, it focuses on the relationship between history, monuments and one's sense of place in the world, and how that comes to be disrupted in war – thus resulting in forms of grief that are not limited to the violence of war and death counts but that seep into the environment of the living. The article argues that for the ancient peoples of Mesopotamia, the loss or destruction of these objects in war would have been understood as the erasure and destruction of memory and history, a loss not limited to personal representation, but a communal loss leading to collective grief and lamentation.

المستخلص

لَقَد عُرِضَت هذه الورقة البحثية كمحاضرة عامة أُلْقِيَت في متحف الميتروبوليتان للفن في نيويورك، ضمنَ سياقِ ندوةٍ أقامَها المتحَف والمُتَعَلِّقة بمعرض *فَن المُدُن الأولى: الألفية الثالثة قبل الميلاد من البحر الأبيض المتوسِّط إلى نهر السِند*؛ وقَد نُشِرَت في *آرت جورنال* (*Art Journal*) في العام التالي . في كُلٍّ من المحاضرة والمقالة، قمتُ بتقديم روايةٍ ذاتيّةٍ عن تجربتي كفتاةٍ في بغداد، تَتَعَرَّف على الفن، والنَّحت والآثار من المجموعة الموجودة في المتحف العراقي. إن العرض الأولي لفحوى هذه المقالة في متحف الميتروبوليتان كان بعد عدة أيامٍ فقط من أول أخبار النَّهْب والدمار الَّذين لَحِقا بالمتاحف والمكتبات العراقية. بالنسبة للمقالة اللاحِقة في *الآرت جورنال*، تم تحديث وتعزيزُ النَّص بمناقشةٍ عمّا كان معلوماً حول الآثار المنهوبة من المتحف العراقي في زمن النَّشر. قَدَّمَت المقالة وَصفاً لبَعض القِطَع بالِغَة الأهميّة التي فُقِدَت، فَضلاً عن تفسيرِها بوَصفِها أعمالاً أثريةً وفنية-تاريخية ضِمن سِياقٍ اجتماعي- تاريخي لِعالَم وادي الرافِدَين القَديم حَيثُ تمَّ إنتاجُها. ركَّزَت المقالة في موضوعِها على العِلاقة بين التاريخ، والآثار وإحساس الفَرْد بالمكان في العالم، وكَيفَ كانَ لذلك أن يتزَعزَع إبانَ الحَرب—مِمّا تَسَبَّبَ بأشْكالٍ من الأسى لا تَقتَصِر على عُنف الحَرْب وأعداد الأرواح التي أُزهِقَت إذ أنَّها امتَدَّت لتَشمِل بيئة الأحياء. تُحاجِج المقالة بأنَّه بالنسبة لِلشُعوب القديمة لوادي الرافِدَين، فإنَّ خَسارة أو هَدْم هذه التُحَف في الحَرب سيُفْهَم حينَها على أنَّه مَحوٌ وتَدميرٌ للذاكرة والتاريخ، وخَسارَةٌ لا تَقتَصِرُ على التمثيل الشَخصي، بَلْ إنَّها خَسارَةٌ مُجْتَمَعيّة تَدَعُنا مع أسىً وألَمٍ جَمْعي.

7

The destruction of cultural heritage in Iraq

Not for Sale: A Swiss–British conference on the traffic in artefacts from Iraq, Afghanistan and beyond, edited by Matt Kimmich, 18–20. Bern: The British Council, 2004

’ تَدمير المَوروث الحَضاري في العِراق‘ في *لَيسَ لِلبَيع:*
المؤتمر السويسري-البريطاني عن الاتجّار باللُّقى الأثَريّة
من العِراق، وأفغانستان وما وَرائِهما، المُحَرِّر مات كيمِش،
18–20، بيرن: المجلس الثقافي البريطاني، 2004.

Synopsis

This paper was presented at Not for Sale, a conference held at the University of Geneva, in the context of a panel titled ‘Politics, Legal Frameworks, Damage and Ethics’, to discuss the pressing issue of antiquities trafficking, which by February of 2004, when the conference took place, was clearly mounting. Antiquities, medieval manuscripts, and works of modern art from recently occupied Iraq were now appearing in the West and in the Gulf countries at levels that were previously unseen. Some were clearly works looted from museum collections and libraries, while others were newly dug up amid the increased looting of archaeological sites. Because I had been in Iraq in the spring and summer of 2003, I here discussed the conditions at the Iraq Museum in Baghdad and at various archaeological sites throughout the country. As the conference was attended by diplomats as well as curators and scholars, I raised the question of the legal frameworks set in place by the occupation, which had so greatly impacted the loss of cultural property. The interconnection of de-Baathification policy, new legal parameters and international free-market ideas permitted or at least eased the export of freshly dug-up antiquities, manuscripts and transportable works – including paintings and sculptures by twentieth-century Modernists, not usually taken into account in archaeological discussions of heritage at that time. Many of the latter artworks in fact ended up in private collections in places like the Gulf countries and Western Europe. The works that were lost during that first year of the war began to be tallied, focusing on the contents of the Iraq Museum, which is the country's main archaeological museum. But within a few months it became clear that the range of works was much greater, and that their appropriation involved an international network of participants.

المستخلص

لقد تم تقديم هذه الورقة البَحثيّة في المؤتمر الذي أُقيمَ في جامعة جنيف، *ليسَ للبَيْع*، في سِياق حَلَقة نِقاش بعنوان ' السياسة، والأُطُر القانونيّة، والضَرَر والأخلاق'، لمُناقَشة القَضيّة المُلِحَّة الخاصّة بالاتِّجار بالآثار، والتي كانَت، حينَ عُقِدَ المؤتمر في شباط 2004، تَتَفاقَم بوضوح. إذ بَدَأَت حينَها الآثار، ومَخطوطات العصور الوسطى، وأعمال الفَن الحَديث مِن العِراق المُحتَل في الآونة الأخيرة بالظُهور في الغَرْب وفي دُوَل الخَليج بمُستَويات غَير مَسبوقة. لقد كانَ واضِحاً بأنَّ البَعض منها كان قَد سُرِقَ من مجموعات المتحف ومن المكتَبات، بينما الأُخرى كانَت قد استُخرِجَت حديثاً وَسْطَ تزايُد أعمال النَّهْب للمواقِع الأثَريّة. ولأنني كنت في العراق في ربيع وصيف عام 2003، فقد ناقشت هنا الأوضاعَ في المتحف العراقي في بغداد وفي مختلف المواقع الأثرية في جميع أنحاء البلاد. بما أنَّ هذا المؤتمر قد شَهد حضور دبلوماسيين فضلاً عن أُمَناء متاحف وباحثين، لِذا أَثَرْتُ مسألةَ الأُطُر القانونيّة التي فَرَضَها الاحتلال، والتي كانَ لها بالِغَ الأثَر في خَسارَة المُلكيّة الثقافيّة. لقد سَمَحت تِلك الصِلة بين سياسة اجتثاث البَعث، والمعايير القانونية الجديدة وأفكار السوق الحُرّة الدوَليّة أو على الأقَل يَسَّرَت تَصديرَ الآثار والمَخطوطات والأعمال القابِلة للنَقْل التي تم استخراجُها حديثاً— بما في ذلك لوحات ومَنحوتات فَنّاني الحَداثة في القَرن العشرين والتي لَم تكُن عادةً لِتَلْقى نصيباً من الاهتمام حينَها في المناقشات التي تدور في مُجتَمَع الآثاريين حول التُراث. إنّ كثيراً من الأعمال الفَنيّة الأخيرة انتَهى بها الأمْر في الواقِع لتُصبِحَ ضِمن مجموعاتٍ خاصّة في أماكن مثلَ دولِ الخَليج وغَرْب أوروبا. تمَّ إحصاءُ الأعمال التي فُقِدت خلال تلك السنة الأولى من الحرب، وقد كان التركيز من نصيب محتويات المتحف العراقي الذي يُعدُّ المتحف الأثري الأساس في البَلَد. إلّا أنّ الأشهُر القليلة التي تَلَت ذلك كَشَفَت عن إن نطاق الأعمال المَفقودة كان أكبر بكثير ممّا تَمَّ إحصاؤه، وأن الاستيلاء عليها قد اشتَرَكَ فيه العديد من المُتَسَبِّبين في تِلكَ الخَسارة من مختلَف الدوَل.

The looting of the Iraq Museum last April was reported widely in the press, and if you will remember, the pendulum swung in both directions. The press first informed us that the entire collection was gone but later insisted that only 33 objects were actually missing. There was a great deal of discussion of where the responsibility lay, and the blame was shifted around between the US and UK military, the Pentagon, the curators of the Iraq Museum, and so on. Likewise, with the second aspect of the destruction of Iraq's heritage, the looting at the archaeological sites, and the appearance of antiquities outside Iraq, the question of responsibility has arisen. Ambassadors Cordone and Bondioli Osio have given the official reports on the situation. But I am told that I am allowed to raise some points for discussion, and rather than going over numbers and figures or summarising the plans being made for the future by the Coalition Provisional Authority or international NGOs, I will instead raise the question of ethical responsibilities involved in the protection of Iraq's cultural heritage from plunder in the postwar situation today, and the theoretical-ideological basis upon which the trade in illicit antiquities from Iraq is functioning. I would also like to suggest that the case of Iraq might make those of us who are experts and professionals in the field of cultural heritage consider new ways of dealing with such disasters when, and preferably before, they arise.

My first point or question therefore is this: How does the legal authority for decision making regarding cultural heritage affect the loss of cultural property? The looting of the museums occurred because there was chaos, there were no guards, and the continuing looting at archaeological sites is, of course, a similar situation. There are thus two aspects of the trade in illicit antiquities coming out of Iraq today. The first, well known from the press and television coverage, is the looting at the museums and libraries in April 2003; the second, covered much less in the press, is the horrendous plunder at the archaeological sites. The truth of the matter is that in the past ten months, the cultural heritage of Iraq has suffered an immense number of losses and it continues today. In fact, the extent of the loss, the theft and looting of cultural property in the past months is unprecedented in Iraq's history. As a historian of antiquity I am painfully aware that there is no historical parallel for the amount of destruction that has taken place over the past ten months. In the Iraqi example of the illicit trade in antiquities, we can circle around the issue of the current looting taking place today, but in the end I think we must confront the fact that it is now primarily a matter of lack of law enforcement.

The rescue efforts that followed the museum thefts of April 2003, and the US military investigation into the looting conducted during the summer months have received a great deal of coverage in the media and the rescue efforts of the US military, as I have said elsewhere, are not only commendable – they can only be described as Herculean. The progress in recovery of objects from the museum has really been tremendous, but the cultural heritage of Iraq continues to be destroyed. Besides the Iraq Museum in Baghdad, the Mosul Museum of antiquities, the Museum of Modern Art and a number of important libraries and collections of manuscripts were also looted and damaged. Although a cursory report on libraries was submitted by a Library of Congress team that was in Iraq for a few days last November, thorough and methodical assessments of losses to these collections have yet to be made. Most of the rescue effort has focused on the Iraq Museum and plans for the renovation of the museum are under way, funded primarily by the US State Department, but a thorough inventory of the collections will take years to complete. Only then can we know the exact amount and nature of missing objects, so that we can stop their movement across borders and repatriate those objects that have appeared outside Iraq.

The other part of the looting is taking place at the over 10,000 archaeological sites in Iraq. The illicit looting at these sites has reached a previously unimagined extent. Several ancient cities have been destroyed completely in this way in recent months. Antiquities from these Iraqi sites are then sold on the international black market. These Mesopotamian or Iraqi antiquities end up in the United States, Western Europe, Israel and Japan. My second point of discussion is this: that we must confront the theoretical, political and ideological basis upon which this market flourishes and upon which collecting illicitly acquired antiquities, far from being socially considered as the international crime that it is, is so often lauded as an elegant humanist pastime of highly cultured individuals.

I would like to stress that the looting of antiquities is an export business. It is not for local museums or private collections in the source country. Museums and collectors, the consumer end of the market, when they are not careful to take steps to check provenance, ought to bear much of the responsibility for the destruction. This destruction is not simply limited to the loss of objects that might be found and repatriated at a later time. What is worse even than the loss of the objects is the destruction of the context in the process of the plundering, buildings, cities, artefacts, scientific information, settlement patterns, archival data. History itself is destroyed.

Ironically, the illicit antiquities trade is ideologically supported by the notion of 'global cultural heritage' itself. Cultural artefacts have been considered the available realm of free market enterprise because, collectors and dealers argue, they belong to all of us, and that they value and protect them when they buy them for their own collections. More importantly now we have the added ideological argument of anti-nationalism. Nationalism has been criticised and for very good reasons; however, the anti-nationalist arguments have been very serviceable for the illicit trade in antiquities. The new situation in Iraq has brought this issue to the fore. I have heard it said, even by seemingly liberal thinkers, that these antiquities are not actually the rightful property or heritage of the people of Iraq since Iraq is an artificial postcolonial nation state with borders drawn by colonial powers after the collapse of the Ottoman empire. Obviously, such arguments work very well in the service of the illicit antiquities trade. These new discussions regarding the allegedly proper or correct identification of the geographical area, Iraq, or Mesopotamia, have had an unacknowledged impact on the illicit trade in antiquities. The exploitation and consumption of other peoples' cultural heritage can thus be articulated in political and economic terms. It is not simply a matter of organised criminal activity, it is a matter of ideological belief in the right of ownership of cultural property.

Then there is the problem in the source country, Iraq. Artefacts are sold in Iraq and are going across the border. Archaeological sites are plundered for antiquities, and entire cities have been destroyed this way. Some archaeological sites are being damaged by development and construction as well as by expanding military installations. Since April 2003, the authority to make decisions about Iraq's cultural heritage has been in the hands of the CPA [Coalition Provisional Authority]. International laws regarding the responsibility for cultural heritage during occupation exist, but it seems to me that the ethical and moral thing to do, regardless of international laws, is to protect the cultural heritage of the world, a heritage which is our joint history and for which we bear the responsibility to future generations to protect. It is also the responsibility of international experts in the field of cultural-heritage management as well as scholars and intellectuals to call for a greater effort in the protection of this cultural heritage. In conclusion my two main points are: first, that the ideological politico-economic basis of the trade in antiquities needs to be confronted and discussed; and second, the ethical and moral duties of occupying authorities in times of war must be clarified. In peacetime it is easy to uphold ideals of culture and its protection; it is precisely when it becomes difficult to do so, in times of chaos or upheaval, that we must make a greater effort to protect cultural heritage.

Figure 1 Arch of Ctesiphon, Taq Kisra, Iraq, 1932.
Public domain (US Library of Congress).

Figure 2 A US tank stationed at the Iraq Museum, Baghdad, 2003.
Photo Zainab Bahrani.

Figure 3 The author with Donny George Youkhanna, Director of the Iraq Museum, Baghdad, 2003.

Photo from the author's collection, reproduced with the kind permission of Steven George.

Figure 4 The author and colleagues assessing the damage in the galleries of the Iraq Museum, Baghdad, 2003.

Photo from the author's collection.

Figure 5 Broken display cases, Iraq Museum, Baghdad, 2003.

Photo Zainab Bahrani.

Figure 6 Damaged statue of Apollo from Hatra (the head was looted), Iraq Museum, Baghdad, 2003.

Photo Zainab Bahrani.

Figure 7 Damaged ancient glass vessels on the storage room floor, Iraq Museum, Baghdad, 2003.

Photo Zainab Bahrani.

Figure 8 Uruk vase, ca. 3300 BC, Iraq Museum, Baghdad.

Photo Osama Shukir Muhammed Amin (CC BY-SA 4.0).

Figure 9 Uruk vase, broken state, 2003.
Photo Zainab Bahrani.

Figure 10 Archaeologist Muzahim Mahmoud Hussein points to the spot where thieves cut away a part of a sculpture at Nimrud, 2003.
Photo Dominique Collon, from the author's collection.

Figure 11 Helicopter over Babylon, 2004.

Photo Zainab Bahrani.

Figure 12 Coalition military base at the site of Babylon, 2004; notice the tanks stationed in the open area to the right of the palace.

Photo Zainab Bahrani.

Figure 13 Coalition military base at the site of Babylon, 2004: military installations in the centre of the archaeological site.

Photo Zainab Bahrani.

Figure 14 Soldiers in Babylon, in the reconstructed area of the Palace of Nebuchadnezzar (sixth century BC), 2004.

Photo Zainab Bahrani.

Figure 15 Soldiers in Babylon, at the remains of the sixth-century BC Ishtar Gate, 2004.

Photo Zainab Bahrani.

Figure 16 The author inspecting damage to the Ishtar Gate, Babylon, 2004.

Photo from the author's collection.

Figure 17 Archaeologists Maryam Omran Moussa and Haider Almamori surveying tank tracks on archaeological ground at Babylon, 2004.

Photo Zainab Bahrani.

Part II
Military occupation and archaeological discourse

القِسم الثاني: الاحتِلال العَسكَري والخِطاب الآثاري

Preface

تمهيد

Synopsis

Part II covers the topic of Iraq's military occupation. The country, its legal framework for the protection of antiquities and heritage sites, and the transport/export of cultural property were all under the authority of the civil administration of the Coalition Provisional Authority (CPA) headed by Paul Bremer. Iraqi museum professionals and archaeologists were marginalised in favour of decisions taken by military officials, the most obvious example being the use of heritage sites as military barracks. As a network of military bases set at heritage sites covered the land, I became increasingly exasperated by the silence, regarding these abuses of heritage sites, in the press, by organisations such as UNESCO, and among many of the archaeologists who specialise in the region. This part addresses these issues both in articles written from a theoretical-scholarly perspective and in newspaper articles in which I hoped to bring these abuses of heritage sites to the attention of a wider audience among the general public.

المستخلص

يقوم القِسم الثاني بتَغطيةٍ لموضوع الاحتلال العَسكَري للعراق. إذ أنَّ البَلَد، والإطار القانوني لِحِماية المَواقِع الأَثَريّة والتُراثيّة، والنَقل/التَصدير لِلمُلكيّة الثَقافيّة كانَت جميعها تحت سُلطَة الإدارة المَدنية لسلطة التحالف المؤقتة برئاسَة بول بريمَر. تم تهميشُ العاملين في المتاحف وعلماء الآثار العراقيين لصالح القرارات التي اتَّخذُها المسؤولون العسكريون، ويَتَجلّى ذلك بوضوح في استعمال المواقع التراثية كثُكَنات عَسكريّة. لَقَد غَدَت المواقعُ التراثيّة أسيرَةَ شَبَكَةٍ من القَواعِد العَسكريّة التي اَتَّخَذَت مواضِعَها فيها.

كانَ غَضَبي بِيَستَشيط إزاءَ ذلك الصَّمت الإعلامي بشأنِ تلك الانتهاكات التي تَتَعَرَّض لها المواقِع التُراثية، الّذي أبْدَتْه مُنَظَّماتٌ كاليونسكو، بَل سادَ كذلك بَينَ العديد من عُلماء الآثار المُختَصّين بهذه المنطقة. يَتناوَل هذا القِسم تلك القَضايا من خِلال كُلٍّ من المقالات المكتوبة من منظورٍ نظري علمي، والمقالات الصُحفيّة التي كُنتُ آملُ أن ألْفِتَ بِها انتباهَ جمهورٍ أوسَع من بينِ عامّة الناس إلى هذه الانتِهاكات للمواقعِ التُراثيّة.

In Baghdad, especially through the spring and summer of 2004, there was a constant background medley of sounds – a composition of gunshots, explosions, sirens and people running. In the Green Zone, where the old Presidential Palace had been turned into the CPA headquarters, there was also laughter, there was the euphoria of victory and total control. A man sat in an office, positioned in the centre of a small room in the palace, his army-issue beige canvas boots propped up on the desk. Before him was a stack of documents of all the public properties in Iraq that he could allocate as he saw fit.

As much as I was shocked by the bombed cityscape of Baghdad and the calamitous condition of the museums and libraries when I returned, I was still unprepared for what I would encounter next: seeing how property and space were allocated by the CPA, including the way that several heritage sites were commandeered as military bases. These decisions reflected Bremer's CPA Order 9, called 'Management and Use of Iraqi Public Property'.[1]

The aftermath of war, and the in-between time of war, was simply a continuation of war. The end of the shock and awe campaign of the spring of 2003 did not bring an end to the destruction of the country or its historical heritage; it was simply the start of a new phase. The death toll continued to rise under the occupation, and heritage sites continued to be occupied and heavily damaged. Before the war, the Bush administration had constructed an image of Iraq as a barren desert that could benefit from development by private contractors. These contractors were slated to take over every aspect of society, including such areas of life as education, the writing of textbooks for schools, and the heritage sector, as well as, more obviously, industries such as petroleum. They also moved into archaeological sites in order to build the massive bases for the Multi-National Forces (MNF).

That spring and summer, as Senior Advisor to Iraq's Minster of Culture, Mufeed al-Jaza'iri, I was able to enter the military base of Babylon, which the MNF called 'Camp Alpha' or 'The Ruins' (Figures 12–15), to survey the wreckage caused by their installation. Much of my time that summer was spent at Babylon documenting the damage of this encampment (see Figure 16). Despite my vociferous opposition to the war, I had agreed to return to Iraq and to work with al-Jaza'iri. He was a member of the Communist Party of Iraq's Central Committee, a journalist who escaped to Kurdistan during the rule of the Baathist regime; he became a prominent member of the Kurdish opposition, though not himself Kurdish. At the time, there was still a glimmer of hope among Iraqis who opposed the war that we might yet be allowed some form of free elections and could perhaps contribute to a better future. These hopes lasted only a brief instant however, as it soon became clear that the occupation would continue for the long term, and that even in the realm of culture, of archaeology and heritage, we could have little say.

At Babylon I worked closely with the Iraqi archaeologist who had been the director of the site before the war, Dr Maryam Omran Moussa and her assistant, Haider Almamori (who was later to become Professor of Archaeology at the University of Babylon) (see Figure 17). Contemptuously, Maryam was not permitted onto the base if she was not in the company of an American. Although later the Western press lauded Western archaeologists for calling attention to this abuse of Babylon, it was in fact Dr Maryam (as I came to know her) who had raised the alarm and who had travelled from Hillah to Baghdad in order to lodge an official complaint with the American authorities there; it was she who had done the arduous and stressful work of confronting the generals in charge of the base in a series of official meetings at Babylon where I was also present. Together, we spent much of that spring and summer surveying the damage, documenting it for the possibility of a future restitution claim. Although neither of us knew much about the laws of war, Dr Maryam pointed out to the generals in charge that using a heritage site as a military base was clearly a violation. Section 2, Category 1 of Order 9 states that CPA decision-making includes 'property that is assigned to, occupied and used by the CPA, Coalition Forces'.[2] By the laws of occupation, the CPA was thus responsible for the decision of using this heritage site as the one of the largest military bases in Iraq. During several meetings and negotiations with the MNF generals, I asked repeatedly for an international and non-aligned team of archaeologists with expertise in Mesopotamian archaeology to be permitted onto the base in order to assess the situation and conduct an independent survey of the damage, but my request was denied. During Babylon's occupation, UNESCO made no condemnation of this MNF practice, either here or elsewhere in Iraq. But in 2009, with Iraq still under occupation, UNESCO produced a report on the use of the base, titled: 'Report on Damage Assessments in Babylon'.[3] The report, described on its front page as the 'final report on damage assessment', was not made by independent archaeologists but by government employees of the countries in the MNF forces responsible for the damage in the first place. Historians of the future will no doubt question the merit and accuracy of such an internal investigation, produced while the country was still under military occupation. It will be read as part of the fog that war creates. The report itself is thus another artefact of the occupation, just as the destroyed archaeological layers and damaged standing structures will bear the traces and scars of this period, into the future. The investigative file was swiftly closed in 2009, but the extensive documentation that remains, and the tangible evidence on site, will nevertheless allow for restitution claims by later generations.

Ever since I first saw it in 2004, I have always thought that the colossal military base, built right on top of ancient Babylon, was in some way emblematic of the entire occupation of Iraq. Both military and corporate power (if they are not one and the same in war) had installed themselves into the heart of the site, quite literally digging through the present and into the archaeological layers of the past. In the words of Frantz Fanon, colonialism 'turns to the past of the oppressed people, and distorts, disfigures, and destroys it'.[4] They had imposed their barbarous cinder blocks and blast walls across the ancient city, their bulldozers cutting away into the historical remains. At military bases like Babylon, the civilising mission of this war, with its claims to the moral high ground, was so clearly ridiculous.

From April 2003 until December 2004, while Babylon, that ancient city of legendary fame, was in use as a major US and coalition military base, things were different. The Bush administration was in its heyday, and few had the courage to speak out against any of its policies. Halliburton and its subsidiary company KBR bulldozed away into the ancient city, dug trenches and paved helicopter pads, piped in water and piped out sewage for their military employers, without any disturbance from outside complaints. Iraqi antiquities and heritage laws were ignored, and international laws on the protection of cultural heritage during armed conflict were dismissed. Even though part of the occupation forces, among them Poland, who held command of the base after the autumn of 2003, are signatory to the 1954 Hague Convention, such minor legal details appeared to be no obstacle to their construction projects. This convention was breached across Iraq at a number of important historical sites. In 2008, four years after the closing of the Babylon base, UNESCO passed a resolution calling for all parties there to respect Iraq's antiquities and heritage law and the international laws on cultural heritage, but it was too little, too late. The destruction had already taken place, and like so many other aspects of the occupation of Iraq, those who broke the law are not likely to be held accountable. In a final noteworthy decree passed by Bremer just before he left the country, CPA Order 100 gave CPA employees and American contractors immunity from Iraqi law.[5]

When the UNESCO report on Babylon appeared in 2009, I remembered well the closing of that base in December of 2004. It was one of the first of the major US bases to be shut down and dismantled. I remember walking through the site in the midday sun, through that long Babylonian summer, looking at destroyed archaeological layers, seeing sixth-century BC walls with their carved magical creatures that had been hacked away in places by the MNF soldiers, some of whom were stopped with antiquities stuffed into their duffel bags. The ancient ritual processional way of the Babylonian New Year, the Akitu festival, was littered with huge concrete blocks cracking the ancient paving. A fleet of helicopters was constantly taking off and landing next to the palace of Nebuchadnezzar, the propellers sandblasting small pebbles into the ancient temple precinct beyond. The area of the theatre of Alexander the Great was taken over by heavy machinery; that is when the theatre was not in use for the pomp and display of the military ceremonies of the conquering army.

The military base was closed at the end of 2004, but Babylon remained a pawn in the occupation and in the continuing colonial attitude towards Iraq, its people and its heritage. And a number of questions continue to trouble me even now. What does it mean to have a 'final assessment of damage' done at an archaeological site in Iraq while the country was under a foreign military occupation, and when no independent archaeological survey had been conducted? Wouldn't it have been more useful if UNESCO had taken an official stance against the military abuses of cultural heritage sites, say in 2003 or 2004, when KBR was filling sandbags and Hesco containers with pottery and cuneiform tablets, literally using antiquity to shield the MNF troops from the natives?

The situation at Babylon and the Western response to it was not an exception in this war. What the military called Camp Alpha can be taken as a metaphor for the entire occupation of Iraq, as I shall explain in the essays included in this section. Basically, what you saw in Babylon in 2004 was a scene of an arrogant colonial conquest led by corporate greed. The heart of the ancient city was literally covered with Halliburton-KBR signs and equipment, military buildings and blast walls, latrines and cafeterias, and all this contemptuous destruction of our history, taking place under the pretext of bringing us freedom from tyranny. You will not read these details in the 2009 UNESCO report, however. The US and its allies continue to speak about democracy and accountability, but what sort of example are they setting? They repeatedly and flagrantly fly in the face of the United Nations, one of the most noble and democratic institutions that the world has set up. They disregard international laws, even those excellent international conventions on cultural heritage that they established themselves, and which they uphold before us as a standard of civilised behaviour.

The first three pieces included in this part discuss the case of Babylon's occupation as a military base. One was written for the press, while two others were published in scholarly editions. I then turn to Baghdad and to other areas of violence and destruction that took place in the first two years of the war. As an American citizen, I could exercise my privilege to enter locations that other Iraqis were denied. And as an Iraqi citizen, I could go places and see things that foreigners, whether occupation forces or journalists, could not; I spent time in the homes of family and friends, and heard their horrific stories of the war. I spent time in the Iraq Museum, in the storage rooms and archives. This movement back and forth between the so-called Red Zone, where normal Iraqis lived (marked red for danger), and the Green Zone, where the CPA occupation had its headquarters, revealed a great deal, including the way that Iraqi citizens were treated by troops – threatened and made to wait for hours on end at checkpoints in their own city, harassed on the streets and dehumanised on a daily basis. With native-level fluency in both Iraqi Arabic and American English, I could hear clearly that among the troops, a common way to refer to an Iraqi was as an 'Ali-Baba', a 'haji' or a 'sand-n----r'. I recorded these experiences and observations into my handwritten notebooks, but when I returned to New York, I soon learned that there was little interest in hearing the Iraqi side of this war.

In the essay titled 'Desecrating history', written on the five-year anniversary of the war and once again published in *The Guardian*, in the UK, I sought to explain that there was no change in Iraq; there was only a continuing and insistent justification of the coalition's role in the destruction of history and heritage. At the same time that I was voicing my experience to the general public, I became increasingly frustrated by archaeologists and intellectuals who were unwilling to consider that the occupation was detrimental to Iraq. Instead, the field of Mesopotamian archaeology in the US and elsewhere in the West became increasingly militarised.[6] The last essay in this part addresses the relationship of archaeology and warfare, while the piece included here under the title 'October questionnaire' addresses the response of Western intellectuals and artists to the war and occupation. A group of writers and Orientalists who one might have expected to be antiwar, had instead used their voices and expertise to support and build the case for war and occupation, and continued to insist on their just cause, even after the news of Abu Ghraib prison and other crimes against humanity emerged.

Likewise, the expatriate Iraqis who had been willing to speak out against the atrocities of the Saddam regime were silent in the face of acts of torture and violence by the coalition troops, and the black sites of the war on terror, all of which were also done in their (our) name and with their support. The antiwar majority in the US and UK had become subdued. In the Middle East and elsewhere in the world, the days of protest seemed to have gone by without much notice. The state of war became ordinary.

Notes

1 CPA/ORD/08 JUN 2003/09: accessible online via the FDLP Electronic Collection Archive. https://permanent.fdlp.gov/lps46372/cpaord9.pdf.
2 CPA/ORD/08 JUN 2003/09, as at n. 1, above.
3 See https://unesdoc.unesco.org/images/0018/001831/183134E.pdf.
4 Frantz Fanon, *The Wretched of the Earth*. New York: Grove Press, 1963.
5 CPA/ORD/28 JUN 2004/100: https://permanent.fdlp.gov/lps50919/20040628_CPAORD_100_Transition_of_Laws__Regulations__Orders__and_Directives.pdf.
6 See Yannis Hamilakis, 'The "War on Terror" and the military-archaeology complex: Iraq, ethics, and neo-colonialism', *Archaeologies* 5 (2009): 39–65; R. J. González, 'Towards mercenary anthropology? The new US Army counterinsurgency manual FM 3-24 and the military-anthropology complex', *Anthropology Today* 23 (3) (2007): 14–19.

8

Babylon: a case study in the military occupation of an archaeological site

in *Of the Past for the Future: Integrating archaeology and conservation.* Congress proceedings of the conservation theme at the 5th World Archaeological Congress, Washington DC, 22–6 June 2003[1]

’بابِل: دراسة حالة عن الاحتلال العَسكَري لموقِع أَثَري‘ في *من الماضي من أجْل المُستَقبَل: تحقيق التكامُل بين عِلم الآثار والصَوْن.* وَقائِع الكونغرس لِمَوضوع الصَوْن في المؤتمر العالمي الآثاري الخامس، واشِنطُن العاصِمة، 22–26 حُزَيران 2003.

Synopsis

This paper was read in absentia at the conference *Of the Past for the Future: Integrating archaeology and conservation*, because I was in Iraq at the time. The paper, which was included in the conference proceedings after my return to New York, addressed the 2003–4 occupation of Babylon (which at the time of the conference was current) and other archaeological sites in Iraq by US-led military forces, and its physical and psychological ramifications for the cultural heritage and people of Iraq. My argument was that, not unlike the bombing of the Bamiyan Buddhas by the Taliban, a well-known and widely publicised case of religious iconoclasm, the occupation of cultural and historic sites in Iraq was a method of cultural warfare. Concerned about the lack of attention to this area of archaeological theory, my paper proposed a close study and analysis of the way in which occupation, demolition and unconstrained construction and development at ancient sites and historical urban centres have become instruments of war, examining what this may tell us about iconoclastic gestures that are not limited to an iconic erasure but serve to justify the conquest of land.

المستخلص

لقَد تمَّتْ قِراءة هذه الورقة البَحثيّة عنّي غيابيا في مؤتمر من *الماضي من أجل المستقبل: تحقيق التكامُل بين عِلم الآثار والصَوْن*، لأنَّني كُنتُ حينَها في العراق. لَقَد تناولَت هذه الورقة البَحثيّة، التي أُدرِجَت في وقائِع المؤتمَر بعدَ عَودَتي إلى نيويورك، احتلال بابل عام 2003–2004 (والذي كان ما زالَ قائِماً أثناءَ انعقاد هذا المؤتمر) إلى جانِب مواقع أثَريّة أخرى في العراق من قِبَل القوّات العَسكَريّة التي تقودُها الولايات المتحدة، وتداعياته الماديّة والنفسيّة على الموروث الحضاري وعلى شعب العراق. كانت مُحاجَجَتي بأنّ ذلِك لا يَختَلِف عَن تَفجير تماثيل بوذا في باميان على يد طالبان، والتي تُعَدُّ إحدى قَضايا تحطيم الأيقونات الدينية الشَّهيرة والتي حَظِيَت بتَغطيةٍ إعلاميةٍ واسعةِ النِّطاق، إذ إنَّ احتلال المواقعِ الثقافيّة والتاريخيّة في العراق من أساليبِ الحربِ الثقافيّة. بدافعِ من القَلَق بشأن عَدَم الاهتمام بهذا الجانِب من النَظريّة الأثريّة، اقتَرَحت ورقتي البحثيّة دراسةً وتحليلاً دَقيقَين للطريقة التي أصبحَ بها الاحتلال والهَدْم والبِناء والتَطوير غير المُقيَّد في المواقعِ القديمة والمراكِز الحَضَريّة التاريخيّة أدواتٍ للحَرب، مُتَقَصِّيةً بذلك ما قد تُطلِعُنا عَليه بشَأنِ مَلامِح التحطيم الأيقوني التي لا تَقتَصِر على المَحوِ الأيقوني بَل تعمل على تَبرير احتِلال الأرض.

The occupation of Babylon

Babylon, one of the most prominent and important cities in Mesopotamian history, has been seriously damaged as a result of war and occupation by US-led coalition forces.[2] Before the 2003 air campaign in Iraq, archaeologists and scholars of Near Eastern antiquity were well aware of the possible dangers to Iraq's archaeological sites and spoke out publicly and with a united voice regarding the need to protect Iraq's museums, monuments and heritage sites in the case of war.[3] What the scholarly community had not foreseen was that the greater part of the damage to cultural heritage would not occur as a result of the bombing campaign or early ground war against the Iraqi regime. Instead, it was to be the result of the subsequent occupation by the coalition forces. This series of events in Iraq ought to be heeded by the World Archaeological Congress, the scholarly community, conservationists and heritage management professionals, because it is an example of cultural destruction of a kind that is not often addressed in discussions of the protection or treatment of cultural property during war. In particular, the Iraq war has brought to the fore significant issues regarding military use of the historic fabric of the enemy's land. If military conflict implies, at least in part, an aspect that is heavily territorial, then the historic environment as enemy terrain or the territory of conquest is a subject that needs to be addressed more directly by archaeological theory. In hostilities such as the 1990s Balkan wars and territorial conflicts in Palestine–Israel and Cyprus, the use of heritage sites in the formation of identities and territorial disputes has been addressed (Abu El-Haj 2001; Kohl and Fawcett 1995). However, these lessons have not been applied to the practices of the coalition forces in Iraq, either by the popular press and media or in academic writing. The conceptual territory of antiquity and the uses of the past in nineteenth-century imperialist discourse is an area that has been discussed specifically in my earlier work (Bahrani 1998; 2003). Here I address a similar semiotic use of the past, but in this case it is not limited to a conceptual historic terrain. In the example of Babylon (as well as a number of other archaeological sites in Iraq), this symbolic use of the past has taken on a material reality in the physical occupation of antiquity, a reality that has extensively damaged the archaeological remains.

The destruction of the Bamiyan Buddhas by the Taliban regime, as a form of direct iconoclasm, was met with international cries of outrage. Yet there has been relative silence in response to the destruction of standing monuments and heritage sites in Iraq. What are the factors that make one type of cultural destruction (iconoclasm of figural images) seem horrendous and unacceptable and another (destruction of nonfigural archaeological sites or standing monuments) more readily acceptable as part of the collateral damage of war? Here I examine the case of Babylon, an ancient city whose fame is of legendary proportion, and consider its treatment as a result of armed conflict, as well as what ought to have been done to avert the extensive damage that has taken place. I also argue that the occupation and destruction of a legendary site such as Babylon can be read along the same theoretical lines as iconoclastic acts.

Through his renowned study, *The Power of Images*, David Freedberg has shown that acts of destruction we call iconoclasm reveal a belief in the power of the image rather than a disregard for it (Freedberg 1989). In response to the destruction of the Bamiyan Buddhas, he wrote convincingly that this was a perfect indication of the Taliban's fear of the power of these magnificent colossal images (Freedberg 2001). The occupation and consequent destruction of Babylon by coalition forces, it can be argued, reveals a similar ambivalence to that manifested in the iconoclastic destruction of more direct forms of pictorial representation. The destruction of the site takes place, not because of a disregard or lack of interest in Babylon or Mesopotamian antiquity, but precisely because Babylon is recognized by its military occupiers as a powerful sign of the occupied land. In the case of the 2003 Iraq war, Babylon as 'sign' became a locus of the investment of military aggression as a form of display. That use of the site reveals an ambivalence not completely unlike that displayed by the Taliban's response to the Buddhas, in that the legendary city associated with decadence, despotism and evil in the biblical Christian tradition was deliberately chosen as a military base, not despite the fact that it is Iraq's most famous, legendary heritage site, but because of its fame and mythical values. The occupation damages the site, seemingly without any respect or concern for its values as a historic site or as cultural property; yet this very same destructive occupation makes use of the efficacious and potent symbolic power of the site.

The bombing campaign of March and April 2003 did not directly hit any museums, religious buildings, or archaeological sites. It was only in the aftermath, during the occupation, that the destruction began. At first, the destruction was considered the result of activities of a mob of local people, even if some blame was initially placed on coalition forces for not guarding civil buildings. The looting of museums and libraries in spring 2003 was well publicized in the media, but it was only the beginning of a more general destruction that was about to take place. It soon became clear that there would be systematic occupation of heritage sites by the military; however, the extensive damage to cultural property that has occurred throughout Iraq since the fall of Baghdad has remained mostly unrecorded and unrecognized because, unlike other recent conflicts such as that in the Balkans, there has been no survey of war damage by international observers or scholars. When the United Nations, the Red Cross, and other international aid organizations pulled out of Iraq in fall 2003 because of the worsening security situation, it spelled an end, in effect, also to international efforts to assist Iraq's museums, libraries, and cultural property in general.

The worst aspect of the cultural disaster is at archaeological sites. Iraq is referred to as Mesopotamia, the so-called cradle of civilization in traditional archaeological terminology. It comprises over ten thousand listed archaeological sites as well as hundreds of medieval and Ottoman Muslim, Christian and Jewish monuments, making it one of the world's richest countries in terms of ancient heritage. While some looting has always gone on in countries rich in antiquities, the archaeological sites of

Iraq are now being looted to an extent that was previously unimaginable anywhere. The looting supplies the appetites of a large international illicit trade in antiquities, as many objects end up in places such as Geneva, London, Tokyo and New York. The lack of border control under the occupation has only added to the ease with which the illegal trade in Mesopotamian artefacts functions, and there is now no real effort, either by coalition forces or by the interim government, to stop the plunder that is taking place.

The destruction of sites by looting is widely known to the world archaeological community. What is not well known is that the coalition military forces now occupy a number of important ancient Mesopotamian cities, Babylon being only the most famous example. The military occupation of archaeological sites is causing ongoing daily destruction of some of the most important heritage sites in Iraq. The structures built for the military camps are dug into the archaeological layers. Heavy equipment tramples across and destroys ancient remains. For example, helicopter flights have rattled the brick walls of Babylon to the point that at least two temple structures of the sixth century BC have collapsed (see Figure 11). There has been no statement or response from UNESCO or any other cultural nongovernmental organization calling for a halt to this occupation of heritage sites or to their destruction by the military. The terms of the Geneva Convention and the Hague Convention, however, would make the occupation of such sites illegal under international law.

Babylon was first occupied by the US Marine Corps in April 2003 (see Figures 12–15). The camp, known as Camp Alpha or 'The Ruins', in military terminology, was ceded to the Polish military command in fall 2003. Much of the infrastructure of this extensive camp, the headquarters of South Central Command, had been installed under US command, for example, the bulldozing and paving of an area for a helicopter pad in the heart of the ancient site. But construction work continued throughout the ancient site under Polish command. Although the United States and Britain have not ratified the Hague Convention of 1954, Poland has signed and ratified it. Article 28 allows for the prosecution of those breaking the convention.

There was initially a tremendous international response to the looting of institutions in April 2003. International meetings were called and pledges were made to assist the museums and libraries of Iraq in restoring and renovating their collections. Plans to protect archaeological sites were discussed by a number of cultural NGOs in Europe and the United States, but few of the international pledges have come through, and international experts, conservators, archaeologists and cultural organizations have been unwilling to risk going into Iraq. Therefore, meetings on Iraq have shifted, usually to Amman, where Iraqi scholars are then requested to travel out by land to meet with the international experts at this safer location. As a result, the world's archaeological and scholarly community has not seen the extent of destruction that has taken place in Iraq. Because places like Babylon are military camps and security is invoked as a reason for limiting access, the international press has had little to say about this. In Iraq itself, as a rule, archaeologists from the State Board of Antiquities and Heritage (SBAH) are not allowed onto sites that have been taken over as military camps. No permission is sought by the coalition forces before any construction work, movement of earth, or changes in the topography are made by the military. Although the Antiquities and Heritage Law of Iraq requires that any construction work at a heritage or archaeological site be authorized by the SBAH, this law has been ignored by the military, whose spokesmen have stated that, for security purposes, all such laws are suspended during the war and the occupation.

Nature of the site before and after the occupation

Although knowledge of Babylon had survived in the Western tradition through references in the Bible and by classical authors, its location was unknown. In the region of Iraq itself, however, the place always retained its name and was called Babil by the locals. Among the names for the grouping of mounds in the area, 'Babil' was still in use locally during the Ottoman era. From 1811 to 1817 Claudius James Rich conducted early excavations at Babylon. Robert Koldewey, the German archaeologist, began extensive work there in 1899. Excavation by Koldewey revealed a city of tremendous proportions. The southern citadel, the processional way, the Greek theater, and a number of temples and residential quarters were all unearthed, and Koldewey's team removed parts of the ancient, glazed brick walls, including the Ishtar Gate, to take to Berlin. The ancient city encompassed about 900 hectares; it was the largest city in antiquity before imperial Rome. Babylon was considered a city of such vast proportions that nothing else could compare. According to Herodotus (*The Histories* 1.191), people in the inner city remained unaware when its outskirts were captured by Cyrus. Aristotle stated that because the city was so large, it took three days for news of the conquest to reach the center (*Politics* 3.1.12).

US military reports, and even statements by representatives of UNESCO in the past year, indicate that there is a lack of awareness with regard to the extent of the site. Military reports and press accounts state that ancient Babylon is limited to the small area where reconstruction work took place under the previous regime. The military's public affairs office thus uses the argument that any damage to Babylon was already done by Saddam's regime and that by the time the US Marines arrived at the site, little ancient heritage remained.

In the 1980s a team of Iraqi archaeologists, under orders from Saddam Hussein, reconstructed the lateral wall of the processional way near the palace, the Greek-Hellenistic theater, and parts of the palace of Nebuchadnezzar. Saddam Hussein also had a palace of his own built on the ancient riverbed, after bringing in earth from outside Babylon to form a large mound or artificial tell (no doubt as a mock ancient site) as a base for the palace. The reconstruction was loudly disapproved of by the world's archaeological and scholarly community because it was located in the ancient area. It was this project that notoriously included bricks inscribed with Saddam's own name in the reconstructed walls of the palace of Nebuchadnezzar II.

Nevertheless, the damage that has occurred as a result of turning Babylon into the South Central headquarters of the multinational coalition force, the largest military camp in the area, is far more extensive than any damage that occurred as a result of the additions ordered by Saddam. The military camp has conducted projects that have required the bulldozing and compacting of earth across the site and in numerous areas. Sandbags and large barrel-like containers used for barricades have been filled with ancient earth from the site. Colossal concrete blocks have been positioned everywhere, compressing the layers below. Tanks and other heavy military vehicles drive across the ancient pavement of the processional way, destroying the surface. A large helicopter landing zone was constructed in the heart of the ancient site, between the palace and the Greek theater. This area was bulldozed and leveled, then paved with asphalt. Dozens of helicopters fly in and out of this area on a daily and hourly basis, over ancient palace and temple walls. The military also began construction of two more helicopter landing zones in Babylon, which were eventually turned into parking lots for large military vehicles and machinery.

When asked why the site of Babylon had been decided on as a military camp, no official was able to give an answer. The modern town of Hilla, where the coalition has another helicopter landing zone and which is close to Babylon, could have been used instead as a location for the camp. In April 2003 press reports stated that US troops likened their entrance into Babylon to that of Alexander the Great and his troops in the fourth century BC. Tanks drove along the ancient processional way and occupation ceremonies took place that were photographed and published by the media. This behavior suggests that the occupation of Babylon was a deliberate symbolic expression of power over Mesopotamia. The occupation of sites such as Babylon and the images of military force at the ancient ruins can be described as an aesthetic of occupation, a display of force that uses the sign of history and its control as a statement of victory.

International response

Some form of international response by the world archaeological community can still take place, but for Babylon and other occupied archaeological sites in Iraq, there can be no solution now. The lack of response may in part be due to the fact that as a military base, Babylon has not been open to either scholars or journalists. As noted earlier, the military cites general security concerns as a reason for both the occupation of Babylon and prohibiting access to the site. Access to the site by archaeologists or by the SBAH director in charge, Maryam Omran Moussa, and her assistants, was considered unnecessary since the Polish troops had brought along their own civil–military cooperation (CIMIC) archaeologists. The US military also has a section called CMO (civic military operations). These officers can be well intentioned, but they themselves were at times responsible for damage to Babylon, because they felt that they could take decisions on construction despite the Antiquities and Heritage Law or requests from the SBAH representative that they do no work at the site.

There have been varied responses from the international academic community. Some intellectuals are reluctant to make statements about the destruction of cultural property in Iraq by the coalition while so many people are losing their lives in the violence of war. Other scholars state a desire to remain politically neutral in the conflict. Remarkably, the Archaeological Institute of America and the College Art Association of America have been more critical and outspoken than have scholarly organizations that specialize in the Middle East. But the occupation of archaeological or heritage sites during war, as a practice or an act of war, still has to be addressed seriously in the archaeological literature. The use of archaeological sites, the deployment of modern architectural construction, and the demolition of older city centers in the name of modernization are well-known tools of colonial occupation. The issue has been discussed by numerous anthropologists, architectural historians, and architects (for example, Abu El-Haj 2001; Segal and Weizman 2002). Archaeologists must also come to understand that the demolition and the reconstruction of ancient sites and older traditional city centers in the name of modernization and security are not purely aesthetic or historical issues. They are related directly to human rights because the manipulation and destruction of the historic and architectural fabric of the occupied land is an instrument of war.

Destruction of cultural property in armed conflict can take several forms. In 'Cultural Warfare', John Yarwood points to four types of such destruction (Yarwood 1998). In the first case, damage is collateral in operations where an enemy occupies an area that includes historic monuments. In the second case, there is deliberate destruction of monuments with the intention of ethnic cleansing. The third type of damage occurs through looting, ultimately for connoisseurs who reside outside the occupied country. While a great deal of looting in Iraq fits into this third category, this form of damage and the illicit antiquities trade are more readily discussed by the archaeology profession. Instead, I am concerned here with the fourth type of cultural warfare: the deliberate destruction of the enemy's patrimony in situations in which, in Yarwood's terms, this assists neither military nor ethnic cleansing operations. Such destruction can be a result of an uncontrolled, unplanned attack, or often, a deliberately planned psychological operation (Yarwood 1998).

After two years of military occupation and martial law, the ancient heritage of Iraq can be classified as seriously endangered. Whereas the extensive looting and damage to sites has been described in the press and in the world archaeological community as falling, more or less, into the category of collateral damage, it can be demonstrated that the occupation of iconic heritage sites such as Babylon are psychological operations of military occupation. That at least six heritage sites have been taken over as coalition military camps indicates that this is not a random choice but the preplanned and systematic use of heritage sites for military operations. It is a psychological operation of warfare because it appears to be a deliberate choice to occupy a famous and iconic site of local cultural mythology. Babylon's symbolic mythical value is not lost here; instead, it is incorporated into the process of the occupation, and its symbolic significance is subsumed in a display of power over this ancient terrain.

Perhaps what is needed now is a new protocol for the protection of cultural heritage during war and occupation. This protocol might underscore the fact that the use of a heritage site as a military base qualifies as a form of direct cultural destruction, directly related to other forms of cultural warfare and ethnic cleansing. Furthermore, since the current political situation has rendered UNESCO an ineffective voice for the protection of cultural heritage in Iraq (and perhaps elsewhere), a nonaligned cultural organization made up of archaeologists and conservationists could be called together, perhaps under the auspices of the World Archaeological Congress, to take on that responsibility. A survey of war damage ought to be conducted as soon as possible under this independent professional group. Finally, an academic study of the practices of the uses of the past and the systematic occupation of heritage sites by the US-led occupation of Iraq could be the subject of future archaeological-theoretical studies on the relationship of archaeology and politics and, more generally, of ideological uses of the past.

Notes

1 *Of the Past for the Future: Integrating archaeology and conservation.* Congress proceedings of the conservation theme at the 5th World Archaeological Congress, Washington DC, 22–26 June 2003, edited by Neville Agnew and Janet Bridgland, 240–6. Los Angeles: Getty Conservation Institute, 2005.

2 This essay is based on my own fieldwork, assessment and documentation of the damage to Babylon under coalition occupation. The work was conducted jointly with Maryam Omran Moussa, director of the site of Babylon, on site, over the course of three months in summer 2004. Reports of this damage were made known by us to the Iraqi Ministry of Culture, to the US Civil Military Affairs Office in Baghdad, to the US Department of State, Office of Cultural Property, and to the British Embassy in Baghdad in July 2004. Requests and negotiations for the removal of the camp, and outlines for the correct procedures to accomplish the removal, were also made over the course of the summer in a joint effort by Dr Moussa and me. As a result of these negotiations, the coalition authorities agreed to remove the camp by the end of 2004. In preparation for the final removal, John Curtis of the British Museum was called to Babylon for a three-day trip, 11–13 December 2004, as a witness and to verify reports of damage. The British Museum posted his preliminary report on damage to the site, 'Report on Meeting at Babylon 11th–13th December 2004'. https://tinyurl.com/mvttuc33. It is important to note that the document did not cover all the damage but was intended as a list of the types of damage that have occurred.

3 A full account of the struggle for Babylon will appear at a later date, elsewhere. This essay presents some preliminary observations only. It is dedicated to Maryam Omran Moussa, with profound admiration.

References

Abu El-Haj, Nadia. *Facts on the Ground: Archaeological practice and territorial self-fashioning in Israeli society*. Chicago: University of Chicago Press, 2001.

Aristotle. *Politics*. Loeb Classical Library Edition. Cambridge, MA: Harvard University Press, 1995.

Bahrani, Zainab. 'Conjuring Mesopotamia: Imaginative geography and a world past'. In *Archaeology Under Fire*, 159–74. London: Routledge, 1998.

Bahrani, Zainab. *The Graven Image: Representation in Babylonia and Assyria*. Philadelphia: University of Pennsylvania Press, 2003.

Freedberg, David. *The Power of Images: Studies in the history and theory of response*. Chicago: University of Chicago Press, 1989.

Freedberg, David. 'The power of wood and stone: The Taliban is not the first to fear the mysterious lure of art'. *Washington Post*, 25 March 2001.

Herodotus. *The Histories*. Trans. A. de Selincourt. Harmondsworth: Penguin, 1954.

Kohl, Philip L. and Clare Fawcett. *Nationalism, Politics and the Practice of Archaeology*. Cambridge: Cambridge University Press, 1995.

Segal, Rafi and Eyal Weizman. *The Civilian Occupation: The politics of Israeli architecture*. Tel Aviv: Verso, 2002.

Yarwood, John. 'Cultural Warfare'. Paper presented at the international conference *Art, Antiquity, and the Law: Preserving our global cultural heritage*. Rutgers University, New Brunswick, NJ, 1998.

9

The battle for Babylon

The Guardian, 16 April 2006[1]

'المَعركة من أجلِ بابِل' *الغارديان*، 16 نيسان، 2006

Synopsis

These two texts (Chapters 9 and 10) have the same title and cover similar ground, but they are different essays. One was written for the British newspaper *The Guardian*, while the other was written as an academic paper. In both, I take the military occupation of Babylon as emblematic of the larger theme of historical destruction by military occupation, which includes several other aspects of the erasure of histories and collective memory in Iraq. I point out that the use of heritage sites as military bases was a breach of the Hague Convention and Protocol of 1954, Chapter 1, Article 5, which covers periods of occupation. Across the country, US and coalition forces disregarded Iraqi antiquities and heritage laws and the pleas of both the State Board of Antiquities and Heritage staff, as well as of international archaeologists and historians. For the academic article, I went further to point out the ways in which the voices of Iraqi archaeologists and museum staff were marginalised or silenced in favour of heroic narratives of Western rescue and protection from the natives – similar to nineteenth-century accounts – in a situation where the reality was rather one of catastrophic destruction and the disregard of Iraqi archaeologists who dared to call attention to this.

المستخلص

إنَّ لِهذَين النَّصَّين (الفَصْلَين 9 و10) العنوانَ ذاتَه ويقومان بتَغطيَة مواضيع مُتشابِهة، إلّا أنَّهُما مَقالَتان مُختَلِفَتان. إحداهُما كُتِبَت للصَحيفَةِ البريطانيّة، *الغارديان*، بينَما كُتِبَت الأخرى كوَرَقةٍ بَحثيَةٍ أكاديميّة. في كِلتَيهِما، تَناوَلْتُ الاحتلالَ العَسكَريَّ لبابِل كرَمْزٍ

للموضوع الأشمَل المُتَمثِّل بالدَمار التاريخي الذي تَسَبَّب به الاحتلال العَسكَري، والذي يتَضمَّن عِدَّة مَظاهِر أُخرى تَستهدِفُ بمُجْمَلِها مَحو التاريخ والذاكِرة الجَمعيّة في العراق. لقد أَشَرْتُ إلى أن استعمال المواقع التُراثيّة كقواعِد عسكريّة يُشكِّلُ خرقاً لاتفاقية لاهاي وبروتوكولها لعام 1954، الفصل 1، المادة 5، التي تغطي فترات الاحتلال. في جميع أنحاء البَلَد، غضَّت القوّات الأمريكية وقوّات التحالُف النَظَر عَن قوانين الآثار والتراث العراقيّة وعن مُناشَدات كُلٍّ من موَظَّفي الهيئة العامة للآثار والتُراث، فَضلاً عن علماء الآثار والمؤرِّخين الدوليين. لقد كُنتُ أرمي إلى أبعدَ من ذلك في مقالي الأكاديمي، مُشيرَةً إلى الطُرُق التي تم بها تهميش أصوات علماء الآثار العراقيين وموظفي المتاحف أو إسكاتِها لصالِح الروايات البطولية عن الإنقاذ الغربي والحماية من السُكّان الأصليين—على غِرار روايات القرن التاسع عش— في وضعٍ كان فيه الواقِع يتَّسِمُ بالأحرى بكونه دماراً كارثياً، وبتجاهُل عُلماء الآثار العراقيين الذين تَجرَّأوا على لفت الانتباه إلى هذا.

A US military spokesman says he would be willing to apologise for the military occupation of an ancient heritage site

Babylon is back in the news as a US military spokesman said that he would be willing to apologise for the military occupation of this ancient heritage site. When asked if he would offer an apology to the director of antiquities in Iraq, Col John Coleman said: 'If it makes him feel good'. But he insisted that anything the military had done at Babylon was carried out in close consultation with the Iraqi state board of antiquities and heritage (SBAH). He explained that, before setting up camp, the US command had 'made an analysis' and had come to the conclusion that it would be best for the site, because it would protect it from looters. This excuse of 'protection' is now being invoked in various contexts across occupied Iraq. In fact, the damage done to Babylon by coalition forces is both extensive and irreparable, and even if US forces had wanted to protect this ancient city, placing guards around the site would have been far more sensible than bulldozing it and setting up the largest coalition military headquarters in the region.

The idea that the military occupation of Babylon was for its own protection simply beggars belief. The US did nothing to guard any heritage site, museum or monument in the country in April of 2003. While the first air strikes of Operation Iraqi Freedom left historical monuments undamaged, the US-led occupation has resulted in a tremendous destruction of history well beyond the museums and libraries looted and destroyed at the fall of Baghdad. Babylon is the most famous ancient site occupied as a military base, but it is certainly not the only one. At least seven or eight heritage sites have been used in this way by US and coalition forces since April 2003, one of them being the historical heart of Samarra, where the al-Askari shrine built by Nasr al-Din Shah was recently bombed.

The use of heritage sites as military bases is a breach of the 1954 Hague Convention and protocol, chapter one, article five of which covers periods of occupation. The United States has not ratified the convention, but a number of the coalition countries (Italy, Poland, Australia) and Iraq are contracting parties. Since 'sovereignty' was returned to Iraq on 1 July 2004, the United States has been in the country at the invitation of the interim Iraqi government, and may be subject to the Hague convention as well as to the Iraqi antiquities and heritage law, which forbids any construction or use of a heritage site without prior permission of the SBAH. But at several heritage sites across the country, the US and coalition forces disregarded Iraqi antiquities and heritage laws, and the pleas of both the SBAH and international archaeologists and historians.

It is not only that museums and libraries were plundered after they were left unguarded in April 2003, and that hundreds of ancient sites are now pitted and destroyed by looters, although that damage is certainly extensive. The occupation of heritage sites, and now the deliberate targeting of monuments can be added to the list of the general destruction of history in the past three years. Obviously, none of this matters, in comparison to the daily slaughter and suffering of the people, but international conventions and laws that protect cultural heritage exist because people's identities are linked to historical monuments and landscapes and this is precisely why monuments become targets of war.

As an advisor to the SBAH and the ministry of culture in Iraq in the summer of 2004, I was a witness to much of this disregard of antiquities laws. During that time, my Iraqi colleague Dr Maryam Moussa and I made the preliminary archaeological assessments of damage to Babylon that became the basis of the SBAH report. We surveyed the damage at the site and documented it with extensive photography over several months, so that the continuing construction by KBR (the American contractors that provides all logistical services for the military) and the coalition command can be seen in an archive of dated photographs. The helicopter pad built by the US was bulldozed into the very heart of the site, between the Hellenistic theatre dating to the era of Alexander the Great and the Palace of Nebuchadnezzar. Parking lots and living installations for the troops were dug into the ancient layers, and hundreds of sandbags had been filled with archaeological earth.

The observations that Maryam Moussa and I had made at Babylon were later corroborated by Dr John Curtis of the British Museum, who went to Babylon for a three-day inspection in December of the same year.

If Babylon had been occupied for its own good, the military commanders would certainly have listened to requests that they stop construction and put an immediate end to helicopter flights (see Figure 11). But for 18 months they dug their heels in and refused. I recall the surreal situation of standing in front of the commander of the base and being told that no damage had been done, while behind his head a crane or a bulldozer could be seen working away into the Babylonian temple precinct. It reminded me of the PR methods of the former Iraqi Minister of Information, al-Sahhaf, who, while Baghdad was burning, continued to claim that there were no troops anywhere near the city. This method was nicely summed up by Groucho Marx when he asked: 'Who are you going to believe, me or your own eyes?'

It was only after a long and arduous campaign by archaeologists that the coalition commanders agreed to work on a schedule for the removal of the base known as Camp Alpha or 'the Ruins', in military jargon. 'The Ruins' was no small base. It was the south-central headquarters of the multinational forces. During 2003 and 2004 the archaeologist in charge of the site made numerous complaints and wrote letters to the commanders stating in no uncertain terms that she refused permission for any kind of construction, the use of helicopters, or the use of the site as a military base. The coalition forces consistently stated that the site was needed for military reasons. For me, the battle for Babylon has always been a metaphor for the occupation of Iraq. The idea that the US took Babylon for its own protection is perhaps similar to the idea that the US invaded Iraq to bring it freedom. If you believe in the second statement, you are likely to believe the first.

Note

1 https://www.theguardian.com/commentisfree/2006/apr/16/thebattleforbabylon.

10
The battle for Babylon

in *The Destruction of Cultural Heritage in Iraq*, edited by Peter Stone and Joanne Farchakh Bajjaly, 165–72. Woodbridge: Boydell Press, 2008

’المَعركة من أجلِ بابِل‘ في *تَحطيم المَوروث الحَضاري في العِراق*، تَحرير بيتر ستون وجوان فارتشاخ باجالي 165–172، وودبرِج: مَطبَعة بويدَل، 2008.

Synopsis

These two texts (Chapters 9 and 10) have the same title and cover similar ground, but they are different essays. One was written for the British newspaper *The Guardian*, while the other was written as an academic paper. In both, I take the military occupation of Babylon as emblematic of the larger theme of historical destruction by military occupation, which includes several other aspects of the erasure of histories and collective memory in Iraq. I point out that the use of heritage sites as military bases was a breach of the Hague Convention and Protocol of 1954, Chapter 1, Article 5, which covers periods of occupation. Across the country, US and coalition forces disregarded Iraqi antiquities and heritage laws and the pleas of both the State Board of Antiquities and Heritage staff, as well as of international archaeologists and historians. For the academic article, I went further to point out the ways in which the voices of Iraqi archaeologists and museum staff were marginalised or silenced in favour of heroic narratives of Western rescue and protection from the natives – similar to nineteenth-century accounts – in a situation where the reality was rather one of catastrophic destruction and the disregard of Iraqi archaeologists who dared to call attention to this.

المستخلص

إنَّ لِهذَين النَّصَّين (الفَصْلَين 9 و10) العنوانَ ذاتَه ويقومان بتَغطيَة مواضيع مُتشابِهة، إلّا أنَّهما مَقالَتان مُختَلِفَتان. إحداهُما كُتِبَت للصَحيفَةِ البريطانيّة، *الغارديان*، بينَما كُتِبَت الأُخرى كوَرَقةٍ بَحثيّةٍ أكاديميّة. في كِلتَيهما، تَناوَلْتُ الاحتلالَ العَسكَريَّ لبابِل كرَمْزٍ للموضوع الأشمَل المُتَمثِّل بالدَمار التاريخي الذي تَسَبَّب به الاحتلال العَسكَري، والذي يتَضمَّن عِدَّة مَظاهِر أُخرى تَستهدِفُ بمُجْمَلِها مَحو التاريخ والذاكِرة الجَمعيّة في العراق. لقد أَشَرْتُ إلى أن استعمال المواقع التُراثيّة كقواعِد عسكريّة يُشكِّلُ خرقاً لاتفاقية لاهاي وبروتوكولها لعام 1954، الفصل 1، المادة 5، التي تغطي فترات الاحتلال. في جميع أنحاء البَلَد، غضَّت القوّات الأمريكية وقوّات التحالُف النَظَر عَن قوانين الآثار والتراث العراقيّة وعن مُناشَدات كُلٍّ من موَظَّفي الهيئة العامة للآثار والتُراث، فَضلاً عن علماء الآثار والمؤرِّخين الدوليين. لقد كُنتُ أرمي إلى أبعدَ من ذلك في مقالي الأكاديمي، مُشيرَةً إلى الطُرُق التي تم بها تهميش أصوات علماء الآثار العراقيين وموظفي المتاحف أو إسكاتِها لصالِح الروايات البطولية عن الإنقاذ الغربي والحماية من السُكّان الأصليين—على غِرار روايات القرن التاسع عشر—في وضعٍ كان فيه الواقِع يتَّسِمُ بالأحرى بكونه دماراً كارثياً، وبتجاهُل عُلماء الآثار العراقيين الذين تَجرَّأوا على لفت الانتباه إلى هذا.

> Colonialism is not satisfied with merely holding a people in its grip and emptying the native's brain of all form and content. By a kind of perverted logic, it turns to the past of the oppressed people, and distorts, disfigures, and destroys it.
>
> (Fanon 1963, 210)

It has been more than two years since I left Iraq. The last time I was there was in 2004 when I spent several months as an advisor to the former Iraqi Minister of Culture. At that time, the Coalition Provisional Authority (CPA) had handed 'full authority' of the ministry back to Iraq and to the State Board of Antiquities and Heritage (SBAH), but the truth was that this was merely a charade. As soon as I left, I was bombarded by requests for interviews from various international newspapers and popular journals. Yet only two or three of the journalists who contacted me wanted to know anything about the condition of archaeological sites, museums or cultural heritage in Iraq. The others wanted to do a personal profile, complete with portrait photo. They seemed mostly interested in my education (was it Western or Iraqi?), ethnicity (are you Kurd or Arab?) and religious background (are you Shiite or Sunni?). I contacted some prominent newspapers in the US and in Britain in an attempt to give them my first-hand account of the damage to monuments, libraries and historical sites, but only *The Guardian* expressed any interest in this issue ('Days of Plunder', *The Guardian*, 31 August 2004). In the end, I gave interviews only to those who would allow me to speak about the damage I had observed at Babylon, the occupation of other heritage sites, and the general destruction that has occurred under the occupation. Now, yet again, rather than being asked to write an essay on the destruction of history, I am asked to write an essay on my experience as an archaeologist in the line of fire and, frankly, I feel that I have nothing to say on the matter. I could write a theoretical paper on the implications of war for the hypothetical universal archaeologist or scholar working on cultural monuments or institutions; I could write on the question of military archaeologists in war based on my personal observations over four months (I am not in favour), but I have had no inclination so far to write on the subject of what it meant for me personally to live and work in Iraq in the days of the so-called transfer of authority from the CPA to the Iraqi Government.

It is not acceptable practice for an academic writing in a scholarly volume to take a stance on war, but for me, writing about this issue was a political act from the start. In April of 2003, when the news of the looting of the Iraq Museum broke, I sat down and wrote an article for *The Nation* in which I laid the blame on the Bush Administration, pointing out that what had happened under their command was in opposition to both the Hague Convention and the principles of the Geneva Convention (Bahrani 2003). As a result I, like anyone who opposed the war at that time, was branded as anti-American by the press in the US and the UK, as if any criticism of the actions of the Bush Administration meant that one must hate democracy, Hollywood cinema, apple pie or rhythm and blues. Little did I know when I wrote on the morning after the looting that the destruction of the museums and libraries in 2003 would be only the tip of the iceberg of an immense historical annihilation that was to come, the processes which I would have the unfortunate privilege of seeing for myself in 2004.

Inside Iraq in the summer of 2004, it had all seemed like a fiasco. The dividing line between the newly designated 'Green Zone' and 'Red Zone' was in the process of being made more emphatic by the erection of a series of massive concrete blocks like those that form the wall between Israel and the Palestinian territory. The Green Zone was in the process of becoming a fortification of foreign rule in the very heart of the city of Baghdad. The hostility and aggression of the coalition forces toward the local population of Iraq was becoming increasingly violent. On the streets one could see the abusive behaviour of soldiers and mercenaries, as if the entire population were prisoners of war in an extensive detention camp. This is the experience I can attest to because I merged as a local and experienced for myself what other Iraqis went through, simply by walking on the street or approaching a checkpoint. I usually went around Baghdad in a local car, or flagged the occasional taxi, and sometimes, I walked over the streets in the so-called Red Zone (all of Iraq outside US bases) on foot and so I have had the unpleasant experience of armed US soldiers at a checkpoint aiming directly for my head, with that 'shoot first, ask questions later' look on their faces, on more than one occasion. One is completely helpless in that situation. Yet the idea that I should write an essay on myself as 'an archaeologist in the line of fire' (as requested here) seems ludicrous to me, given the horrors of that time and even more so in the face of the current massacres and destruction that have become the day-to-day existence of the average Iraqi. Archaeology and libraries have received some attention by various NGOs and government ministries, more so than the civilian death count or the contaminated drinking water or the hospitals full of dying children.

Since the first news of the looting of the Iraq Museum broke in the press, there has been a barrage of reports, of soundbites from self-styled experts on Iraq's history or cultural heritage, reports from journalists who sat in the Rashid or Palestine hotels in Baghdad while their Iraqi employees went out on the streets, reports of coalition government representatives who minimise the effects of the damage or shift the blame to the previous regime, and reports of representatives from various governments, each claiming to have done the most, or making a pledge to do the most, for the rescue of cultural heritage in Iraq while they remain silent about the civilian deaths that the US government refuses to count as if they were not those of sentient beings. Living in Iraq itself, one saw precious few of the projects that have been announced as the valiant rescue of lraq's heritage. These are mostly paper promises. Worse yet, some of the projects and funding agencies appear to be geared more for the benefit of European and North American consumption rather than being of much use to heritage in Iraq itself. In a country taken over by violence one can expect no more.

In reality, only a handful of scholars or cultural preservationists made the dangerous journey into Iraq in the first years after the fall of Baghdad, and even fewer have spent more than a few days there, or attempted to venture outside the Green Zone without a convoy of armoured SUVs, flak jackets, helmets and the now proverbial South

African bodyguard. After the United Nations building collapsed in a 2003 bombing, the UN pulled out of Iraq and other NGOs followed suit, stating that it was simply too dangerous for their employees to remain. A number of institutions began working on projects to reconstruct the museums and libraries or to train Iraqi scholars from the safety of the distance provided by Amman, London or New York. In addition, some of the accounts that I have read on cultural heritage issues in Iraq are more in the genre of sensationalising narratives that set out to portray the western protagonist as an heroic figure and give either little or no credit to the Iraqi archaeologists and scholars who have been doing all the work inside Iraq. As a result of some of these accounts, one might say that the destruction of cultural heritage in Iraq becomes salvaged into a narrative of rescue and reconstruction, where in fact there is nothing but catastrophic loss. This appropriation of the very narrative of the events, of the historical account of what has happened to historical sites and cultural institutions and who has been working to rescue and preserve these, is a facet that I could not foresee in March and April of 2003. Cultural heritage is a pawn in this game of war in more ways than one.

In 2003 I went to Iraq with two colleagues, Elizabeth Stone and Paul Zimansky, driving the long road from Amman to Baghdad. This trip was a personal rather than a professional journey, even if it was aimed at providing equipment and assistance to the Iraq Museum. In the same way, returning to Iraq alone in 2004 was a decision taken out of personal anguish. I felt compelled to act in the face of the unceasing destruction of the cultural heritage of my own country, its ancient civilisations, its magnificent golden domed and turquoise mosques, its cruciform and box-like churches like ancient reliquaries, its remarkable tradition of early bold and linear modernist arts and architecture, its libraries filled with scrolls and codices, and its centuries and millennia of historical archives. It was only after I had gone and returned that I ever thought of danger, and even then it was only because others, outside Iraq, became rather vocal in pointing it out to me. It is only now that I can see that I acted without being consciously aware of any potential dangers or consequences, let alone caring about them, so I did not see or experience my time there as an act of bravery.

In academia, the general stance has been that notions of cultural heritage and history, the relation of people to monuments, well, that is not to be universalised like the human subject, whose rights we fight for; that attitudes to history are culturally constructed, which is perhaps an obvious point. But furthermore, the currently favoured view in archaeology is that this kind of a relation of people to the past is a

Western one, and as such it is part of a Western order that we impose on others. My own scholarly view diverges from these current positions and the Iraq war has only made this clearer to me. The appropriation of the notion of historical consciousness for the West, currently favoured by certain camps in the discipline of archaeology, is simply a continuation of past colonial attitudes under a new liberal guise. The historical accounts of antiquity make clear that the relationship of people to monuments, to natural and constructed landscapes, and to historical narrative itself is a very ancient one, certainly as old as the Early Dynastic Mesopotamian cities of the third millennium BC.

In my view, having lived in the midst of this war and seen its violence on a daily basis, the horror of war is not the horror of body counts alone. Wars and occupation cause damage to the living that cannot be quantified. One of the forms of violence that Iraqis continue to endure is the destruction of their rich history. Psychologically, the loss of history can and does have a devastating effect on people. That is why such destruction is calculated into the strategies of war and is discussed quite openly as an aspect of military strategy known as a 'psy-op'. This is why iconoclasm and destruction and relocation of monuments have occurred as deliberate acts of war throughout recorded world history, why ethnic cleansing works through the annihilation of people by means of eradicating any trace of their past. This is why international legal conventions were written in opposition to such acts, especially after World War II.

In 2004 I had been Senior Advisor to the former Minister of Culture, Mufeed al-Jaza'iri, a member of the communist party who had opposed the Saddam regime. Being opposed to the war, I was reluctant to go, but I had naively hoped that the ministry would become independent of the occupation authority. It soon became clear to me that the US forces held authority over use of land and public buildings, including heritage sites. In a number of publications I have attempted to explain how the occupation, demolition and construction of ancient sites and historical urban centres have become instruments of war. A case in point is Babylon, occupied as a US military base in the summer of 2003. By way of conclusion I will explain why, for me, the occupation of Babylon is emblematic of the entire US war and occupation of Iraq. It is perhaps for that reason that I focused all my energies, in 2004, on the removal of the military base from this archaeological site.

In late 2006, Colonel John Coleman, speaking to the BBC, insisted that anything the military had done at Babylon was carried out in close consultation with the SBAH (BBC News 2006). He explained that before setting up camp, they (the US command) had 'made an analysis' and had come to the conclusion that it would be best for the site, because it would protect it from looters. In fact, during the dozens of meetings that I had with US officers on the matter of Babylon, in 2004, there was no one who could answer the question of who it was that had taken the decision to occupy Babylon, or why. There was no-one who had any information about a decision, a plan or a strategy. Later, after we had exposed the story through the press, the idea of 'protection' emerged. This excuse of 'protection' is now being invoked in various contexts across occupied Iraq. In fact, the damage done to Babylon is both extensive and irreparable, and even if US forces had wanted to protect it, placing guards around the site would have been far more sensible than bulldozing it and setting up the largest coalition military headquarters in the region.

The idea that the military occupation of Babylon was for its own protection simply beggars belief. The US did nothing to guard any heritage site, museum or monument in the country in April of 2003. In fact, while the air strikes left historical monuments undamaged, the occupation has resulted in a tremendous destruction of history, well beyond the museums and libraries looted and destroyed at the fall of Baghdad. While Babylon is the most famous site that was occupied as a military base, it is certainly not the only one. At least seven or eight historical sites have been used in this way by US and coalition forces since April 2003, one of them being the historical heart of Samarra, where the al-Askari Shrine built by Nasr al Din Shah was bombed in 2006.

The use of heritage sites as military bases is a breach of the Hague Convention and Protocol of 1954, chapter 1, article 5 of which covers periods of occupation. While the United States has not ratified the Convention, a number of the coalition countries (Italy, Poland, Australia, the Netherlands) and Iraq are contracting parties. Since 'sovereignty' was returned to Iraq on the first of July 2004, the United States has been in the country at the invitation of the Iraqi government, and may be subject to the Hague Convention as well as to the Iraqi Antiquities and Heritage law, which forbids any construction or use of a heritage site without prior permission of the SBAH. But across the country, the US and coalition forces disregarded Iraqi antiquities and heritage laws, and the pleas of both the SBAH and international archaeologists and historians.

In 2004, I was a witness to much of this disregard of antiquities laws. During that time, my Iraqi colleague Dr Maryam Moussa and I made the preliminary archaeological assessment of damage to Babylon that became the basis of the SBAH report. We surveyed the damage at the site and documented it over several months, so that the continuing construction by KBR (the American contractors that provide all logistical services for the military) and the coalition command can be seen in our archive of dated photographs. The observations that Maryam Moussa and I had made at Babylon were later corroborated by John Curtis, who went to Babylon for a three-day inspection in December of the same year (https://www.theguardian.com/world/2005/jan/15/arts.iraq).

If Babylon had been occupied for its own good, the military commanders would certainly have listened to the repeated requests that Maryam Moussa and I personally made that they stop construction and put an immediate end to helicopter flights (see Figure 11). But for 18 months, they dug their heels in and refused. I recall the surreal situation of standing in front of the commander of the base and being told that no damage had been done, while behind his head one could see a crane or a bulldozer working away into the Babylonian temple precinct. It reminded me of the PR methods of the former Iraqi minister of information, al-Sahhaf, who while Baghdad was burning in March and April of 2003 continued to claim that there were no US troops anywhere near the city. This method was nicely summed up by Groucho Marx when he asked: 'who are you going to believe, me or your own eyes?'.

It was only after a long and arduous campaign that the US and coalition commanders agreed to work on a schedule for the removal of the base known as Camp Alpha, or 'the Ruins' in military jargon. 'The Ruins' was no small base. It was the South Central Headquarters of the Multi-National Forces. We had made numerous complaints and Maryam Moussa wrote letters to the commanders stating in no uncertain terms that she refused permission for any kind of construction, the use of helicopters, or the use of the site as a military base. The officers we spoke to consistently stated that the site was needed for military reasons. For me, the battle for Babylon is a metaphor for the occupation of Iraq. The idea that the US took Babylon for its own protection is perhaps similar to the idea that the US invaded Iraq to bring it freedom. If you believe in the second statement, you are likely to believe the first.

Bibliography

Bahrani, Zainab. 'Looting and conquest', *The Nation*, 14 May 2003. https://www.thenation.com/article/archive/looting-and-conquest.

Bahrani, Zainab. 'Days of plunder', *The Guardian*, 31 August 2004. https://www.guardian.co.uk/comment/story/0,,1293931,00.html.

BBC News. 'US Marines offer Babylon apology', 24 October 2007. https://news.bbc.co.uk/1/hi/world/middle_east/4908940.stm.

Fanon, Frantz. *The Wretched of the Earth*. New York: Grove Press, 1963.

11
Desecrating history

The Guardian, 9 April 2008[1]

’تهديمُ التاريخ‘ *الغارديان*، 9 نيسان، 2008،

Synopsis

This piece was written for *The Guardian* at the five-year anniversary of the war. In the first few days after the end of the shock and awe campaign, between 10 and 12 April 2003, Iraq's main museums, libraries and archives were looted and extensively damaged by fire. A Bradley tank and a number of US troops were in the area. At one point a curator from the Iraq Museum staff walked over and asked for assistance but was told by the tank commander that no orders had been given to help. At the time, Donald Rumsfeld appeared on our television screens in the US and declared these events to be a positive sign of the liberation of an oppressed people: 'stuff happens', he said. Those of us who opposed the war from the start, and who implied that the US bore some responsibility for its negligence, were dismissed as anti-American radicals and 'Yankee bashers', even in the mainstream press. But by 2007, Barbara Bodine, the US Ambassador at the time, revealed to Charles Ferguson, in his documentary film *No End in Sight*, that direct orders had come from Washington stating that no one was to interfere with the looting. The looting spree in the museums and libraries was just the tip of the iceberg of the catastrophic-scale historical destruction that was to come in the following five years, and it was not simply the result of poor planning or the inadvertent damage of war.

المستخلص

لقَد كُتِبَت هذه المقالة لصحيفة *الغارديان* في الذكرى الخامسة للحرب. إبان الأيام القليلة الأولى بعدَ انتهاء حَملة "الصدمة والرعب"، ما بين يَومَي 10 و 12 نيسان 2003،

كانت المتاحف، والمكتبات، والكتب النادرة والوثائق التاريخية العراقيّة المهمة قد تَعَرَّضت للنَّهب فضلاً عن التّلَف الكبير الذي تَسبَّبَت به الحرائق. كانت هناك دبابة برادلي مع مجموعة من القوات الأمريكية في المنطقة. في خِضَمِّ ذلك، عندما حَثَّ الخُطى إلَيهم أحَد أُمَناء المتحف العراقي طَلَباً للمُساعَدة، كانَ رَدُّ آمِر الدَبّابة بأنَّهم لَم يَتَلَّقوا أوامِراً بالمساعدة. آنَذاك، كان دونالد رامسفيلد يُطِلُّ علينا من شاشات التِلفاز مُعلِناً أنَّ هذه الأحداث ما هيَ إلّا دَلالة إيجابية على تحريرِ شَعْبٍ مُضطَهَد قائلاً: ' -هكذا- أشياء تَحدُث '. أولئِكَ الَّذين وَقفوا ضِدَّ الحَرب مِنّا منذ البدايةِ، والَّذين لَمَّحوا بأنَّ الولايات المُتَّحِدة تَتَحمَّل بَعض المَسؤوليّة عن إهمالِها، تمَّ إقصاؤهم باعتبارهم مُتَطَرِّفين مُناهِضينَ لأمريكا ووُصِفوا بأنَّهم ' مُهاجِمي اليانكي -أي الأمريكان- ' حتى في الصَحافة السائِدة. لكن بحلول عام 2007، كَشَفَت سفيرة الولايات المتحدة حينَها، باربرا بودين، لتشارلز فيرجسونِ في فِلمِهِ الوثائِقي *لا نهاية على مَدِّ البَصَر* بأن الأوامِر المُباشِرة القادِمة من واشنطُن كانت تَنُصُّ على ألّا يتَدَّخَل أحدٌ فيما يخص أعمالَ النَّهب. لقد كانَت موجَةُ النَّهب في المتاحف والمكتَبات مُجرَّدَ غَيضٍ من فَيضِ الدَّمار التاريخي المَهول الذي جاءَ في السنوات الخَمْس التي تَلَتْها، ولم يكُنِ الأمْر مُجَرَّدَ نتيجةٍ لسوءِ التَخطيط أو ضَرَر غير مَقصودٍ للحَرْب.

Iraq's cultural treasures have been ransacked since 2003. This is no mere side issue: it undermines a key part of the country's collective identity

In the first few days after the end of the 'shock and awe' campaign, from 10–12 April 2003, Iraq's main museums, libraries and archives were looted and extensively damaged by fire. A Bradley tank and a number of US troops were in the area. At one point a curator from the Iraq Museum staff walked over and asked for assistance but was told by the tank commander (who to give him credit, actually radioed his superiors to request permission) that no orders had been given to help.

At the time, Donald Rumsfeld appeared on our television screens in the US and declared these events a positive sign of the liberation of an oppressed people: 'stuff happens', he said.

Those of us who opposed the war from the start, and who implied that the US bore some responsibility for its negligence were dismissed as anti-American radicals even in the mainstream press. But by 2007, Barbara Bodine, the US ambassador at the time, revealed to Charles Ferguson, in his documentary film *No End in Sight*, that direct orders had come from Washington stating that no one was to interfere with the looting.

The events of that April are still lamented everywhere as the unfortunate collateral damage of war, another consequence of the occupation that was not foreseen, like so many other aspects of the occupation, due to the lack of foresight of the Bush administration. But the looting spree in the museums and libraries was just the tip of the iceberg of a catastrophic destruction of historical treasures that was to come in the following five years, and it was not simply the result of poor planning or the inadvertent damage of war.

Even if the original looting of the museums and libraries could not have been avoided, or was not foreseen (an excuse that I personally find rather weak given the fact that numerous archaeologists and other scholars had warned both US and UK governments against exactly such a scenario months before the war), there are areas of cultural destruction that were entirely avoidable and sometimes preplanned.

First, there was the Pentagon's strategic decision to use the main cultural heritage sites of the country as military bases. These sites include Ur, the legendary birthplace of Abraham; Babylon, the famed capital of Mesopotamian antiquity; and Samarra, the Abbasid Islamic imperial city. The digging, bulldozing, filling of sand bags and blast-barricade containers, the building of barracks and digging of trenches into the ancient sites; all this has destroyed thousands of years of archaeological material, stratigraphy and historical data. Walls and standing structures have collapsed as a result of shootings, bombings and helicopter landings.

At the risk of repeating myself, I would like to remind readers that such activities are against both Iraqi cultural heritage law and against international laws of war and occupation. In other words, like human rights abuses, the destruction of a people's cultural heritage and history has elsewhere been regarded as a war crime. To be precise, similar to the case of torture, international law has regarded such activities as war crimes when people or states other than the US have been responsible for them.

Imagine, if you will, that Stonehenge was taken over as a military barracks that housed thousands of troops and required the digging of the earth in order to provide plumbing and sewage in the middle of the ancient site itself, while trenches were dug around the megaliths and perhaps some of the smaller monoliths were relocated, and used as blast walls to protect the troops at the checkpoint entries to the base. When leading archaeologists came to point out the damage, they were asked: 'Are you suggesting that we risk the lives of our troops?'. This is the situation today at some of the most important cultural sites of Iraq.

At other locations we have a second type of massive but preventable destruction. This is the ongoing looting of countless Mesopotamian archaeological sites, looting that continues because the state board of antiquities and heritage has little money or equipment for site guards like those in other countries rich in antiquities such as Egypt, Italy, Turkey or Greece, and because the US and UK governments have had little interest in including such site protection in the multi-trillion dollar budget of the occupation. Despite the noble pledges of commitment to the rescue of cultural heritage and rebuilding of the museum and libraries that were made in 2003, the reality is similar to that of the situation with electricity and water. Almost nothing has been done. The Iraqi government is no better. It has shown a remarkable lack of interest in preserving historical sites, whether they are of the pre-Islamic or Islamic eras. More recently, the Maliki government has actually cut what little money had been allocated for these sites. Worse yet, last summer Iraqi troops marched into the National Library and physically assaulted librarians and other staff.

At the time when the first news of the Iraq Museum looting emerged, there were also allegations made in the western press and media that the curatorial staff had been responsible. These charges were never substantiated, although people's lives and reputations were seriously damaged as a result. In the de-Baathification plan of Paul Bremer, qualified curators, archaeologists and professors were removed from their positions. In the following five years, many more scholars left the country, forced into exile because of direct threats to their lives; others were not so fortunate and have just become part of the collateral damage of war.

So on this fifth anniversary of the looting, I will repeat what I wrote in April 2003. The destruction of history, which has become a prominent aspect of this violent occupation, is not simply the unfortunate damage of some art objects.

As in other wars at other times and places, the destruction of monuments and historical archives works to erase the historical landscape and the realms of memory around which people define their collective identities. The fact that people's relations to monuments, history and landscape are always and everywhere constructed does not make cultural destruction any more ethical or legal. It is precisely through such destruction that empires have usually remapped space.

The continuing destruction of historical sites in Iraq must be addressed more seriously as one of the distinctive aspects of the current occupation of Iraq. History and archaeology are never untainted by politics. If ethnic groups or nations construct identities through monuments and historical narratives, the opposite is also true. In the words of George Orwell: 'Who controls the past controls the future: who controls the present controls the past'.

Note

1 https://www.theguardian.com/commentisfree/2008/apr/09/plunderingiraq

12

October questionnaire

October 123 (Winter 2008): 11–13

’استبيان أوكتوبر‘ *أوكتوبر* 123 (شِتاء 2008): 11–13.

Synopsis

The journal *October*, widely regarded as one of the foremost journals of modern and contemporary art, and a pathbreaker in its theoretical engagement with contemporary issues, invited a number of scholars to reflect upon the seeming absence of visible opposition to the Iraq War in the years between 2003 and 2008, within what the editors described as ‘the milieu of cultural producers working in the sphere of contemporary visual culture’. I was invited to present my thoughts on this question. Therefore, while the essay is not concerned with archaeology or antiquity, it addresses the roles of public intellectuals, artists and academics during this period. It points out that while the 2003 antiwar protests were a significant and spectacular international show of resistance in the face of state power, they held the promise of an oppositional force that did not materialize. Among those who opposed war, most academics were not prepared to speak openly, while others, specialists in the Middle East, could be counted among the main architects of the war. It was their expertise and knowledge of ‘the Arab mind’ that formed part of the intelligence for making the case for war. And like Napoleon in Egypt, the military also had its own artists in tow at the start of the invasion, producing images from the perspective of tanks rolling into the streets of Baghdad. In the US and UK, other leading intellectuals went so far as to openly support the state’s increasing surveillance and internment without charge of those who appeared to be of Middle Eastern or South Asian origin. The essay also addresses contemporary visual media and the depiction of Arabs and Muslims at that time, arguing that there was, as yet, no US–UK defeat in the ‘image war’, despite the pictures of the horrors of Abu Ghraib and Bush's infamous 'mission accomplished' moment. I suggest that Abu Ghraib, Falluja and Guantanamo also underscore this 'in-your-face' hegemony, similar to some ancient text of the Assyrian or Roman Empire that effectively declares: 'we will torture and slaughter as a sign of victory; the people will consent'. Nor do these kinds of images bring state violence completely into the realm of the visible. Camp X-Ray was anything but transparent. It was a secret detention camp, which we were nevertheless permitted to glimpse or hear of through whispers, as was also the case with the secret rendition flights and the black sites of torture. The essay thus addresses the ethical responsibilities of public intellectuals and academics in times of war.

المستخلص

قامَتْ مجلةُ أوكتوبَر العلمية، وهي مجلةٌ ذائعةُ الصيت كونَها من أهم المجلّات العلمية المُتَخَصِّصة بالفَن الحَديث والمُعاصِر والرائِدة في إسهاماتِها النَظَريّة عن القَضايا المُعاصِرة، بدَعوَةِ عَدَدٍ من الباحثين ليُدلوا بدَلوِهِم فيما يخُص ذلك الغِياب المَلحوظ لمَعالِم مُناهَضَةِ حَرب العراق في السَنَوات ما بين 2003 و2008، ضِمنَ ما وَصَفَه محرِّرو المجلّة على أنَّه ' الوَسَط الخاص بالمُنتِجين ثَقافِياً العامِلين في مَجال الثقافة البَصَريّة المُعاصِرة'. وقَد دُعيتُ لأُقدِّم أفكاري حول هذه المسألة. لِذا، ورُغم إن هذا المقال لَم يُعنَ بعلم الآثار أو الآثار، إلا أنَّهُ تناولَ أدوار المُفَكِّرين، والفنّانين والأكاديميين خلال تِلك الحِقبة. إذ يشير إلى أنّه بينما كانت الاحتجاجات المناهِضة لحرب 2003 تمثِّل عَرضاً دولياً مهماً ومُذهلاً في مواجهة سلطة الدولة، إلا أنّها اتَّخّذَت وَعداً بقوَّة معارَضةٍ لم يتَحَقَّق. من بَين الَّذين عارَضوا الحَرب، لم يكُن مُعظَم الأكاديميين مُستعدِّين للحديث بصراحة، بينما كان الآخرون، المُتَخَصّصون في الشَّرق الأوسَط، بالإمكان عدُّهم من بين مُهندسي الحرب الأساسيين. فقَد كانت خبرتهم ومعرِفتهم بالـ ' العَقل العَربي' قَد شَكَّلَت جُزءا من المعلومات الاستخبارية التي هيَّأَت لملَف الحَرب. وكما كان الحال مع نابليون في مصر، كان للجَيش في مَطلَع الغَزو، فنّانون خاصون به لأغراض الدعاية، يُنتِجونَ صوراً من منظورِ الدبّابات وهي تزحَفُ نحو شوارع بَغداد. في الولايات المتحدة والمملكة المتحدة، كان هناك فِئةٌ أخرى من المُثَقَّفين البارزين الَّذين دَعَموا علانيةً رقابةَ دُوَلِهم المتزايدة والاعتقال بدون تُهمة لِمَن يبدو أنَّهم من أُصولٍ شَرق أوسَطيّة أو جنوب آسيوية. تتناول المقالة كذلك وسائل الإعلام المرئيّة وأسلوب تصوير العَرَب والمسلمين في ذلك الوقت، مُجادلةً بأن لم يكن هناك، حتى ذلك الحين، هزيمةٌ أمريكية- بريطانية في ' حَرب الصوَر'، على الرَّغم من الصور التي تكشِف أهوالَ أبي غريب وتلك اللحظة سيئة الصيت لبوش التي أعلن فيها بأنَّ ' المهمَّة قد أُنجِزَت'. في رأيي بأنَّ أبو غريب، والفلّوجة، وغوانتنامو قد عملت كذلك على تأكيد سياسة الهيمنة العِدائيّة السافِرة، بما يُشابِه ما وَرَدَ في بعض نُصوص الامبراطوريّة الآشوريّة أو الرومانية والتي تُصَرِّح عَلناً 'إنَّنا سَنُعَذِّب ونَذبَح إيذاناً بانتِصارنا؛ سيوافقُ الشَّعب'. لم يكُن لتِلكَ الصوَر أن تنقل عنف الدولة تماماً على مرئى من الجميع. لقد كان مُعسكر إكس رَي (Camp X-Ray) بعيداً كلَّ البُعد عن الشَفّافيّة. لقَد كان مُعسكَر

اعتقالٍ سِرّي، مع ذلك سُمِحَ لنا لبلمحَةٍ أو سماع هَمَساتٍ عنه، كما هو الحال مع عمليّات الترحيل السِريّة ومواقع التعذيب السَّوداء. لذا تناوَلَت هذه المقالة المسؤوليّات الأخلاقيّة للمُثَّقَفين والأكاديميين البارزين في أوقات الحرب.

Questionnaire

1. In what ways have artists, academics (faculty, staff, and students), and cultural institutions (including collectors, dealers, and magazines) responded to the US-led invasion and occupation of Iraq? Can you offer examples of significant oppositional practices? How would you assess the forms, visibility, and efficacy (or lack thereof) of opposition?

2. Are there examples of an active counter-public sphere in which protest against the war in Iraq is conducted with an intensity comparable to the protests organized during the era of the Vietnam War? What, if anything, demotivates the current generation of academics and artists from assuming positions of public critique and opposition against the barbarous acts committed by the government of the United States against a foreign country? Do you consider the absence of the draft the sole significant factor?

3. Can we speak of the 'professionalization' of the artist (as a highly paid and market-dependent provider of infotainment) as having reduced or eliminated political consciousness from cultural production? Have academics and those working in cultural institutions been subject to similar processes of professionalization, and if so, what have been the effects of this professionalization? What have been the political effects of the increasing marginalization of the humanities in American academic institutions? Do artists and academics still regard cultural production as a socially and politically communicative, transgressive, or critical activity?

4. Antiwar opposition seems most visible on the Internet, where information is distributed, money is raised, and demonstrations are organized. How does this electronic-technological public sphere compare to the public protests of the Vietnam era, during which agitprop cultural activities were organized through word of mouth, flyers, and planning meetings, and demonstrations were staged in the streets, in museums (for example, by Guerrilla Art Action Group), in theaters (Bread and Puppet Theater, The Living Theatre), and in a variety of print media (from pamphlets to weekly magazines)?

5. Does this condition imply a fundamental transformation of the sense of a public political subject? Do advanced technologies (and more specifically, the ease with which we consume them) serve simultaneously as universally accessible tools of communication and as spaces of social confinement and depoliticization?

6. What, if anything, do you think can be done to make intellectual and artistic opposition to the war more active and effective?

The antiwar protests of 2003 were a significant and spectacular international show of resistance in the face of state power, but they held the promise of an oppositional force that did not materialize. For those who opposed war, the shock and awe campaign produced a sense of futility that defeated dissent, while in the US and UK, the absence of the military draft meant that most people continued to live in a dream world of consumer distraction in which they viewed the military activities of their governments as distant events, unrelated to their own lives. In the US, steadfast academics, writers and artists continue to oppose the war and occupation through their work, and in a public way, but most are not prepared to speak openly. As a result, during the past five years, the majority of academic voices in the public sphere have not been oppositional; instead they form an integral part of a new military-industrial-information complex. Some academics, such as Kanan Makiya and Fouad Ajami, number among the main neocon architects of the war. It was their expertise and knowledge of the 'Arab mind' that formed part of the intelligence in making the case for war. And like Napoleon in Egypt, the military also had its own artists in tow at the start of the invasion, producing images from the perspective of victorious Bradley tanks rolling into Baghdad, ready to paint murals over Saddam's face and recast the bronze from his statues into images of American heroes.

In the UK, the situation is much the same. There is mostly silence, but some (such as Anthony Giddens and Martin Amis) have openly supported the state's increasing surveillance and internment without charge of those who appear to be of Middle Eastern or South Asian origin.

One place where there was international public agreement among academics, artists and cultural institutions was the issue of cultural heritage in Iraq. Lists of monuments, libraries, and historical sites and calls for their protection were posted on the websites of the Archaeological Institute of America and the College Art Association. These institutional public statements may be taken as examples of collective opposition, but they were not necessarily an antiwar position. A large number of the scholars, collectors and dealers who called for the protection of cultural heritage in the event of war were in favor of war, so the two positions cannot be conflated. These groups continued to speak out on matters of cultural heritage long after antiwar protests had effectively ended.

In my opinion, the silence of intellectuals is partly a result of the stance (also promoted by the liberal Left) that being apolitical is correct academic form. Mesopotamian antiquity, seen as global cultural heritage, received attention only because it is defined as a humanist concern, beyond war. But we can think of this concern the opposite way around. Even if it is not always overtly stated, the call for protecting world heritage is often presented as the enlightened counterposition to indigenous destruction and neglect, an argument that has certainly been used to make the case for custodial superiority by dealers and collectors, as well as some academics, who are more concerned with bringing the system of the antiquities market into the global economy than with the violence of war.

The case is often made that current technologies permit more information and images to circulate, allowing numerous voices and dissent, but there are large blackouts nevertheless. What do we ever see or hear of Iraqis other than Maliki and Sadr, or the weapon-wielding kidnapper-terrorist with his kaffiyeh-covered face? Visual media and the patterns of dissemination may be changing, but it would be a mistake to think of this simply as the advent of a more liberating and inclusive public sphere. It is a greater dissemination of the same, not of different images and voices. I am also not convinced that greater visibility enrages the forces of power. There is, as yet, no US–UK defeat in the image war, despite the pictures of the horrors of Abu Ghraib or Bush's 'Mission Accomplished' banner. Abu Ghraib, Falluja, and Guantanamo also underscore the in-your-face hegemony – similar to some ancient text from the Assyrian or Roman Empire – that effectively declares, 'We will torture and slaughter as a sign of victory'. The people will consent, perhaps even gloat. It is not only the acts that were considered amusing by the perpetrators at Abu Ghraib; the photographs they made of these acts were taken by the soldiers for pleasure, for their own amusement and that of others. Nor do these images bring state violence completely into the realm of the visible. Camp X-Ray is anything but transparent. It is a secret detention camp, which we are nevertheless permitted to glimpse or hear of through Chinese whispers, as is also the case with the secret rendition flights and the black sites of torture.

Why is this practice, which they claim is for the sake of gaining information, undertaken in secret places, the existence of which we are nevertheless allowed to know and glimpses of which reach our newspapers and television screens on a daily basis? An image of torture is a statement of victory in and of itself. It is a symbol of triumph over the body of the other. It is no mere technique of war, but a statement and signal of absolute power. Torture summarizes state terror and absolute sovereign power as displayed through the control of the body and life; the act of bringing the victim close to death but not quite, a life that is a prolonged death, without the release of death itself. Thus the practice of torture circulates in the media, but is kept hidden at the same time. This public secret of torture is very similar to the technique of fear Saddam Hussein used. In order for it to work as a deterrent to dissent, we need to be made aware of it through rumors and fleeting looks, but never see it clearly.

A similar system of fear and secrecy circulating through mass-media representations holds true for the battle of Falluja, a massive slaughter of a civilian population that, in a perfect Chomskian case of manufactured public opinion, we applaud as the defeat of terrorists. Control of opinion is very successful, despite new, more accessible media (as I write this, the *Guardian* reports that in the week before the war, Tony Blair telephoned Rupert Murdoch several times). And the overwhelming bombardment of what are nevertheless select and repeated images (such as Saddam's capture) leaves little space or energy for critical consciousness and thought.

What was also disturbing for many of us in the antiwar movement was the significant shift in the images of state power in 2001–3. In the US, we observed the abandoning of any pretense of a subtle propaganda of liberal democracy in favor of an imagery and rhetoric that was clearly more akin to the propaganda of totalitarian regimes. But the imagery of US power in the New World Order was nothing new. For example, Bush's performance on the aircraft carrier was a direct borrowing of Vladimir Putin's appearance as a fighter pilot in the 1999 Chechen war. Flag waving and military parades, usually the standard fare of the overt propaganda of dictatorship, became common on American streets, and television news began to display targets, military maps, and the banners of unwavering patriotism. Since this imagery has now become normal on US television screens, it is difficult to imagine that it will not continue after the next presidential election.

The Left has been waylaid by the promises of liberating technologies, but the YouTube public sphere encourages a fast-food version of political engagement. An example of this politics bereft of political consciousness is the way in which the early popular support of the war in the US has now been replaced by a popular swing toward its opposition. This growth in the antiwar movement is primarily a reaction to the rising numbers of dead American troops. But it is a movement whose anger is directed at the Bush administration in particular, not at the neoliberal ideologies of global capital or the Manichean rhetoric that enabled the waging of war. The Internet as public sphere is also becoming increasingly monitored not only by the state but by self-appointed censors like Campus Watch, leading not so much to a marginalization of any real oppositional voices or serious critique, but to ever more self-censorship and silence. Just as the ideology of global capital depends upon liberal myths of diversity and inclusion, so too the idea of an unrestrained multiplicity and reality of visual images, snapshots taken by people on mobile phones and digital cameras, is not something we can afford to leave unquestioned. Despite these fast-paced changes, public intellectuals do continue to speak out, write, and make works of art in acts of resistance and dissent, yet it will require more and more energy and courage to do so, and the support of a larger network of oppositional voices and groups. The antiwar movement needs to recover the strength and the momentum of 2003, opposing the war not because of the returning body bags, but because of the fundamental injustice of the war and continuing occupation of Iraq.

13

Archaeology and the strategies of war

in *The Cultural Cleansing of Iraq*, edited by Raymond W. Baker, Shereen T. Ismael and Tareq Y. Ismael, 67–81. London: Pluto Press, 2010

‘علم الآثار واستراتيجيات الحَرب’ في *التطهير الثَقافي للعِراق*، تحرير رَيموند و. بَيكَر، وشيرين ت. إسماعيل، وطارق ي. إسماعيل، 67–81، لندن: مطبعة بلوتو، 2010.

Synopsis

The destruction and looting of cultural heritage in the Iraq War and occupation were the subject of a great deal of press reports and academic journal articles and conferences. The discussions had remained mostly at the level of unease over the unfortunate collateral damage of war and occupation, damage that included a patrimony that was seen not as a loss for Iraq as a state or for its people but as ‘global cultural heritage’. Most of the attention that this subject had received at that date concerned the ‘cradle of world civilization’ and circumvented the impact on the people of the land that was under military occupation. This paper takes into account the aspects of heritage destruction that do not fall under the category of collateral damage, addressing the theoretical issues of historical erasure and collective memory. It surveys a range of forms of military destruction that were taking place in occupied Iraq, arguing that although such forms had been addressed carefully by scholars in the fields of cultural heritage, archaeology and preservation in the context of the former Yugoslavia, similar activities had taken place in occupied Iraq – and thus demanded comparable scrutiny. The essay also calls attention to the Pentagon's strategic decision to use the main cultural heritage sites of the country as US and coalition military bases. At least eight major historical heritage sites were used in this way; in addition, satellite imagery studied by archaeologists for looting patterns revealed that an early second-millennium BC site had been levelled to accommodate a US military base nearby. The idea that there was no preplanning in the selection of these sites is difficult to accept.

المستخلص

إنَّ الدَّمار والنَّهْب اللَّذَين تعرَّض لهما الموروث الحضاري إبانَ حَرب العراق واحتِلالِه كانا موضوعاً لعَدَدٍ كبيرٍ من التقارير الصحفية والمقالات البحثية الأكاديمية والمؤتمرات. أبدَت المُناقَشات في الغالب مستوىً من عدم الارتياح لتَبِعات الحرب والاحتلال من أضرارٍ مؤسفة، تلك الأضرار التي شَمَلت إرثاً لا يُعدُّ خسارةً للعراق كدولة أو لشعبه فحَسبُ، بل إنَّه يتعدى ذلك كونه ' تراثاً حضارياً عالمياً'. انصبَّ معظم الاهتمام الذي حظيَ به هذا الموضوع حينَها على كونِهِ يَخُص ' مَهد الحَضارة العالميّة' والالتفاف على أثَرِه في شَعبِ تلك الأرضِ التي غَدَتْ تحت سَطوة الاحتلال العسكري. تضَع هذه الورقة البحثية في الحُسبان تلك النواحي من التدمير الحضاري التي لا تَندَرج تحت مُسَمّى الأضرار الجانبية، لتُعالِجَ القَضايا النَّظرية للمَحو التاريخي والَّذاكرة الجمعية. تَستعرِضُ هذه الورقة البحثية مجموعةً من أشكال التَّدمير العسكري التي جَرَت عِند احتلال العراق، مُحاجِجَةً بأنَّ على الرُّغم من العناية التي أبداها الباحثون المختَّصون في الموروث الحَضاري، وعلم الآثار والحفاظ في دراسة مثل هذه الأشكال ضمن سياق يوغُسلافيا السابقة، إلا أنَّ مُمارَسات مُماثِلة قد حدَثَت في العراق المُحتَل— وبالتالي يتطلَّب ذلك تَمحيصاً مُماثِلاً. دَعَت المقالةُ كذلك إلى إيلاء الانتباه إلى القرار الاستراتيجي للبنتاغون باستعمال مواقع التُراث الحَضاري في البلاد كقواعِد عَسكريَّة للولايات المتحدة ودول التحالف. لقد تم استغلال ما لا يَقِل عن ثمانية مواقِع تاريخية تراثية رئيسية بهذه الطريقة؛ هذا وقَدْ كَشَفَت دراسة أجراها علماء آثار على صورٍ مُلتقَطة من الأقمار الصِّناعيّة لأنماط النَّهب، بأنَّ مَوقِعاً يعودُ إلى مَطلع الألف الثاني ق.م قَد تَمَّت تسويتَهُ لاستيعاب قاعدة عسكريّة أمريكيّة بقُربِه. إنَّ فكرة عدم وجود تخطيط مُسبَق في اختيار تلك المواقع يصعب قبولُها .

The destruction and looting of cultural heritage in the Anglo-American war and occupation of Iraq has been the subject of a great deal of press reports and discussions in academic journals and conferences in the past five years, ever since the initial invasion of 2003 culminated in the widespread plundering of museums and libraries. These discussions, however, have remained at the level of unease over the unfortunate collateral damage of the war and occupation; damage that has included a patrimony, which is seen not as a loss for Iraq as a state or for the people of this land but primarily for what is described as 'our global cultural heritage'. Since ancient Iraq is the land that archaeologists and ancient historians refer to as Mesopotamia, the cradle of civilization, the place of the rise of urbanism, the invention of writing and complex social structures, Iraq's ancient past is therefore considered to be of great importance to the entire world.[1] However, this international outcry over the destruction and theft of antiquities as a global heritage is a double-edged sword. On the one hand there is no doubt in the importance of raising public awareness on the matter of the particular importance of Iraq's archaeological profile to the world. On the other hand the academic conferences, papers and publications that have emerged from it, as well as general popular press books and the endless news articles on the matter have all circumvented a major point. Cultural destruction in war is not always a result of accidental or 'collateral' damage. It is not just a loss of the world's global heritage. It is a destruction of history in a country under occupation.

The assault on Iraqi history and collective memory

Most of the attention that this subject has received has been mainly phrased as a concern for 'the cradle of world civilization'. However, as in other wars in other times and places, the destruction of monuments and historical archives works to erase the historical landscape and the realms of memory around which people define their collective identities. There has been a remarkable silence on this aspect of the cultural and historical destruction in Iraq. Yet as an area of research and of scholarly and political public discussions and publications, this type of destruction has been recognized and analysed when such acts have taken place in other countries, and when they were perpetrated by other peoples. For example, the attacks on monuments and architectural structures that were conceived to be markers of a particular ethnic group's presence in a region – for example, minarets, orthodox churches, and the famous bridge at Mostar – have now become dominant aspects of the historical accounts of the breakup of the former Yugoslavia, perhaps even iconic of that war in some ways.[2] These standing monuments, stone, brick and mortar, came to be equated to linguistic or religious-ethnic groups or nationalities, their presence unwanted and erased from the landscape at the same time that people were either forcefully relocated or killed, each group considering that their ethnic identity and historical relation to place were made tangible or intangible by the presence or absence of monuments.

The earliest course of events in the 2003 war, in terms of the destruction of the ancient Mesopotamian past, is well known. In the first few days following the end of the US 'shock and awe' campaign on Iraq, when Baghdad was under US military control, Iraq's main museums, libraries and archives were looted and extensively damaged by fire. Most of the damage to museums and libraries occurred between 10 and 12 April 2003.[3] Due to the focus of the international press, it was the Iraq Museum that received the greatest amount of attention. This museum is generally considered to be one of the three or four most important museum collections in the world as it houses a remarkable range of excavated antiquities and Islamic art and manuscripts from Iraq itself rather than being a collection formed by market-bought objects or antiquities acquired through imperial wars and colonization (such as the British Museum in London or the Louvre Museum in Paris, for example).

During the event of the looting of the Iraq Museum in Baghdad, a Bradley tank and a number of US troops were in the area, some meters away from the main entrance. At one point, a curator from the museum staff walked over and asked for assistance but was told by the tank commander (who, to give him credit, actually radioed his superiors to request permission) that no orders had been given to help. At the time, Donald Rumsfeld appeared on our television screens in the US and declared that these events were a positive sign of the liberation of an oppressed people; 'stuff happens', he said. In the United States, those of us who opposed the war from the start, and who implied that the US bore some responsibility for its negligence were dismissed as anti-American radicals, even in the mainstream press. But by 2007, Barbara Bodine, the US Ambassador at the time, revealed to Charles Ferguson in his documentary film *No End in Sight* that direct orders had come from Washington stating that no one was to interfere with the looting.

In the press and among most archaeologists, the events of that April are still described as another consequence of the occupation that was not foreseen and was, like so many other aspects of the occupation, due to the lack of foresight of the Bush administration.[4] The looting spree in the museums and libraries was just the tip of the (proverbial) iceberg of a catastrophic scale of historical destruction that was to come in the following five years, and it was not simply the result of poor planning or the inadvertent damage of war. Even if this could not be avoided, or was not foreseen (an excuse that I personally find rather weak given the fact that numerous archaeologists and other scholars had warned both the US and UK governments against exactly such a scenario months before the war), there are areas of cultural destruction that were entirely avoidable and sometimes preplanned.

First, there is the Pentagon's strategic decision to use the main cultural heritage sites of the country as US and coalition military bases. These sites include (among others) Ur, the legendary birthplace of Abraham; Babylon, the famed capital of Mesopotamian antiquity; and Samarra, the Abbasid Islamic imperial city. The digging, bulldozing, filling of sand bags and blast-barricade containers, the building of barracks and digging of trenches into the ancient sites have destroyed thousands of years of archaeological material, stratigraphy and historical data. Walls and standing structures have collapsed as a result of shootings, bombings and helicopter landings. The idea that there was no preplanning or high-level military decision making in choosing these ancient sites as major camp installations is difficult to believe.

Despite the commonly held view, these activities are not only ethically questionable because they inadvertently damage cultural heritage sites during an otherwise ethically conducted act of jus belli. On the contrary, they are against both the Iraqi Cultural Heritage Law and against international laws of war and occupation. In other words, like human rights abuses, the destruction of a people's cultural heritage and history has elsewhere been regarded as a war crime. To be precise, similar to the case of torture, international law has regarded such activities as war crimes when people or states other than the US have been responsible for them. The war which was presented as a jus belli but was launched on the basis of a series of false claims publicized by the G. W. Bush administration, has disregarded international law in several arenas and cultural heritage is another one of them. This kind of abuse of heritage sites is perhaps difficult to understand when the historical sites are unfamiliar. A simple reversal may help illustrate the needless destructive acts of the occupation forces.

Imagine if you will, if, say, Stonehenge were to be taken over as a military barracks that housed thousands of troops and required the digging of the earth in order to provide plumbing and sewerage in the middle of the ancient site itself, while trenches were dug around the megaliths and perhaps some of the smaller monoliths were relocated, and used as blast walls to protect the troops at the checkpoint entries to the base. When leading archaeologists come to point out the damage, they are asked: 'Are you suggesting that we risk the lives of our troops?'. This is the situation today at some of the most important cultural heritage sites of Iraq.

At other ancient sites, we have a second situation of massive but preventable destruction. This is the looting of countless Mesopotamian archaeological sites. The looting occurred because the State Board of Antiquities and Heritage has a dearth of funding or equipment for site guards like those in other antiquities-rich countries such as Egypt, Italy, Turkey or Greece, and because the US and UK governments have had little interest in including such site protection in the multi-trillion-dollar budget of the occupation. Despite the noble pledges of commitment to the rescue of cultural heritage and rebuilding of the museum and libraries that were made in 2003, the reality is similar to that of the situation with electricity and water. Almost nothing has been done. The Iraqi government is no better. It has shown a remarkable lack of interest in preserving historical sites, whether they are of pre-Islamic or Islamic eras. For example, the ancient area of the ninth-century Abbasid royal city of Samarra was chosen as the place for building an Iraqi police barracks. More recently, the Iraqi government has actually cut what little money had been allocated for these sites. Worse yet, in the summer of 2007 Iraqi troops marched into the National Library and physically assaulted librarians and other staff, when they wished to take over the National Library as an observation point.[5]

At the time when the first news of the Iraq Museum looting emerged, there were also allegations made in the Western press and media that the curatorial staff had been responsible. These charges were never substantiated, although people's lives and reputations were seriously damaged as a result. In the de-Baathification plan of Paul Bremer, any qualified curators, archaeologists and professors who had remained in Iraq through the terrible years of the embargo, were removed from their positions. In the following five years, many more scholars left the country, forced into exile because of direct threats to their lives; others were not so fortunate and have just become part of the 'collateral damage' of war.

Another seriously disturbing development is apparent when it comes to the account of the destruction of Iraq's cultural heritage. A situation has arisen now that the voices of Iraqi archaeologists are mostly dismissed as politically motivated whereas the archaeologists who work with the US or UK government and military are now taken as the unbiased and objective assessors of the situation. In addition to the destruction and erasure of history therefore, we can add the silencing of the voices of Iraqi scholars.

What has happened under the US command of Iraq with regard to cultural heritage, museums and libraries was in opposition to both the

1954 Hague Convention and the principles of the Geneva Conventions. When I first pointed this out, writing on the morning after the looting and destruction of the museums and libraries in 2003,[6] I did not realize that the looting of the museums and libraries would be only the beginning of an immense historical annihilation that was to come, the processes of which I would have the unfortunate privilege of seeing for myself in 2004 while working on the closing of the military camp at Babylon with my colleague Maryam Omran Moussa.[7] [Figure 17] Yet given the horrors of that time and in the face of the current death and destruction that have become the day-to-day existence of the average Iraqi it is difficult for me, as an archaeologist from Iraq, to focus on issues of cultural heritage alone. After all, archaeology and libraries have received some attention by various non-governmental organizations (NGOs) and government ministries, more so than the civilian death count or the contaminated drinking water or the hospitals full of dying children. Yet the destruction of history as an act of war is no small matter.

In academia, the general stance has been that notions of cultural heritage and history, the relation of people to monuments, is not to be universalized like the human subject, whose rights we fight for, because attitudes to history are culturally constructed. Furthermore, the currently favoured view in archaeology and anthropology is that this kind of a relation of people to the past is a Western one, and as such it is part of a Western order that we impose on others. My own scholarly view diverges from these current positions and the Iraq war has only made this clearer to me. The appropriation of the notion of historical consciousness for the West is simply a continuation of past colonial attitudes under a new liberal guise. The historical accounts of antiquity make clear that the relationship of people to monuments, to natural and constructed landscapes, and to historical narratives themselves is a very ancient one, certainly as old as the Early Dynastic Mesopotamian cities of the third millennium BC. In my view, having lived in the midst of this war and seen its violence on a daily basis, the horror of war is not the horror of body counts alone. Wars and occupation also cause damage to the living that cannot be quantified. Historical destruction must be seriously assessed as an act of war.

In the United States and Great Britain, the constant debate about the exact amount of looted archaeological sites or stolen antiquities continues in the press and among archaeologists. Since the first days of the war in 2003 there has been a barrage of reports, of sound bites from self-styled experts on Iraq's history or cultural heritage (many having never been in Iraq), reports from journalists who sat in the Rashid or

Palestine hotels in Baghdad while their Iraqi employees went out on the streets, reports of coalition government representatives who minimize the effects of the damage or shift all the blame to the previous regime, and reports of representatives from various governments, each claiming to have done the most, or making a pledge to do the most, for the rescue of cultural heritage in Iraq while they remain silent about the civilian deaths. Living in Iraq itself one saw precious few of the projects that have been announced as the valiant rescue of Iraq's heritage. Worse yet, some of the projects and funding agencies appear to be geared more for the benefit of European and North American consumption rather than being of much use to heritage in Iraq itself. In a country taken over by violence, one should expect no more.

After the United Nations (UN) building collapsed in a 2003 bombing, the UN pulled out of Iraq and other NGOs followed suit, stating that it was simply too dangerous for their employees to remain. A number of institutions began working on projects to reconstruct the museums and libraries or to train Iraqi scholars from the safety of distance provided by cities such as Amman, London and New York. In addition, some of the accounts that I have read on cultural heritage issues in Iraq are more in the genre of sensationalizing narratives that set out to heroize the Western protagonist and give either little or no credit to the Iraqi archaeologists and scholars who have been doing all the work inside Iraq itself. As a result of some of these accounts, one might say that the destruction of cultural heritage in Iraq becomes salvaged into a narrative of rescue and reconstruction where in fact there is nothing but catastrophic loss. This appropriation of the very narrative of the events, of the historical account of what has happened to historical sites and cultural institutions and who has been working to rescue and preserve these is an aspect that I could not foresee in March and April of 2003. Cultural heritage is a pawn in this game of war in more ways than one.

The people of Iraq continue to endure many forms of violence on a daily basis. Some of these are direct forms of physical violence, while others are psychological forms of violence. The loss or destruction of historical monuments can and does have a devastating effect on people. That is why throughout history such destruction has been calculated into the strategies of war. This is the reason that iconoclasm and destruction or the relocation of monuments have occurred as deliberate acts of war throughout recorded world history, and why ethnic cleansing works through the annihilation of people by means of eradicating any trace of their past. The recognition of cultural destruction as an act of warfare is not new. It was the reason that international legal conventions were written in opposition to such acts, especially after World War II.

Today, as I write this chapter while I sit at my desk in New York City, the death toll for US troops in Iraq stands at 4,183; we see the latest count on the scrolling text at the bottom of our television screens. Conversely, the rising numbers of Iraqi dead never appear in our news reports; the Pentagon does not keep count, and neither does the Iraqi government for that matter. Meanwhile in Iraq itself, water and electricity infrastructures still have not been repaired after over five years of occupation. Hundreds of thousands of people have been killed, exiled or forcibly displaced, women's rights have been obliterated and the rich cultural heritage and historical archives of the country have been extensively looted and destroyed.

At the same time, a new US government initiative that designates $14 million for the assistance of Iraq's historical patrimony, its museums and libraries, was announced. Speaking in early October 2008 at the Iraqi embassy in Washington, DC, then first lady Laura Bush publicized this generous grant made in order to remedy the unfortunate collateral damage done to cultural heritage, and the years of neglect of archaeological sites and cultural institutions under Saddam Hussein's regime.[8] However, a large part of this is money that has already been distributed to American universities in the US, and a great deal of it will actually go to institutions in the US rather than to repairing things that were destroyed under the watch of the occupation or even wrecked directly by the US military in Iraq.

Of course there are good things about this grant and it will certainly be put to positive use in American universities, for example in providing Iraqi scholars with training in the latest technological and scientific methods. The irony here is not to be missed. Part of the money is specifically designated for educating Iraq Museum professionals in curatorial expertise in the US, an offer of lessons in how to be good custodians of your cultural heritage from the country that was responsible for its destruction.

In the US little is heard about the placing of American or Multi-National Force military bases on ancient heritage sites, or about the bulldozing and digging by US forces at legendary historical places like Babylon and Samarra. Satellite images show that one ancient site dating to the early second millennium BC was totally levelled in order to accommodate the expansion of the US base nearby.[9] While different sectarian factions in Iraq bombed each other's mosques and churches because of religious prejudices and intolerance, the occupation's forces participated in the destruction of the historical sites of ancient Mesopotamia in their own way.

The looting of the museums and the torching of the libraries in April of 2003 were famously explained by Rumsfeld as an act of democratic freedom by a previously oppressed population: 'freedom is messy', he said. Speaking for the Bush administration in 2003, he also told the American public that the looting could not have been foreseen by anyone. Rumsfeld knew very well when he said this that the looting was indeed foreseen, since dozens of archaeologists, other academics and museum professionals had warned of exactly such a scenario. Some had actually gone to the Pentagon to be assured by US government officials that guards would be placed at museums and libraries as soon as US forces took over the country. Even if we take Rumsfeld at his word and accept that the looting in April 2003 could not have been predicted, he still needs to explain the Pentagon decisions, made under his command, that involved direct US destruction of ancient sites or the removal of national archives, against the wishes of the Iraqi people and government. In addition, the occupation of a number of archaeological and historical sites as US and coalition military bases continues today. These acts are clear violations of the international conventions on the safeguarding of cultural heritage of occupied territories.

In October of 2008 the Pentagon launched another 'public relations' initiative that would allocate US$330 million for pro-American propaganda inside Iraq. This operation would pay for such things as pro-American television and radio programs as well as print news spun from pro-US occupation perspectives. It is clear that this propaganda is aimed at the Iraqi people, but we should realize that some of this spin is also aimed at consumers here in the West, so that we might believe that the humanitarian intervention in Iraq was a success.

Part of the new campaign, seemingly aimed specifically at academics, includes something called the Minerva Initiative, funded by some US$50–75 million. A website by that name has been set up by the Pentagon, in conjunction with the Social Science Research Council.[10] According to its website, the Minerva Initiative aims to provide a new military-academic interface, calling on all academics to submit proposals for research and articles to this site. The major lure of the Minerva Initiative appears to be not only potential financial support for research projects (to be peer reviewed by the Social Science Research Council in conjunction with the Department of Defense) but for the select few, there will be access to the contested Iraqi archive, now housed in the Hoover Institution at Stanford University.

As the destruction of historical sites and occupation of these sites as military bases continues, despite the constant requests of the State Board of Antiquities and Heritage of Iraq, the attitude towards the stolen archives demonstrates a general policy of disregard for the people and their history. The US continues to refuse the return of archives that were taken out of Iraq and shipped to the United States. As Saad Eskander the Director of the National Library and State Archives of Iraq put it, rather than improving their stance on the protection of cultural heritage, there has in fact been 'an escalation in its [US] violations of international conventions that goes against the principles of the rule of law, self-determination and human rights that are supposed to govern the so called free world'.[11] The archive at the Hoover Institution is reported to consist of tens of millions of records kept by Saddam Hussein's regime on the Iraqi people: all of the records on private citizens who may have been dissidents, records of those who disappeared, records of human rights abuses, the collective punishments and murdering of the population. Iraqis did not have access to these documents under the violent and repressive regime of Saddam; they are denied access to them now in a so-called free and independent Iraq.

In April 2003, Rumsfeld also described the plundering of the museums and libraries as the 'messy birth pangs of democracy'. But we now know that at the Iraq Museum that houses one of the world's most important collections of antiquities, no less important historically than any of the major museums in Western capitals, the looting was at least partially inspired by the concept of antiquities as free-market goods. These are not the ideals of democracy, but of financial profit. It seems that at least one group of looters that entered the museum were professional art thieves who knew exactly what to take, the difference between a real antiquity and a plaster copy, and what objects would fetch the highest prices in the international illicit art market. The former Director of the Iraq Museum, Donny George Youkhanna, has written that months before the war he heard reports from the UK and elsewhere in Europe of people boasting that the war would enable better-qualified Western custodians to take over the antiquities of Iraq, which were, after all, global cultural heritage (he now lives in exile, having been forced to leave when threats were made against his family because they are Christians).[12] Of course there were other looters at the Iraq Museum; many were like the people who went into various government buildings, took furniture and equipment wherever they could find it, and plundered because of their hatred of the regime. However, there is no question that professional art thieves were involved at the museum. A large number of artefacts from the Iraq Museum collections were found later in Western Europe and the United States, as well as several countries in the Middle East, stopped by border control. These objects had obviously been smuggled out of Iraq for sale in the lucrative international market of stolen antiquities.

In the years that followed the museum looting, we also saw an increase in the pillaging of archaeological sites, especially in the south of Iraq, the heartland of ancient Sumer and Babylonia, where there are thousands of ancient sites. Some amount of looting already existed there in Saddam Hussein's era, especially during the days of the embargo, but the rate of the looting increased dramatically after the invasion and occupation of Iraq. Like the major museum thefts, this kind of looting is not for local consumption. It feeds the appetite of the illicit international market in antiquities. The looting has now somewhat subsided, thanks to the appointment of more site guards and the distribution of patrol cars to them, organized and funded in part by the US Department of State as well as by the Italian government. The destruction of the record of the past through the damage done to archaeological sites, whether in the era of Saddam Hussein and the embargo or in the first years of the occupation, can never be repaired.

The wilful violence of cultural destruction

In comparison to the continuing violence in Iraq, the deaths, the forced relocations and exile of the population, the destruction of cultural heritage and the confiscation of archives seem like a minor detail of war, the loss of some bits of paper and old artefacts, but we should not forget that such forms of destruction do great violence to the inhabitants of the land. To Americans, the looting and destruction of museums and libraries that took place soon after the fall of Baghdad is most commonly seen as an example of the phenomenal lack of foresight of the Bush administration. We dismiss much of what happened during the invasion of 2003 and under the continuing occupation as poor planning or, at worst, the stupidity and ineptitude of the early days of the invasion. In fact, however, a large part of the cultural destruction took place not in the first days of the invasion, but during the last five and half years of occupation. Clearly, not all of it was accidental.

The occupation of heritage sites as military bases that I have discussed above is a clear example of a strategic and preplanned use of historical landmarks and monuments. Besides the legendary city of Babylon, which was turned into the headquarters of South Central

Command of the Multi-National Forces, at Samarra, the top of the ninth-century minaret was blown off by a rocket-propelled grenade while it was in use as a US sniper post. When such acts occur in other wars and are perpetrated by other people we have no qualms about speaking of them in terms of historical erasure and calling them crimes of war. Why do we not do the same now?

There is also now the potential of historical destruction in the current plans for the demolition of old city centres, for example in the historical heart of Kerbala and Najaf. The planning by the Iraqi government in collaboration with international construction firms is presented in terms of modernization and reconstruction, but these plans will reshape the medieval city centres, just as the blast walls and checkpoints have reorganized the urban space of Baghdad and facilitated the forced relocation of the population.

The building of 'enduring bases' across Iraq and the colossal US embassy in Baghdad should also be taken into account in that they are part of a construction program that contributes to the militarization of urban space, the demolition of historical areas, and the extensive erasure and rewriting of the historical fabric of the land. How can we think of the larger issue of territoriality and control in Iraq without taking into account the continuing obliteration of the past and memory through the removal and suppression of archives, or the erasing and reconfiguration of the historical terrain through the destruction of ancient monuments and historical sites? These things should not be dismissed as accidental collateral damage; they are direct acts of war and it is precisely through such destruction that empires have always remapped space.

Notes

1 For a history of ancient Mesopotamia, see Marc Van De Mieroop, *A History of the Ancient Near East, ca. 3000–323 BC* (Oxford: Blackwell, 2004).

2 See Robert Bevan, *The Destruction of Memory: Architecture at war* (London: Reaktion Books, 2006).

3 See Zainab Bahrani, 'The battle for Babylon', *The Guardian*, 16 April 2006 (included in Chapter 9, this volume); K. Nashef, *The Destruction of Iraqi Cultural Heritage* (in Arabic), Beirut: Dar al Hamra, 2004; and Donny George, 'The looting of the Iraq National Museum', in *The Destruction of Cultural Heritage in Iraq*, edited by Peter G. Stone and Joanne Farchakh Bajjaly (Woodbridge: Boydell Press, 2008), 97–108.

4 For example, see the discussion 'Robbing the cradle of civilization: Five years later', Salon, 20 March 2008 https://www.salon.com/news/feature/2008/03/20/iraq_roundtable/print.html. Accessed December 2008.

5 Saad Eskander, personal communication with the author in 2007.

6 Zainab Bahrani, 'Looting and conquest', *The Nation*, 14 May 2003 (included in Chapter 1, this volume).

7 Maryam Moussa, 'The damages sustained to the ancient city of Babel as a consequence of the military presence of coalition forces', in *The Destruction of Cultural Heritage in Iraq*, edited by Peter G. Stone and Joanne Farchakh Bajjaly (Woodbridge: Boydell Press, 2008), 143–50.

8 Laura Bush, 'Remarks at the launch of the "Iraq Cultural Heritage Project"', 16 October 2008, https://web.archive.org/web/20081021100912/https://www.whitehouse.gov/news/releases/2008/10/20081016-1.html. Accessed 30 August 2024.

9 See Elizabeth C. Stone, 'Patterns of looting in Southern Iraq', *Antiquity* 82 (2008): 125–38.

10 See Thomas Asher, 'Making sense of the Minerva controversy and the NSCC', Social Science Research Council, October 2008. https://items.ssrc.org/the-minerva-controversy/making-sense-of-minerva-controversy-and-the-nscc/. Accessed 30 August 2024.

11 Saad Eskander, 'Minerva research initiative: Searching for the truth or denying the Iraqis the rights to know truth?', Social Science Research Council, 29 October 2008, https://web.archive.org/web/20100630170753/http://essays.ssrc.org/minerva/2008/10/29/eskander/. Accessed 30 August 2024.

12 Donny George, 'The looting of the Iraq Museum', in *The Destruction of Cultural Heritage in Iraq*, edited by Peter G. Stone and Joanne Farchakh Bajjaly (Woodbridge: Boydell Press, 2008), 97–108.

Part III

Aftermath: erasing/writing

القسم الثالِث: العَواقِب: المَحو/ الكِتابة

Preface

تمهيد

Synopsis

Part III examines the issues of the trafficking of cultural patrimony, the removal and control of archives and documents and the impact of such activities on the subsequent writing of history. The part opens with the text of a lecture that I delivered at UCL in 2011, the year of the withdrawal of US troops from Iraq. The following essays, therefore, cover the long-term aftermath of decisions taken during the war and occupation regarding not only the archaeological sites but also the relocation of archives, the greater reach of the global trade in antiquities, historical manuscripts, and works of modern art from Iraq (many works were also looted from the Museum of Modern Art in Baghdad) and the justifications for such acquisitions in humanist notions such as 'global cultural heritage'.

المستخلص

يُناقِش القسم الثالث قَضايا الاتِّجار بالتراث الحضاري، ونَقل الوثائِق والكُتُب النادِرة والمستندات وفَرْض السيطرة عليها وأثَر مثل هذه المُمارَسات في كِتابة التاريخ لاحِقاً. يُفتَتَح القسم الثالث بنَصٍّ محاضَرةٍ كُنتُ قد ألقَيتُها في جامعة كُليَّة لَندَن في عام 2011، العام الذي شَهد انسحاب القُوّات الأمريكية من العِراق. لِذا فإنَّ المقالات اللاحِقة تُغَطي التَبِعات طويلة الأمَد للقَرارات التي تم اتِّخاذُها إبانَ الحَرب والاحتلال ليس فقط فيما يتَعَلَّق بالمواقِع الأثريَّة، وإنَّما أيضاً بما يتعَلَّق بنقل الوَثائق والكتب النادِرة، وذلك القَنص العظيم للتجارة العالميّة في الآثار، والمَخطوطات التاريخية، وأعمال الفَن الحديث من العراق (إذ أنَّ العديد من الأعمال في متحف الفَن الحَديث في بغداد قد تعرَّضَت هي الأخرى للنَّهب) لتأتي مُبَرِّرات ما تمَّ الاستحواذ عليه هكذا بهيئة مفاهيم إنسانية كمفهوم 'التراث الحضاري العالمي'.

The three essays included in this part were written in the short period between 2011 and 2013, in the context of the withdrawal of US troops from Iraq, bringing the occupation to an official end by December 2011. The first of these is the text of a lecture delivered at the start of that year at UCL, while Iraq was still under occupation. It was never published. At the time, the leading archaeological journals showed little interest in critical assessment of the soldering of the link between archaeological knowledge production and military interests. Any criticism of their increasing interdependence was seen as unpatriotic or worse, and, due to the prevalent atmosphere, the borders of academic publications were controlled to keep out critique.[1] The language and terminology of the military became commonplace in archaeological and heritage studies reportage about Iraq; military officers became the source of unquestioned authority and expertise on academic panels.[2] It was as if the field and its scholarship had become a reserve branch of the Multi-National Forces (MNF) without anyone taking notice. At the same time, leading Assyriologists in the US and Britain, esteemed for their expertise in the cuneiform script of ancient Mesopotamia, authenticated looted tablets and artefacts for the global market in Iraq's heritage, and they published them without heed for either legal or ethical concerns.[3]

I was spending that academic year (2010–11) at All Souls College, Oxford, as the Slade Professor, and I was in the midst of writing a series of art historical lectures that I delivered there under the title *The Infinite Image: Art and ontology in antiquity*. These Slade Lectures were later published as a book where I presented my argument that, in ancient Mesopotamia, images and monuments were ontologically figured to break through the boundaries of time, effecting a survival of the past into the present. Integrated into specific spaces and environments, into the lived experience of the day to day by means of forms of carving and shaping, and by performative rituals, they are thus better understood as a participatory *methexis* rather than mimesis, to use the Ancient Greek Platonic terms.[4] What I argued was in many ways the opposite of one of the dominant art historical methodologies of the time, which followed object biographies through acquisition, collection and movement across the globe, and through theories of reception. I pushed away from this method, which despite its very important contributions to the study of collecting practices and reception histories, de-emphasised the context of such works within their own environments and histories.

In my academic writing and lectures during that final year of occupation, I was deeply immersed in issues of time, memory and the presence of the past – the way that it inheres and manifests itself in artworks and monuments, in rock reliefs carved in the mountains, and in historical architecture. Scientific archaeology, as it strengthened its methods in the first half of the twentieth century, categorised these things as artefacts and documents of particular sociocultural realities of an ancient polity or economic system. Art historians of the same period often saw them in the formal terms of an art object, or as part of the histories of iconographies and style that could be charted or classified. In both cases there was a disinclination to think with any depth or seriousness about how the artwork as a thing, or how the aesthetic dimension as a philosophical concept, was understood in the ontological framework of that ancient world. In thinking with and through objects and ancient texts, I sought an alternative way of looking and seeing – to paraphrase John Berger – and found inspiration and solace in the ancient works themselves. They became artefacts through which I could think about and address the contemporary matters with which I was grappling – uncomfortable matters that surrounded us and threatened the democratic ideals that we had learned to take for granted.

A few years earlier I had returned to the Codex Hammurabi to explore the concept of justice and the law through the oldest surviving monument of law that comes down to us from antiquity, one that documents our human aspiration to justice (ca. 1760 BC). The insight that came out of my study of this early monument of law was that for justice to be just, the law cannot be secret. Accusations cannot be made without presenting evidence, nor can prisoners be held without charge. The fact of the monument itself, the large basalt monolith that Hammurabi had placed in the public sphere, was a statement about the nature of justice.[5] The monument itself, as monument, promulgates the decree of the accessibility of the law. All of the most basic human ideas of justice present in Hammurabi's monument, such as the legal concept of habeas corpus, were at that time being systematically dismissed in the so-called global war on terror. Prisoners were abducted, hooded, shackled and held in black sites of torture, whose secret locations were known to exist, though we knew not where. At the same time, the occupation of Iraq continued, and, after 2006, sectarian violence threatened to consume the land. The beautiful al-Askari mosque and mausoleum in Samarra, with its golden dome and its elegant fine columned façade, was bombed on 22 February 2006, in a targeted terrorist attack meant to destroy this structure in particular. It was an act of war against a building, and it prefigured the horrors that were yet to come in the next decade.

The al-Askari mosque, one of the four major Shia shrines of Islam, was first built in the tenth century AD. Throughout the centuries, various rulers had it restored and repaired so that much of what one sees today dates to the Safavid period, in the seventeenth century, with Ottoman-era repairs. The mosque stands in Samarra, a medieval Abbasid capital city known for its massive spiralling minaret, dating to the ninth century AD, which Western travellers and artists often mistook for the biblical Tower of Babel. The top of the minaret had already suffered from a targeted strike by US forces in 1991, during the First Gulf War. Later, from sometime in 2004 until March 2005, the spiral minaret was occupied by US troops, and the site itself was used as a base, with military berms and trenches dug into it. It is unclear how the terrorists who bombed the mosque in 2006 were able to enter the shrine and set up explosive devices inside, but they somehow managed to do so, according to the Iraqi official who inspected the site the following day.[6]

The art market benefited from these disasters of war. In December of 2007, a small leonine figure carved in crystalline limestone was auctioned at Sotheby's in New York (Figure 19); the Guennol Lioness, as it was called, sold for the highest price ever paid for a sculpture, US$57 million.[7] The problem was not whether it was seen as a work of art, inserted into a Western aesthetic discourse of fine arts or as an artefact of an ancient civilisation divorced from that archaeological discourse. The problem was that the small sculpture – however one chose to define it – was a market commodity in a worldwide antiquities bazaar of neoliberal acquisition. It had been taken out of Iraq decades earlier, but the astronomical price it fetched meant that looting would only increase in the following years.

Since the occupation began in 2003, and relentlessly continuing throughout it, museums and libraries were ransacked and archaeological sites plundered. The land was devastated. These events once again brought to mind the Sumerian poetic laments where war's violent destruction and looting is described, including mournful passages about the plundering of works of art:

> The great door ornament of the temple was felled; its parapet was destroyed; the wild animals that were intertwined on its left and right lay before it like heroes smitten by heroes; its open-mouthed dragons and its awe-inspiring lions were pulled down with ropes like captured wild bulls and carried off to enemy territory.[8]

As David Wengrow has noted, this kind of act can also be understood as a desacralisation and removal of divine protection.[9] His observation regarding the ontological shift that such spoliation indicates is also applicable to the recent looting, as these ancient works are ripped from their context, and while declared global heritage, are transformed into monetised commodities.

While the UCL lecture had been written before the final withdrawal of US troops, the two essays that follow it in this part were written in its aftermath. They reflect on the remains and ruination that we can now begin to understand as the permanent traces and scars of the war and occupation. Such ruination is typical of the aftermath of colonial experience, for imperial violence does not end at the moment of the withdrawal of the occupiers; rather, its forms of damage endure and become inscribed into the environment and into the upheaval and trauma of people's lives. In Iraq, this long-term damage to culture and heritage was marked in other ways. It could be seen in the flourishing global art market, as I have already said, where both looted antiquities and modern art from Iraq circulated, and in the mounting rhetoric of 'global cultural heritage' that supported it.[10] It could also be seen in the academic milieu of Iraq, or what remained of it after the intensive campaign of assassinations that targeted intellectuals and university professors.

While the destructive market in looted antiquities received some attention in the press and in academia, the loss of thousands of works of the Iraqi Modernists, artists of the twentieth century, was barely noticed. The Museum of Modern Art in Baghdad had been pillaged and set on fire on 9 April 2003, according to reports of the time. Almost 8,000 works of modern art, including paintings, sculptures, prints and photography, were lost. This collection held some of the best-known works of the leading artists of the mid-twentieth-century Iraqi Pioneers (al-Ruwad) and the Baghdad Modern Art Group (Jama'et Baghdad lil Fen al-Hadith), including Jewad Selim, Faiq Hassan, Khalid Rahal and Mohammed Ghani Hikmet. Some of these works began to appear in galleries and private homes across the world. Demand for the works of Iraqi Modernist artists has only increased in the market since then.[11] The art world has now started to see the value of these works and their historical significance as postcolonial Modernist works, but ironically some in the West began to speak of 'discovery', using the same terminology of colonial archaeology; as provenance is difficult to document due to the destruction of the museum's archives, the eventual repatriation of these works to Iraq's Museum of Modern Art seems unlikely.

The second text in this part (Chapter 15) begins to address this long-term ruination of Iraq, the devastation that the war and occupation left for us in its wake. In addition to the looting of art and antiquities and the killings of the scientists and professors, the control of archives seized and removed from Iraq while it was under occupation remained in question long after the end of the occupation. They continued to be retained by the United States despite numerous requests for their return.[12] The titles of the two essays in this section, 'Tabula rasa' and 'Amnesia in Mesopotamia', both refer to the presumption of a clean slate of history in Iraq, an idea that was bound to fail in this land of great antiquity, which already in the ancient Epic of Gilgamesh is characterised as a land of deep time.

In August of 2003, Edward Said wrote, in what would be one of his final essays, that many Western scholars had helped justify the case for war with their Orientalist ideas, but that 'history cannot be swept clean like a blackboard, so that "we" might inscribe our own future there and impose our own forms of life for these lesser people to follow'. He continued:

> It is quite common to hear high officials in Washington and elsewhere speak of changing the map of the Middle East, as if ancient societies and myriad peoples can be shaken up like so many peanuts in a jar. But this has often happened with the 'orient', that semi-mythical construct which since Napoleon's invasion of Egypt in the late 18th century has been made and remade countless times. In the process the uncountable sediments of history, and dizzying variety of peoples, languages, experiences and cultures are swept aside or ignored, relegated to the sandheap along with the treasures ground into meaningless fragments that were taken out of Baghdad.[13]

In Iraq itself, the director of the National Library and State Archives, Saad Eskander, continued to demand the return of materials airlifted out by the US military, reminding us of the Orwellian phrase that control of the archive is the control of history.[14] The erasure of monuments and history, we soon saw, could become horrendous acts of direct warfare, as 2014 brought the horrors of ISIS/Daesh to Iraq and Syria.

Notes

1 There were a few exceptions among academic journals; they include the *Journal of the World Archaeological Congress*, *Archaeologies*, and *Public Archaeology*.

2 Yannis Hamilakis, '"The War on Terror" and the military-archaeology complex', *Archaeologies* 5 (2009): 39–65, refers to specific examples of this militarisation. He also notes that he

withdrew from one such conference at Cambridge University in 2008, along with two other colleagues, because a UK Army General still actively in charge of British forces in Iraq at the time was on the same panel. I was one of the other two that withdrew.

3 The first-time publication of an unprovenanced tablet provides a scholarly authentication and inclusion into the scholarly corpus. It is considered an unacceptable and unethical practice in the field of archaeology and is not accepted by the leading archaeological organisations, including the Archaeological Institute of America, which will not publish any looted material as a first-time publication.

4 Zainab Bahrani, *The Infinite Image: Art, time and the aesthetic dimension in antiquity* (London: Reaktion, 2014).

5 See Zainab Bahrani, *The Infinite Image: Art, time and the aesthetic dimension in antiquity* (London: Reaktion, 2014), 173–90 (chapter 6, 'The monumental force of the law'); see also Bahrani, *Rituals of War* (Philadelphia: University of Pennsylvania Press, 2008), 101–30.

6 According to the description by Iraq's Construction Minister, Jassem Mohammed Jaafar. See Imad Khadduri, 'Who benefits from the Samarra attack? A short "history"', 26 February 2006. https://www.uruknet.info/?p=m21047&l=i&size=1&hd=0.

7 Sotheby's, *Antiquities*, 5 December 2007, lot 30. https://www.sothebys.com/en/auctions/ecatalogue/2007/antiquities-n08373/lot.30.html?locale=en.

8 Translation after Piotr Michalowski, *Lamentations over the Destruction of Sumer and Ur* (Winona Lake, IN: Eisenbrauns, 1989), 63 (translation emended). These laments date to the third millennium BC. Quoted and discussed in Zainab Bahrani, *Rituals of War* (Philadelphia: University of Pennsylvania Press, 2008), 166.

9 David Wengrow, 'Art and material culture', in *A Companion to the Ancient Near East,* edited by Ann C. Gunter (Hoboken, NJ: Wiley, 2019), 37.

10 The main proponent of this widespread argument was James Cuno, who at the time was the director of the Art Institute of Chicago and would later head the J. Paul Getty Trust. See Cuno, *Who Owns Antiquity* (Princeton, NJ: Princeton University Press, 2008), which came out while Iraq was under occupation and was widely read and cited; see also Cuno, 'Art museums, archaeology, and antiquities in the age of sectarian violence and nationalist politics', in *Acquisition and Exhibition of Classical Antiquity*, edited by Robin F. Rhodes (Notre Dame, IN: University of Notre Dame Press, 2008), 9–26.

11 See interview with the Iraqi art historian Nada Shabout, who has been at the forefront of the work that documents and seeks to locate the looted modernists works: Isis Nusair, 'The cultural costs of the 2003 US-led invasion of Iraq: Conversation with art historian Nada Shabout', *Feminist Studies* 39 (2013): 119–48. Also see Shabout, 'The free art of occupation', *Arab Studies Quarterly* 28 (2006): 41–53; Shabout, 'Historiographic invisibilities', *International Journal of the Humanities* 3 (9) (November 2006): 53–64; Shabout, 'Bifurcations of Iraq's visual culture', in *We Are Iraqis: Aesthetics and politics in a time of war*, edited by Nadje Al-Ali and Deborah Al-Najjar (Syracuse, NY: Syracuse University Press, 2012), 5–23.

12 See Wisam H. Alshaibi, 'Weaponising Iraq's archives', in *Middle East Report* 291 (Summer 2019): 3–9; Nabil al-Tikriti, '"Stuff happens": A brief overview of the 2003 destruction of Iraqi manuscript collections, archives, and libraries', *Library Trends* 55 (3) (Winter 2007), 730–45; Rebecca Abby Whiting, 'Destruction and displacement: The 2003 war and the struggle for Iraq's records', in *Archives: Power, truth and fiction*, edited by Alison Prescott and Andrew Wiggins (Oxford: Oxford University Press, 2023), 455–70.

13 Edward W. Said, 'A window on the world', *The Guardian*, 1 August 2003.

14 cf. George Orwell, *1984: A Novel* (New York: Harcourt Brace, 1949), 35: 'Who controls the past … controls the future: who controls the present controls the past'.

14

Archaeology, global cultural heritage and Iraq

UCL Institute of Archaeology, 27 January 2011

’علم الآثار، التراث الحضاري العالمي، والعراق‘ جامعة كلية لندن، قسم الآثار، 27 كانون الثاني، 2011.

Synopsis

In 2011 the end of the US occupation of Iraq was officially declared by the US under the Obama administration. Forces were withdrawn, leaving only a smaller number behind in the more long-term US bases set to remain in Iraq. Early in the same year, I was invited to speak at UCL's Institute of Archaeology. In the lecture that forms the basis of this chapter, I chose to discuss the concept of 'global cultural heritage', which by that time I had begun to see as a term that permitted the appropriation of cultural artefacts from the Global South into free-market economies that regarded them as commodities of social distinction. My argument is framed around a particular episode: in 2007, a small alabaster lioness (known as the 'Guennol Lioness' after the Welsh form of the name of the modern owner, Mr Alastair Bradley Martin) was sold at Sotheby's for US$57.2 million. It was the highest price ever paid for a sculpture.

المستخلص

في عام 2011، تمَّ إعلان انتهاء الاحتلال الأمريكي للعراق رسميّاً من قِبَل الولايات المُتَّحِدة بإدارة أوباما. انسَحَبَت القُوّات، تارِكةً وَراءَها عدداً أقل من الجنود في القَواعِد الأمريكية طويلة الأمَد التي أُنشِأَت لتَبقى في العراق. قَبلَ ذلك بقليل في العام ذاته، كُنتُ قَد دُعيتُ للحَديث في قسم علوم الآثار التابع لجامعة كلية لندن. في المحاضَرة

الّتي تُشكّل أساسَ هذا الفَصل، اختَرْتُ أن أُناقِش مفهوم ’التُراث الحَضاري العالَمي‘، إذ كُنتُ حينَها قَد بدأتُ أراه كمُصطَلَح يَسمَح بالاستيلاء على التُحَف الحضاريّة من الجَنوب العالمي وزَجِّها في اقتصاديات السوق الحُرَّة التي تتعامل معها على أنَّها سِلَع التَّميُّز الاجتماعي. تَتأطَّر حُجَّتي حول حَلَقة مُعَيَّنة: في عام 2007، تم بَيع لَبوة سومَريَّة من حجر الألَباستَر (تُعرَف بـ ’لبوة غوينول‘ وهو الاسم الذي أُطلِقَ عليها نِسبةً للكُنية الويلزية لمالكِها الحديث، السيد أليستَر برادلي مارتن) في دار سوذبي للمزادات بمبلغ 57.2 مليون دولار أمريكي. لَقَد كان هذا أعلى سِعر على الإطلاق بيعَت به مَنحوتة.

In the seventh century BC, the Assyrian king Esarhaddon restored the sanctuary of the goddess Ishtar at Uruk (Figure 18). That sanctuary, we know from archaeological evidence, was built at some point in the mid fourth-millennium BC, almost 3,000 years before the height of the Assyrian Empire. The time interval between Esarhaddon's restoration and the building of the original sanctuary is similar to that between our own day and the era of the Greek city-states. It was several centuries longer than the interval of time between the formation of the modern nation of Iraq after the fall of the Ottoman Empire and the reign of Nebuchadnezzar II in Babylon (604–562 BC). What today, then, leads us to believe that interest in the past, together with monument preservation or restoration, is a modern invention? We do have our own archaeology with its modern epistemology and methods, but as Alain Schnapp and Yannis Hamilakis have each shown us in different ways, we are certainly not the first people to relate to traces of the past.[1]

There are many forms of scholarly interaction with the ancient past, which we might call archaeologies, and many ways to engage with antiquity. The past is a parallel dream-time to some, and to others it is a constant presence, crossing over into our everyday existence. The end of this enchanted vision of the world in which the past and the present are parallel, interlaced realms may form the basis for our own scientific archaeology, but perhaps not completely. We now think of archaeology in terms of excavating, of recording and preserving all traces of the past as thoroughly as we can, and we see these activities as distinctively modern.

Esarhaddon was neither the first nor the last ancient Mesopotamian ruler who set out to preserve and repair ancient buildings and restore sculptures and monuments. Throughout Mesopotamian history, as in many other cultures across the world, the practice of preserving the past was ideologically embedded in the idea of correct and sacrosanct rule. It was also a way of honouring dead ancestors and establishing ties to place by means of monuments and sacred sites, creating what Pierre Nora would, in more recent years, come to call *lieux de memoire*.[2] It is by some hubris or artifice of modernity that we take the concern with the past to be an invention of our own time. That hubris becomes even more egregious when the claim is made – as it often is today by some camps in archaeology and anthropology – that the concern with the past (and even the ability to have a conceptual projection of a future time, as some archaeologists suggest) is not only modern but also Western, and that it was only the Western imperial enterprise that taught the native about his past. These are old arguments that clearly emerge from the discourse of that civilising mission called 'empire', but their ghosts remain with us. These spectres of imperial archaeology seem to be haunting us in more than one way in our own time. They have re-emerged in our own current global wars.

The destruction and looting of ancient sites and museums in the war and occupation of Iraq has certainly become a prominent subject in archaeology over the past seven years, but these discussions have mostly remained at the level of how we can rescue antiquities in the midst of conflict. Many people, archaeologists and others, have given us competing accounts in public lectures or in statements to the press, in blogs and in academic journals, each one claiming to provide the most accurate story of the events as they unfolded in March and April of 2003, and later.

Right from the beginning of this war, in both Britain and the United States, the news of the looting of the museums in the spring of 2003 quickly turned into a heated debate circling around, above all else, the exact amount of stolen objects from the Iraq Museum in Baghdad. What I would like to speak about today is somewhat different. I am not here to recount the story of the looting of the museums and libraries of Iraq, or to give you a list of numbers of things that were lost or things that were found. From my point of view, that kind of tallying and attempt at quantification of the loss of antiquity is of little use. Worse yet, it is (in my opinion) a distraction from the real issues at hand. As scholars, we might rather address the question of what these current events of cultural destruction in Iraq, and the response to them, mean to the disciplines of archaeology, anthropology and art history, in terms of both archaeological practice and theory.

Let's begin with the obvious. What has the response of archaeologists and archaeological organisations and institutions been to the extensive destruction of archaeological sites and historical material in Iraq? Since Iraq is the region of Mesopotamia, the so-called 'cradle of civilisation', its ancient past is of great importance to the entire word, and in the West we say that we are the recipients of that heritage.

This nineteenth-century idea still carries a lot of weight today. For example, recently the three most prominent museum collections of antiquities in Europe – the Louvre in Paris, the British Museum in London and the Pergamon Museum in Berlin – all presented an exhibition of antiquities from Babylon, unproblematically, as a part of European history. At the same time, the relationship that the nation-state of Iraq has to its Mesopotamian past is described, by this same scholarly discourse, as a construction, an invented tradition, which is of course a correct observation, but no less so when applied to the European appropriation of that past. This is also the old story whereby other people's relations to the past are invented and constructed, whereas ours are historical fact.

Even though it has now been almost eight years since the first days of the museum looting in Iraq, our discussions on the fate of historical sites or antiquities have remained at the level of unease over the unfortunate 'collateral damage' of war and occupation (to use that grim Pentagon phrase). This damage, we always hear, included some 'important cultural heritage', a patrimony that is seen not so much as a loss for Iraq as a state or for its people, but for 'our global cultural heritage'. As archaeologists, we are the stewards in charge of that heritage. In any case, this is what the Archaeological Institute of America (AIA), along with 21 other leading organisations, like the American Anthropological Association (AAA) and the Society for American Archaeology, declared on our behalf in 2003: in a letter sent to the US government, they commended the military for the protection of heritage sites, which the letter describes as being 'in contrast to the inhuman regime that has just ended'.[3] This kind of rhetoric of a bipolarity of civilisation and barbarism has had, as you all know already, a tremendous resurgence in the past decade, reviving the old Orientalism into a reloaded, remixed version of itself. While much of this rhetoric has been on the doorstep of archaeology, the discipline has had very little to say about it.[4]

At the same time, ironically, during the past decade there has been a great resurgence of the concept of historical memory in the fields of art history and historical studies. From Émile Durkheim's and Maurice Halbwachs's ideas of historical consciousness and collective memory to the works of Pierre Nora and others, the idea that collective memory, history and identity are sustained by a relationship to things and places, by means of rituals and commemorative rites, has been at the forefront of art historical and archaeological thought.[5] These discussions, however, have not addressed the concept of global cultural heritage, the encyclopaedic art museum and the destruction of history in Iraq. To my mind the field of ancient Near Eastern archaeology has failed terribly here, because it remains shackled to its insistence on interpreting all ancient Mesopotamian art and cultural production as reflecting Oriental despotism. In several of my previous works, I have tried to point out the serious intellectual flaws and even racist overtones of that paradigm. Intellectually, that kind of straightjacketed thinking leaves no space for any more nuanced understanding of ancient works or of ancient people's relationships to the things in the world in which they lived, and the idea that global cultural heritage is a neutral and apolitical concept continues to be upheld in the midst of war and looting.

With a couple of important exceptions, exhibitions, websites and academic conferences (along with the papers and publications that have emerged from these conferences) have mostly circumvented the more unpleasant issues of the relationship between archaeology, cultural heritage and the act of war. What are these issues?

The first is archaeological practice and the question of ethics in relation to war and military archaeology. This subject was taken up in 2008 by the World Archaeological Congress, which has now posted a statement explaining that group's stance on the matter, a stance that is antiwar.[6] It has likewise been addressed by the Anthropological Association of America. The Archaeological Institute of America, on the other hand, has a different attitude: its focus over the past seven years has been mostly on the need to protect the archaeological sites from looting. On the bright side, the looting of Iraq has raised public awareness about the illicit trade in antiquities in general, and this has perhaps helped to slow this down in other places with antiquities-rich terrains, like Greece and Italy. This call for the protection of sites from looting, as well-meaning as it is, has heavily relied on the idea of 'our shared global cultural heritage'. But we don't acknowledge that this is also the idea used by those in favour of the market in antiquities. They claim that if antiquity is global cultural heritage and that modern nation-states are constructions that have no relations to their past, then who is to say that antiquities cannot become merchandise available to a free and open market, to be bought by the highest bidder?

It is perhaps not insignificant that at the same time that these discussions were taking place, a small marble lion-demon statue was sold at Sotheby's for US$57.2 million (Figure 19).[7] It was the highest price ever paid for a sculpture of any kind – yes, including works by Michaelangelo or Rodin. Although scholars have always identified the lion figure as being probably from Iran, it was advertised everywhere as a Mesopotamian statue.

The opposing view to the free market one has been that the trade in ancient objects and works of art destroys scientific information needed for study purposes. These are the two sides of the debate as we have it today. In our pragmatic world, we think of these things as commodities for our own use, either marketable goods or scientific objects for our own reseach, forgetting the archaeology of memory that we teach and write about, as well as our own scholarly theories of the materiality of the past – how things assert their presence, or how inanimate objects organise the temporality of the animate world. We say nothing about how the destruction of history can be an attempt to destroy people's collective memory, that collective memory is the basis of group identity, and that its erasure is a historically well-known means by which people seek to eradicate each other in acts of war. The implied position of that silence, as well as the silence about the deaths of hundreds of academics, is that artefacts are separate scientific things, and that archaeological work somehow does not involve living people. This silence is even more distressing when it is the silence of field archaeologists, because fieldwork depends on a relationship with the local community. Whether they are willing to admit it or not, archaeologists, like anthropologists, deal with things that are relevant to living people, their cultures and histories. Although the official stance is that silence on the matter of civilian death in this war is correct academic form, because it is apolitical and objective, we know from our own scholarship that silence in the face of such acts is always a political statement in itself in a historical record. I am thinking of scholars like Walter Benjamin and Maurice Halbwachs, whose works I have turned to in thinking about things and memory, and whose tragic deaths in the Second World War are addressed now in academic writing.[8]

The question of the place or the idea of ethics in archaeological and anthropological practice has now begun to receive some attention because of the active recruiting of social scientists by the military; but of course the relationship of archaeology (or the social sciences) to war is not a new thing. The revival of the closer ties between the military (military personnel, and even military technologies) and the field of archaeology is one of the spectres of imperial archaeology, returned.

Just this last month the Archaeological Institute of America, under the presidency of Brian Rose, a classicist, has made its relationship with the Pentagon unambiguous. It has set up a new arm of the AIA it called CHAMP (Cultural Heritage Archaeological Military Panel), and a link on the AIA website explains how archaeology can serve in the war effort.[9]

Among the recommended readings on the link, none of the articles of scholars who have been openly critical of the war and occupation are included, while articles by active and reserve members of the military are. Needless to say this is not only a stance that alienates many scholars, but it also removes any possibility of archaeology being anything but embedded and militarised.

The second unpleasant issue that has been circumvented is the archival record and the politics of perception: we have not thought about the system of divisions and boundaries that define, among other things, what is visible or sayable within a particular regime (to paraphrase the philosopher Jacques Rancière).[10] How do these affect the production of the record of these acts? We have not addressed the issue of the truth claims of the official accounts regarding the damage of cultural heritage. We don't apply any critical or analytical thinking to these accounts, even though that is what we are trained to do, and we would consider it faulty and incompetent not to do so with any other historical information or official statements. It is clear that some accounts of the situation with cultural heritage are given voice as 'objective', while others are sidelined or considered 'biased'. As a result of some of the most publicised accounts, one might say that the destruction of cultural heritage in Iraq has become salvaged into a narrative of rescue and reconstruction, where in fact what we have before us is a catastrophic loss. This was most obvious in the public-relations ploy of the whirlwind exhibition of the Nimrud gold.[11] This was displayed in Baghdad in July 2003 and presented as having been rescued by the US military, when in fact it survived because it had been stored in a vault by the curators in prepartion for the war – something I witnessed Donny George Youkhanna trying to point out several times, his remarks falling upon deaf ears. This domination of the very narrative of the events, of the historical account of what has happened to historical sites and cultural institutions, and even who has been working to rescue and preserve these, is a facet that was not forseen in March and April of 2003, even though it repeats events from the early-twentieth century. Cultural heritage becomes yet one more pawn in the game of war.

The third unpleasant issue that has been circumvented concerns the broader theoretical implications of such large-scale cultural destruction in war. And, for me, this is a remarkable silence among art and architectural historians, archaeologists and anthropologists who are otherwise keen to analyse such destruction in historical cases and in other regions (such as the former Yugoslavia); thus, I will spend the remainder of my discussion on this third point.

First of all, at the risk of stating the obvious, I would point out that destroying monuments and other material historical objects and documents in war is not always accidental. In my own university in New York, a number of us in the departments of art history, anthropology and other fields have published books on the ambivalence of iconoclasm, and the agency of art objects and monuments.[12] Destruction and iconoclasm in general have been acts of war throughout history. As archaeologists and historians, we recognise and readily acknowledge them in the acts of others in the historical past. We have also seen them clearly, recorded and analysed them in other wars of more recent years; but when it comes to Iraq, that same critical thinking has become clouded. No analytical thought has been put to this cultural destruction, nor have there been any scholarly theoretical studies of these acts and events. What we have seen instead is a number of scholars or institutions that have set out to objectively document the extent of the damage to archaeological sites by looting, using satellite imagery, or to create databases of museum collections from published images available here in the West. These attempts are laudable, but the idea of an objective documentation of destruction in war (funded by governments that instigated the war in the first place) is problematic to say the least.

Documenting the destruction of ancient sites and museums in Iraq is an unachievable task at this point in time. Iraq is still a land under a military occupation; the violent conditions that pervade it, and the extensive military access-limitations of blast walls and checkpoints, make any on-site surveys of damage impossible. The idea that we can document cultural destruction with any thoroughness, while sitting in an armchair in New York or London amassing digital images, compiling databases and lists of things, is perhaps more of an illusion that is comforting for our own sense of order in the world outside Iraq. I will leave aside, for now, the issue that government funding for the so-called rescue and repair of Iraq's cultural heritage is mostly channelled to institutions in Europe and the United States rather than being used for actual preservation or repairs in Iraq, but this is a problem that we also need to address openly.

As in other wars at other times and places, the destruction of monuments and historical archives in Iraq works to erase the historical landscape and the realms of memory around which people define their collective identities, but this has not been discussed. Has there simply been a sort of intellectual delay in our field? Is it that we have just not had the time to address this issue directly? Or is there an implicit argument here that in the current occupation of Iraq, the destruction of heritage over the past seven years all falls under the category of accidental damage?

Before the 2003 air campaign in Iraq, archaeologists and scholars of Near Eastern antiquity were well aware of the possible dangers to Iraq's archaeological sites, and they spoke out publicly and with a united voice regarding the need to protect museums, monuments and heritage sites in the case of an invasion. What no one had foreseen was that a great part of the damage to cultural heritage would occur not as a result of the bombing campaign or the ground war but under the subsequent occupation by the US and coalition forces.

If military conflict and occupation implies, at least in part, an aspect that is heavily territorial, then the historic environment as enemy terrain or the territory of conquest is a subject that needs to be addressed more directly by archaeological theory. The conceptual territory of antiquity and the uses of the past in nineteenth-century imperialism is an area that has been discussed specifically by some. Others have written on antiquity as 'symbolic capital' for nation-states, cultures or ethnic groups. But these uses of the symbolic capital of the past for reconfiguring colonised lands has taken on a new kind of material reality through the physical occupation of antiquity, a reality that has, by the way, extensively damaged the archaeological remains.

This was the case with the archaeological site of Babylon (see Figures 11–17). Babylon was first occupied by the US Marines in April 2003. The camp, known as Camp Alpha, or 'the Ruins' in military terminology, was ceded to the Polish military command in the autumn of 2003. Much of the infrastructure of this extensive camp, housing thousands of troops as the headquarters of South Central Command, had been installed under the US military: for example, the bulldozing and paving for a helicopter pad in the heart of the ancient site, between the area of the Neo-Babylonian palace and the Hellenistic theatre, the provision of plumbing or sewage disposal for the troops digging into the site, and the use of the site for construction projects under KBR, a private, US-based engineering firm. Construction work continued throughout the ancient site under Polish command. As an aside, I would like to point out that although the United States and the UK have not ratified the Hague Convention of 1954, Poland has signed and ratified it.[13] Article 28 allows for the prosecution of those breaking the convention.

Because places like Babylon are military camps and security is invoked as a reason for limiting access, the international press had little to say about this. In Iraq itself, as a rule, archaeologists from the State Board of Antiquities and Heritage were not allowed onto sites that had been taken over as military camps. No permission was sought by the coalition forces before any construction work, movement of earth, or changes in the topography made by the military. Although the Antiquities and Heritage Law of Iraq requires that any construction work at a heritage or archaeological site be authorised by the State Board of Antiquities and Heritage (SBAH), this law was ignored by the military, whose spokesmen stated to me that, for security purposes, all such laws are suspended during the war and the occupation. As a result, only a handful of archaeologists have seen the site while it was a military camp. I was one of the unfortunate few. I spent several months in the summer of 2004 negotiating with military commanders in Babylon for the removal of the military base from the site. The base was finally closed down in January of 2005.

In late 2006, Colonel John Coleman, speaking to the BBC, insisted that anything the military had done at Babylon was carried out in close consultation with the SBAH.[14] He explained that before setting up camp, the US command had 'made an analysis' and had come to the conclusion that it would be best for the site because it would protect it from looters, given what had happened at the museum in Baghdad. In fact, during the dozens of meetings that I had with US officers on the matter of Babylon in 2004, there was no one who could answer the question of who it was that had taken the decision to occupy Babylon, or why. There was no one who had any information about a decision, a plan or a strategy. And no Iraqi on the SBAH staff had been consulted. In fact, the representative of the SBAH at Babylon repeatedly complained that the coalition had no right to occupy the site, and we certainly have the written correspondence to show that Coleman's account was not entirely accurate. Later, after we had exposed the story through the press, the idea of 'protection' emerged from the Public Affairs Office of the US Department of Defense and the Coalition Provisional Authority.[15] This excuse of 'protection' is now being invoked in various contexts across occupied Iraq. In fact, the damage done to Babylon is both extensive and irreparable, and even if US forces had wanted to protect it, placing guards around the site would clearly have been far more sensible than bulldozing it and setting up the largest coalition military headquarters in the region.

The idea that the military occupation of Babylon was for its own protection in any case does not explain the larger question. While Babylon is the most famous site that was occupied as a military base, it is certainly not the only one. At least seven or eight historical sites were used in this way by US and coalition forces since April 2003, one of them being the historical heart of Samarra, the city where the beautiful al-Askari mosque was bombed in 2006.[16]

The 2001 destruction of the Bamiyan Buddhas by the Taliban regime, as a form of direct iconoclasm, was met with international cries of concern and dismay.[17] Yet there has been relative silence in response to the destruction of historical sites in Iraq. What are the factors that make one type of destruction seem horrendous and unacceptable and another more readily acceptable as part of the inevitable damage of war? Can we read the occupation and destruction of a legendary site such as Babylon along the same theoretical lines as iconoclastic acts?

Twenty years ago David Freedberg wrote that acts of destruction we call iconoclasm reveal a belief in the power of the image rather than a disregard for it.[18] More recently, in response to the destruction of the Bamiyan Buddhas, he argued convincingly that this was a perfect indication of the Taliban's fear of the power of these magnificent colossal images.[19] The occupation and consequent destruction of Babylon by coalition forces, one might say, reveal a similar ambivalence. The occupation of the site was not undertaken, as the Pentagon's Public Affairs statement has it, to protect it from looting, or even because of an unfortunate disregard or lack of interest in Mesopotamian antiquity, but precisely because Babylon was read by its military occupiers as a synonym of the occupied land; its occupation, then, became a sign of military might and power over that subjugated land. In a very real way, Babylon was also the place for military aggression as a form of theatrical display. It was chosen for this purpose – not despite the fact that it is Iraq's most famous, legendary heritage site, but because of its fame and mythical value.

If we consider the military victory ceremonies that took place when the base was established, this is fairly clear. In April 2003, press reports stated that US troops likened their entrance into Babylon to that of Alexander the Great and his troops in the fourth century BC.[20]

Tanks drove along the ancient processional way in a victory parade, and occupation ceremonies took place that were photographed and published by the media. The occupation of sites such as Babylon and the images of military force at the ancient ruins can be described as part of a visual semiotics of occupation, a display of force that uses the sign of history and its control as a statement of victory.

But the occupation of archaeological or heritage sites during war, as a practice or an act of war, still has to be addressed seriously in the theoretical work of archaeologists. The use of archaeological sites, the deployment of architectural construction, and the demolition of older city centers in the name of modernisation are well-known tools of colonial occupation in previous eras and in other lands. In Iraq, the establishing of vast so-called 'enduring bases', along with the militarisation of urban space in Baghdad and elsewhere by the erection of countless concrete blast walls and checkpoints, has not been addressed. These are not just aesthetic issues or theoretical questions, obviously. They are related directly to human rights. The lived experience of people in a land characterised by tells, monuments and historical architecture is disrupted, becoming a form of erasure of people and their environments of daily life. While this damage has not been considered in a theoretical way in the context of the US and coalition war in Iraq, the manipulation and destruction of the historical and architectural fabric of occupied land has elsewhere been seen as an instrument of war.

The events of April 2003 are still lamented everywhere as the unfortunate collateral damage of war, as another consequence of the occupation that was not foreseen and was, like so many other aspects of the occupation, due to the lack of foresight of the Bush and Blair administrations. But even if the original looting of the museums and libraries could not have been avoided or was not foreseen (an excuse that I find rather weak, given the fact that numerous archaeologists and scholars had warned both the US and UK governments against exactly such a scenario, months before the war), there are areas of cultural destruction that were preplanned.

The Pentagon's strategic decision to use some of the main cultural heritage sites of the country as US and coalition military bases is an example. In addition to Babylon, these sites include Ur, the legendary birthplace of the biblical Abraham; Kish, the city where in Sumerian legend, kingship descended to the world; and Samarra, an Abbasid royal city; as well as Early Christian sites such as Dair Mar Eliya. The digging, bulldozing, filling of sand bags and blast-barricade containers, the building of barracks and hollowing of trenches into the ancient sites, destroyed archaeological material, stratigraphy and historical data. Walls and standing structures have collapsed as a result of shootings, bombings and helicopter landings, but we have not even addressed these events at the level of scientific destruction, let alone considered the impact on people's lives.

The fact often cited by those wishing to dismiss the importance of cultural destruction (on both sides of the war debate, in support and in opposition), that people's relations to monuments, history and landscape are always and everywhere constructed, does not make cultural destruction any more ethically acceptable or even legal in international law. Those on the Left have dismissed the issue of the destruction of cultural heritage as a frivolous Western humanist concern in the midst of war and the plight of the people struggling to live day to day. Those on the Right have dismissed it as accidental collateral damage, unfortunate but necessary for the greater good. But as historians and archaeologists know, it is precisely through such destruction that empires have usually remapped space. It is the way that they have dislocated, expelled, forcibly removed and attempted to erase populations. It is the way they have taken over lands and rewritten histories. If groups of people or nation-states construct identities through monuments and historical narratives, the opposite is also true. The destruction of monuments and archives, the reconfiguration of urban space and forced relocation of groups of people, and the erasure and rewriting of historical accounts have long been aspects of war.

Notes

1 Alain Schnapp, *La conquête du passé: Aux origines de l'archéologie* (Paris: Éditions Carré, 1993); Yannis Hamilakis, 'Indigenous archaeologies in Ottoman Greece', in *Scramble for the Past*, edited by Zainab Bahrani, Zeynep Çelik and Edhem Eldem, 49–69 (Istanbul: Salt, 2011).

2 Pierre Nora, 'Between memory and history: Les lieux de mémoire', *Representations* 26, special issue: *Memory and Counter-Memory* (Spring 1989): 7–24.

3 See the full letter addressed to then-president George W. Bush, at https://www.archaeological.org/pdfs/home/USICOMOSletteronIraq.pdf.

4 There are a few exceptions: see Khaled Nashef, *Tadmir al Turath al Hadhari al Iraqii* (Beirut: Dar al Hamra, 2004; in Arabic); Yannis Hamilakis, 'Iraq, stewardship and the record', *Public Archaeology* 3 (2003): 104–11; Reinhardt Bernbeck, 'Structural violence in archaeology', *Archaeologies* 4 (2008): 390–413; Yannis Hamilakis, 'The "War on Terror" and the military-archaeology complex', *Archaeologies* 5 (2009): 39–65.

5 See, among others, Émile Durkheim, *The Elementary Forms of Religious Life*, translated by Karen E. Fields (New York: Free Press, 1995 [1912]); Maurice Halbwachs, *On Collective Memory*, translated by Lewis A. Coser (Chicago: University of Chicago Press, 1992 [1950]); Pierre Nora, 'Between memory and history: Les lieux de mémoire', *Representations* 26, special issue: *Memory and Counter-Memory* (Spring 1989): 7–24.

6 Media release at https://worldarch.org/wp-content/uploads/2008/06/cultural_heritage_in_iran_under_threat.pdf (14 July 2008).

7 Sotheby's, *Antiquities*, 5 December 2007, lot 30. https://www.sothebys.com/en/auctions/ecatalogue/2007/antiquities-n08373/lot.30.html?locale=en.

8 See, for example, Walter Benjamin, *The Arcades Project*, translated by Howard Eiland and Kevin McLaughlin (Cambridge, MA: Harvard University Press, 2002 [edited from an unpublished project written between 1927 and 1940]); Maurice Halbwachs, *On Collective Memory*, translated by Lewis A. Coser (Chicago: University of Chicago Press, 1992 [1950]).

9 An announcement of the site's 2011 launch can be viewed at https://www.archaeological.org/cultural-heritage-by-aia-military-panel-announces-website-launch/. At the time of publication of the present volume, the CHAMP site is no longer active.

10 See Jacques Rancière, *The Politics of Aesthetics*, translated by Gabriel Rockhill (London: Continuum Press, 2004).

11 See Shaila K. Dewan, 'After the war: Baghdad; Iraq Museum reopens with Assyrian treasures', *New York Times*, 4 July 2003. https://www.nytimes.com/2003/07/04/world/after-the-war-baghdad-iraq-museum-reopens-with-assyrian-treasures.html.

12 See, for instance, David Freedberg, *The Power of Images* (Chicago, IL: University of Chicago Press, 1989); Zoe Strother, 'Iconoclasm by proxy', in *Iconoclash*, edited by Bruno Latour and Peter Weibel, 458–9 (Cambridge, MA: MIT Press, 2002); Zainab Bahrani, *The Graven Image* (Philadelphia: University of Pennsylvania Press, 2003); *Rituals of War* (New York: Zone Books, 2008); Andreas Huyssen, *Present Pasts: Urban palimpsests and the politics of memory* (Stanford: Stanford University Press, 2003); Michael Taussig, 'Iconoclasm dictionary', *TDR: The Drama Review*, 56 (1) (Spring 2012): 10–17.

13 The articles of the convention and the list of participating nations are accessible at https://en.unesco.org/protecting-heritage/convention-and-protocols/1954-convention.

14 For a summary of the interview, see Jonathan Charles, 'US Marines offer Babylon apology', BBC News, 14 April 2006. https://news.bbc.co.uk/2/hi/middle_east/4908940.stm.

15 As expressed by Coleman in the BBC interview cited above (n. 14).

16 For the history of the al-Askari mosque, see A. Northedge, 'Samarra', *Encyclopaedeia of Islam*, new edition, vol. VIII (Leiden: Brill, 1995), 1039–41; see also https://www.archnet.org/sites/5525.

17 See, for example, Luke Harding, 'Taliban blow apart 2,000 years of Buddhist history', *The Guardian*, 3 March 2001. https://www.theguardian.com/world/2001/mar/03/afghanistan.lukeharding.

18 David Freedberg, *The Power of Images* (Chicago: University of Chicago Press, 1989).

19 David Freedberg, 'The power of wood and stone', *Washington Post*, 25 March 2001.

20 See Nicholas Mirzoeff, *Watching Babylon: The war in Iraq and global visual culture* (New York: Routledge, 2005).

15 Tabula rasa

New York University, 11 October 2012

’الصفحة البيضاء-اللَّوح الفارغ-‘ جامعة نيويورك، 11 تشرين الأول، 2012.

Synopsis

This essay derives from a 2012 lecture at New York University in which I addressed the systematic targeting of the academics and scientists of Iraq that took place especially between 2003 and 2006. It begins with a discussion of cultural sites such as the Monument of the Unknown Soldier in Baghdad, where troops had deliberately damaged or covered over the names of the Iraqi conscripts who had died in the Iraq–Iran war, and whose names were inscribed into this monument to the war dead. It then takes up the issue of the now-forgotten series of deliberate assassinations of hundreds of intellectuals that was recorded in those years by a leading Iraqi academic, who was himself assassinated in 2006 (after which the record ceased to be maintained). Since there is no memorial or recognition of this immense tragedy, the chapter includes images from a list of the names of the assassinated academics, along with their affiliations and date of assassination. This is based on a series of slides presented during the original lecture as a visual statement.

المستخلص

إنّ هذه المَقالة مُستَمدَّة من مُحاضَرة ألقَيتُها عام 2012 في جامعة نيويورك والتي تناوَلتُ فيها الاستهداف المُمَنهَج للأكاديميين والعُلماء في العراق والذي حدَثَ تَحديداً ما بين عامَي 2003 و2006. بَدأتْ هذه المقالة بمُناقَشة بَعض المواقع الثَّقافيّة مثل نَصْب الشهيد لاسماعيل فتاح في بغداد، حيثُ قامَ جُنودٌ عَمْداً بإتْلاف أو تَغطية أسماء الجنود العراقيين الَّذين استُشهِدوا في الحَرب العراقيّة الإيرانيّة، واللّذين نُقِشَت أسماؤهُم

في هذا النَّصب التِّذكاري لشُهداء الحَرب. ثُمّ تناولَت قضيَّة سلسلة من الاغتيالات المُتعمَّدة والتي باتَت في طَي النسيان حاليّاً للمئات من المُثقَّفين والتي قام بتسجيلها في تلك السنوات أكاديمي عراقي بارز، والذي بدورِهِ كان قد أُغتيلَ أيضاً في عام 2006 (بعد ذلك توقَّفت عملية التسجيل رغم عدد الذين تم اغتيالهم بعده). نَظراً لعدَم وجود أي نصبٍ تذكاري أو اعتراف رسمي بتلك المأساة المَهولة، فَقَد تضَمَّن هذا الفَصل قائمةً بأسماء من تمَّ اغتيالَهم من الأكاديميين، موَضَّحاً فيها أماكن عملهم وتواريخ اغتيالهم. اعتمدَت هذه المقالة على مجموعة من الشَّرائح التي تمَّ عَرضُها ضمنَ المُحاضَرة الأصليَّة كبَيان مَرئي.

What is the cultural legacy of the Iraq War? This legacy can no doubt be described in many ways, some of which are more likely to be heard than others. But in Iraq itself, one way we might describe it is as something like a legacy of erasure, or rather an erasure of legacy. The Oxford English Dictionary describes 'legacy' as 'gift left by will, something handed down by predecessors'. The Iraq War started almost ten years ago now, and during that time, in the last twenty years or so, there has been a growing interest in historical scholarship, cultural studies and art history in collective memory practices, especially in the relationship of memory, recorded histories and trauma, to the point that we now speak of a 'memory boom' in scholarship. It should be remarkable, then, that the processes of obliteration and erasure, and the related trauma of loss that ensues when memory is taken away and denied to an entire population, have received such little scholarly attention in relation to the Iraq War. This scarcity of scholarly interest might be explained as due to the general lack of interest and overlooking of the war in public discourse, which has been pointed out already on this panel by Marita Sturken. But there is also a visual and discursive economy of war that erases and deploys information and images; we may also wonder if there is something here of a *damnatio memoriae*, a collective punishment or damnation of memory for Iraq, similar to the ancient Roman practice of erasing people from the historical record.

The extensive destruction of cultural and scholarly institutions, museums and archives during the 2003 war and the following occupation is well known, I am sure, to this audience. The museums of Iraq were looted and destroyed, including, most famously, the Iraq Museum in Baghdad – a museum that caught Donald Rumsfeld by surprise, in that it contained more than one ancient vase from the 9,000 years of history its collection houses.[1] Was he really unaware that Iraq is ancient Mesopotamia, the world's oldest urban civilisation? We laugh at him for a moment, but does our laughter fall under what anthropologists call rituals of reversal, where the king becomes a buffoon for a day and then everything goes back to normal, and he can go back to having power over the lives of others?

We know about the museums and libraries destroyed in 2003, but the destruction and damage of historical sites and monuments continued in occupied Iraq for eight more years. Part of this destruction is a direct result of the occupation's plan to recast the city of Baghdad through the redistribution of spaces and people: creating an architecture of separation, using blast walls and checkpoints in order to control movement, and dividing people according to ethnic groupings, a new geographically organised taxonomy according to the scientific vision of the victors.

At the same time, throughout the country, major monuments and heritage sites were damaged when they were restructured into military bases for US and coalition troops. The most famous case is the use of the ancient city of Babylon for one of the largest US and coalition bases in Iraq, where victory parades likened themselves to the entry of Alexander into Babylon in the fourth century BC (yet somehow forgetting that Alexander met his death in Babylon, a death that was predicted by the Babylonian priests of Marduk, reading the astronomical signs). But Babylon was by no means the only site of historical significance to be used in this way.

So what is this practice of taking historical sites of collective memory and reconfiguring them into military bases for the occupation? I will not have time to present all of these sites of occupation to you tonight. I will mention just one that will open up the other points I want to make here: the war memorial to the 200,000 dead soldiers of the Iraq–Iran war, designed by Ismail Fattah and erected in 1983 in Baghdad (Figures 20 and 21). It is a well-known monument, having been published in art historical survey books on the history of Islamic art and thus familiar in the West well before the 2003 war began; it is still considered an excellent example of contemporary public art in the Islamic world. Similar in function to the Vietnam Veterans Memorial in Washington DC, this monument serves as a memorial for the war dead – soldiers from an army of conscripts forced into service, not volunteers, who lost their lives in a war that had little support among the local population. When Baghdad fell to US troops in 2003, this monument was one of the first places to be used as a military base within the city of Baghdad. Ranks and columns of tanks and Humvees drove into it, and soldiers' barracks were established inside. The US soldiers, who were apparently so culturally alienated as to occupy this site of collective mourning, posted signs and banners across the walls, covering the names of the dead carved in the memorial with their own graffiti, army mottos, paraphernalia and signs of victory, thus creating a victory monument out of a memorial to the dead of war. The iconoclastic gesture of occupying a memorial to the war dead, as an opening gambit of the war, ought to have told us something of what was to come in the following eight years.

The transformation of the Ismail Fattah memorial into a victory monument for the US occupation is a similar iconoclastic recycling to that of the Saddam statues that used to stand throughout the land. The large bronzes of the despotic ruler were melted down, and the metal was recast into statues such as one representing an American Marine mourning the life of his deceased comrade and being comforted by a small Iraqi girl.

In the United States, we speak of those who died in the Iraq and Afghanistan wars. We have numbers. As of November 2012, we know that 4,488 US soldiers and 1,487 contractors have died in Iraq, along with 319 soldiers from other coalition countries. In Afghanistan, we recently reached ten years and the loss of 2,000 US soldiers. How many Iraqi soldiers died in the initial 2003 war? Unlike the US and British armies, it was an army of conscripts, not volunteers, so that almost every family lost a young man. How many civilians, women and children died during the war and occupation? We have no official numbers on record. Independent organisations like the Iraq Body Count database in the UK and the *Lancet* reports have estimated anywhere from hundreds of thousands to close to a million dead civilians.[2]

Almost ten years on, we have stopped asking. Perhaps we don't want to know. In addition to the dead, an estimated two million people have been displaced. Among the displaced are many artists and academics whose work often engages with these issues in powerful ways, but I will not speak about these works today.

In the midst of all that chaos of the last nine years, most of it only known to us through a jumble of snippets of information, combined with the knowledge of the suppression of information, there is one community we can look at more closely: the community of our colleagues, university professors and researchers across Iraq. We know that academics, scholars, professors and intellectuals have been targeted in very direct and deliberate ways from the first days of the war. We have the catalogued names, university affiliations and dates of death of about 500 professors who were killed between 2003 and 2006. Issam al-Rawi, a professor of geology at the University of Baghdad and chairman of the Iraqi Union of University Professors, founded the register of assassinated academics in the wake of the US and coalition invasion.

Every time a colleague was killed, he made a record and logged it in his ledger. By September 2003, in the first six months of the occupation, he had recorded the assassination of about 250 colleagues, and in the first three years of the war and occupation he recorded the deaths of hundreds more scholars, men and women, experts across various fields in the arts and sciences, and of all religious and ethnic backgrounds.

As there has never been any acknowledgement of our war dead, academic or not, and certainly no memorial to them of any kind, I am projecting a translation of the register onscreen with the names of the dead (Figure 22). If it had not been for al-Rawi's dedicated effort to provide a record of some kind, however limited, we would not know these names, and we would probably not imagine such a list; we would have a silent elimination and erasure of all these intellectuals and scientists, almost as if they never existed. When the names are taken together as a catalogue, it appears to be a systematic attack on the intellectuals and scientists of Iraq. On 30 October 2006, Professor al-Rawi himself was assassinated. He also then became a part of the list that he had started.

How can we understand these acts: on the one hand, the occupation of the memorial to the war dead and, on the other, the seemingly unrelated murder of scholars? Both of these situations fit into a larger cultural picture. In an unrelated but quite remarkable event, one of the main architects of the war removed the archive of Mukhabarat secret-service files – so equivalent to the Stasi files – and literally took them home to his residence in the Green Zone, from where they were then shipped to the US; they are now kept at the Hoover Institution of Stanford University.[3] The oxymoronically titled Iraq Memory Foundation was set up as an organisation that is founded upon the principle of erasure.[4] And if my cynicism is misplaced and it is indeed an accurate name, then what does it mean for the Hoover Institution to relocate and control the memory of Iraq? There can be no truth and reconciliation process in Iraq since the archives of the twentieth century are in the US, where Iraqis have no access to them.

When future generations look back at the beginning of the twenty-first century and the disastrous war that dominated its first decade, they will be confronted with a remarkable paradox. In the age of internet communication, when everyone is said to be able to see and reach a global audience through social media and so on, we will find a startling void and an absence of the voices of the people of Iraq. They remain silent not only about what happened in the last decade but also about their own earlier past, because it has been removed from them. In the land where written historical accounts first appeared, no voices are heard, no words can be written, and no one may have access to this past.

Notes

1 'My goodness, were there that many vases? Is it possible that there were that many vases in the whole country?' As quoted in Brian Whitaker, 'Free to do bad things', *The Guardian*, 12 April 2003. https://www.theguardian.com/world/2003/apr/12/iraqbriefing.iraq.

2 Iraq Body Count: https://www.iraqbodycount.org. *Lancet* reports: Les Roberts, Riyadh Lafta, Richard Garfield, Jamal Khudhairi and Gilbert Burnham, 'Mortality before and after the 2003 Invasion of Iraq: Cluster sample survey', *The Lancet* 364 (9448) (20 November 2004): 1857–64; Gilbert Burnham, Riyadh Lafta, Shannon Doocy and Les Roberts, 'Mortality after the 2003 invasion of Iraq: A cross-sectional cluster sample survey', *The Lancet* 368 (9545) (11 October 2006): 1421–8.

3 https://www.hoover.org/library-archives/collections/iraq.

4 https://www.iraqmemory.org/en/. Site no longer active.

16

Amnesia in Mesopotamia

Document Journal 50 (March 2013): 50–3

’فقدان الَّذاكرة في وادي الرافِدَين‘ دوكيومنت جورنال 50 (آذار 2013): 50–53.

Synopsis

Written on the 10-year anniversary of the war, this piece considers the fate of the National Archives and National Library of Iraq as a reminder that memory and history were in danger of erasure. One of the debates at that time involved the transportation of the Iraqi-Baathist regime's secret-police files, including those compiled on the civilian population of Iraq, which had been transported to the United States and housed at the Hoover Institution, at Stanford University in California. The head of the National Library and State Archives in Iraq, Dr Saad Eskander, made repeated demands for the return of the archive to Iraq. Although it consisted of twentieth-century police files kept on average citizens, this appropriated archive came to stand for the control of historical evidence necessary for the writing of history. The underlying theme of the essay, therefore, involves the relationship between archives and power.

المستخلص

كُتِبَت هذه المقالة في الَّذكرى العاشِرة للحَرب، وهي تعُدُّ بأنَّ المصير الذي آلَت إليه الوثائق الوطنية والكُتُب النادرة فَضلاً عن مكتَبات العراق هو تَنبيه بأنَّ الَّذاكِرة والتاريخ كانا يواجهان خَطَر المَحو. إنَّ إحدى المُناقَشات حينَها تَضمَّنَت نَقل ملَفّات جهاز المخابرات للنظام السابق، بما في ذلك تلك التي جُمِعَت من تقارير السُكّان المدنيين في العراق، والتي تم نقلها الى الولايات المتحدة لتستقِرَّ في معهد هوفَر في جامعة ستانفورد في كاليفورنيا. لقد طالَبَ الدكتور سعد إسكندَر المدير العام لدار الكُتُب والوثائق العراقية مِراراً وتِكراراً بعَودَة هذه الوثائق إلى العراق. على الرغم من أنَّه يتألَّف من مَلَفّات

جهاز المخابرات التي تم الاحتفاظ بها عن المواطنين العاديين، إلّا أنَّ هذا الأرشيف المُعتَمَد جاءَ ليَدعَم السَيطرة على الأدِلَّة التاريخيّة الّلازِمة لكتابة التاريخ. لِذا تَضمَّن الموضوع الأساسي لهذه المقالة العلاقة بين الأرشيف والقوّة.

In 2003, Baghdad's National Library was reduced to rubble, eradicating a complex culture, whose ghosts loot the Iraqi psyche indefinitely. Art historian and archaeologist Zainab Bahrani shares her story.

Burned books transformed to ashes, drenched and pulverized fragments of documents scattered on the ground. This is what remained of the greater part of The National Library and State Archives of Iraq after the US invasion of Iraq in the spring of 2003 (see Figure 23). A centuries-old archive of not only state events and political concerns but also the Ottoman-era documents of people's lives, of land deeds and marriages, of inheritance and kinship ties, had been both burned in fire and damaged by water. The buildings in which they were housed transformed into burned-out shell-like structural ghosts of iron beams, soot and ashes (see Figure 24). Soon after the invasion, some archival material of historical importance was either removed or confiscated by the US. At the same time, it became clear that finely made old books – hand calligraphy Medieval manuscripts – were also stolen by looters for an international market in rare books and manuscripts. At the Iraq Museum of Archaeology, clay tablets bearing cuneiform writing, thousands of years old, were stolen along with the other looted archaeological artifacts and works of art; and even today, cuneiform tablets continue to be smuggled out of the country.

All of these written documents, letters, books, manuscripts, legal and official papers, and even the files that the surveillance-obsessed police state of Saddam Hussein kept on its own population (similar to the Stasi files), are what form the stuff of documents in a literate culture. And Mesopotamia, let us remember, is the world's first literate culture. The damage, destruction, erasure and theft of its written archives, no matter how seemingly mundane, whether it is a matter of police surveillance records or land deeds, is poignant to those who are aware of world history. History begins in Sumer, as the great American scholar Samuel Noah Kramer once said, and the French philosopher Jacques Derrida reminds us that the word archive has its roots in the Greek word for beginning and for authority. Without control of the archive there is no political authority, he said.

In Iraq of 2003, the loss of the archives was the first step to the loss of a national collective memory.

In 2003 and 2004 while working on the preservation of cultural heritage in Iraq, I first encountered the destroyed remains of the National Library and State Archives, an institution which is equivalent to the Library of Congress in the United States. The war had induced in me a fixation, a type of archive fever that led me to Iraq in the first two years of occupation, where I had hoped to do whatever I could to save what remained of monuments, archaeological sites and museum collections after the destruction of the 2003 ground war. When I arrived in Iraq I quickly realized that I shared this archive fever with the head of the National Library, Dr Saad Eskander, and with a number of other Iraqi intellectuals, students and museum professionals, each of whom applied her or himself as if driven by some Medieval genie let out of a bottle from the *One Thousand and One Nights*. We had in common a reckless obsession with preserving history, things and documents. Many told us we were misguided, that we should not focus on inanimate things when people were dying, but we saw these forms of annihilation as two sides of the same coin.

The first two years of war and occupation were a violent time of horrendous destruction. I remember driving through the streets of Baghdad searching for any buildings still standing that we might reappropriate for housing what remained of the collections of the library, since the library building itself had turned to ruins. At one point, the remains of mildewing historical papers had to be kept frozen so that continuing damage could be stalled until conservators could come, and proper paper conservation methods applied. Dr Eskander had found an abandoned freezer in the kitchen of bombed-out remains of the private club where formerly the Baathist elite officers had gathered for an evening's entertainment. There was of course no electricity, so he acquired a generator to keep the freezer going, and hired a guard to stand in front of the generator. The remains of the Ottoman archive, the history of Iraq for over 400 years, were for a time stored in this bombed building, held together by an old kitchen freezer. This is the kind of bricolage and creative thinking that went into the conservation work of people like the director of the National Library, when little help came from the outside world and from the occupying authority. There are many such stories to tell about heroic efforts by what remained of the Iraqi scholars and intellectuals in the first years of the war. Hundreds of university professors and intellectuals were also assassinated in those years, and, like other Iraqi War dead, no official record has been kept of their deaths.

The Baathist secret-police archive was airlifted out of Iraq by US forces and is now housed in the Hoover Institution at Stanford University. Destruction of archives incites a collective amnesia, an eradication of memory by means of erasing its documentary and historical apparatus, consigning it to the flames. Because of the destruction of documents and the record of the history of kinship and ties to place that all the peoples and religions of Iraq have, those who wish to incite ethnic hatred and religious intolerance can rewrite history as they please. When documents are confiscated by foreign powers the result is similar; without them there can be no reconciliation for Iraq, and there can be no peace.

Figure 18 Archaeological site of Uruk (Eanna sanctuary of Inanna), 2016.

Photo Haider Almamori (reproduced with permission).

Figure 19 Limestone lioness, probably Proto-Elamite, ca. 3000 BC, private collection, current location unknown; formerly referred to as 'the Guennol Lioness'.

Photo © Brooklyn Museum; courtesy Metropolitan Museum of Art (reproduced with permission).

Figure 20 The Shaheed Monument, war memorial, Baghdad, designed by the Iraqi artist Ismail Fattah, 1983.

Photo Husseinalalie1 (CC BY-SA 4.0).

Figure 21 A US HH-60H helicopter flying over the Shaheed Monument, 30 November 2003.

Public domain (US Navy photo by Aviation Electrician's Mate 1st Class Rex Sackett).

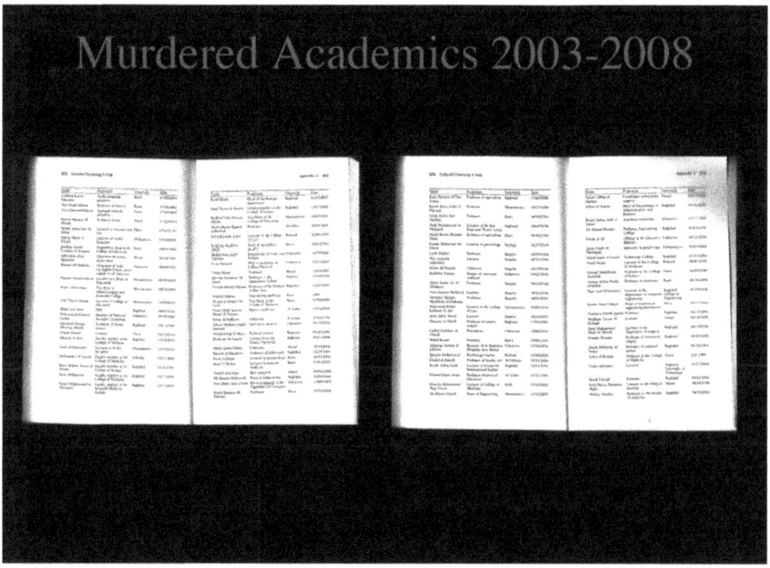

Figure 22 One of several slides shown to the audience of 'Tabula Rasa', listing academics murdered in Iraq from 2003–8 (from *Cultural Cleansing in Iraq*, edited by Raymond W. Baker, Sheeren T. Ismael and Tareq Y. Ismael. London, Pluto Press, 2010. Reproduced with permission).

Figure 23 Burnt books and archival documents, National Library and State Archives of Iraq, Baghdad, 2003.

Photo Roger Lemoyne (reproduced with permission).

Figure 24 Destroyed staircase, National Library and State Archives of Iraq, Baghdad, 2003.

Photo Roger Lemoyne (reproduced with permission).

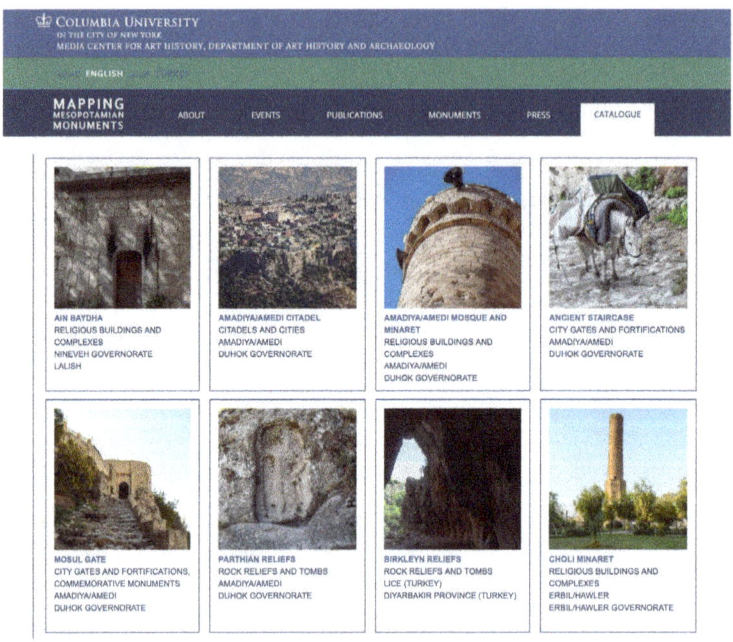

Figure 25 Screenshot of the Mapping Mesopotamian Monuments website.

Courtesy Columbia University, Department of Art History and Archaeology, Media Center for Art History.

Figure 26 Limestone monument of Eannatum of Lagash, ca. 2450 BC. Louvre Museum, Paris.

Photo Eric Gaba (CC BY-SA 4.0).

Figure 27 Portal Guardians at the Northwest Palace, Nimrud (ca. 865 BC), 2008.

Public domain (US military photo by Staff Sgt. JoAnn Makinano).

Figure 28 Palmyra, Syria, 2010.

Photo Bernard Gagnon (CC BY-SA 4.0).

Figure 29 The archaeological site of Umma after looting, following the 2003 US military invasion.

Public domain (US Department of Defense).

Figure 30 Corona satellite images of Ur (left: October 1959; right: May 1969).

Public domain (National Archives Records Administration).

Figure 31 Jean-Léon Gérôme, *The Snake Charmer* (ca. 1879). Oil on canvas, 83.8 × 122.1 cm (32.9 × 48 in). Clark Art Institute, Williamstown, Massachusetts.

Public domain.

Figure 32 Photograph (above) and film still (below) from the 2016 multimedia work *Drone Hits the Great Ziggurat of Ur*, by Hanaa Malallah (reproduced with permission).

Figure 33 Courtyard of the Bughday Khatoun shrine in Kirkuk (fourteenth century with later restorations), 2019, showing rubble from the 1991 bombing still in place.

Photo Zainab Bahrani; courtesy Columbia University, Department of Art History and Archaeology, Media Center for Art History.

Figure 34 Lamassu discovered below the Nabi Yunis shrine, Mosul.

Photo Stefan Maul and Peter Miglus, University of Heidelberg (reproduced with permission).

Part IV
ISIS/Daesh

القسم الرابع: داعش/ISIS

Preface

تمهيد

Synopsis

The concerns of 'amnesia in Mesopotamia', the techniques of destruction and erasure, and the constructions of purified pasts, cleansed of historical or archaeological evidence that could challenge the views of a military rule, were taken up by the group known as ISIS (Islamic State in Iraq and Syria) or Daesh (*Dawla Islamia fi al Iraq wa al Sham*) in its Arabic acronym. ISIS had captured large swathes of land in Syria and Iraq, and it occupied Mosul in northern Iraq in June 2014; the city remained under its control until July 2017. About half a million citizens of Mosul were immediately displaced in the summer of 2014, as they fled the city towards Erbil, in Iraqi Kurdistan (where many continue to live today in the refugee camps designated for internally displaced people (IDP camps). Many others, who did not manage to flee, were killed under this brutal regime. During the years of ISIS control, a massive destruction of the city of Mosul took place, including its shrines, mosques, churches and museums. Many of the targeted locations were sites that countered the claims of sectarianism, such as shrines traditionally serving as sites of worship for several faiths.

المستخلص

إنَّ التركيز على موضوع' فقدان ذاكِرة وادي الرافِدَين'، وتقنيّات التدمير والمَحو، وإنشاء ماضٍ مُطَهَّر، خالٍ من الأَدِلَّة التاريخية أو الأثرية التي قَد تتعارَض مع آراء الحُكم العَسكَريّ، قَد تَمَّ تَبَنِّيها من قِبَل مجموعة تُعرَف بداعش (الدولة الإسلامية في العراق والشام) أو (ISIS) (Islamic State in Iraq and Syria) وهو ما يُقابلُها

في اللغة الإنكليزية. لقَد استَولَت داعش على مساحات شاسِعة من أراضي سوريا والعراق، وقد احتَلَّت الموصل في شَمال العراق في حُزَيران عام 2014؛ بَقِيَت المدينة تحت سيطرة داعش حتى تموز عام 2017. في صَيف عام 2014، كان قد نَزَح في تَوِّها قُرابة نصف المليون من سَكَنة الموصل، إذ فَرّوا إلى أربيل، عاصِمة كُردستان العراق حيثُ استمرَّ العديد منهم بالعيش فيها حتى يومِنا هذا في مُخَيَّمات اللاجئين التي تمَّ تخصيصُها للنازحين من داخل البلد. كما إنَّ العديد من الَّذين لم يتمكَّنوا من الفِرار، قُتِلوا تحت سَطوةِ هذا النظام الغاشِم. خلال سنوات سَيطرة داعش، حدثَ دمار مَهول في مدينة الموصل، بما فيها من مَراقِد، وجوامع، وكنائس، ومتاحف. لقد كانت العديد من المَواضِع المُستَهدَفة مواقِعاً عارَضَت مَزاعِم الطائِفيّة، كما في المراقد التقليدية التي تخدم كمواقع عبادة لِعِدَّة أديان.

In the years after the 2011 withdrawal of US troops, a large expanse of Iraq and Syria was taken over by the armies of a group known as ISIS or Daesh, who terrorised the land. By June 2014 they had captured the city of Mosul and declared it to be the capital of their new caliphate.[1] They began a systematic campaign of murder and genocide that was accompanied by the demolition of historical and sacred sites throughout the region that they controlled, with the apparent aim of a total obliteration of the rich interreligious history of this land. At that time, I was in the second year of a fieldwork project called Mapping Mesopotamian Monuments (MMM), and I was working in Iraqi Kurdistan with my team.[2] Half a million people from Mosul and surrounding towns and villages escaped to the largest cities in Iraqi Kurdistan, Erbil and Dohuk, where IDP camps were quickly set up to house them, and where many remain today as internally displaced people unable to return to the rubble that is left of their homes. In addition to the Iraqis fleeing from Mosul and the surrounding area, there were also many refugees from Syria coming into the parts of Iraq that ISIS did not control. They were the fortunate ones, as those who remained in the cities and villages that fell under ISIS rule were brutalised and slaughtered. ISIS launched a genocidal attack on the Yazidi minority of north-western Iraq. They killed the men, young and old, and enslaved the women and children. They forced women and young girls to become sex slaves for ISIS fighters. They murdered anyone who did not fit their distorted and violent vision of Islamic rule. Between 2014 and 2017 the sprees of violence increased to include the demolition of more shrines, churches and mosques, more ancient sites and things in museum collections. What was not destroyed by ISIS was then turned into rubble by the war to defeat them. Hundreds of historical buildings, religious and secular, were destroyed in the historical heart of Mosul. Thousands of civilians were killed.[3]

In the fields of art history and archaeology, some began to write about the ISIS destruction in academic writing and in the press. I could not. I was simply unable to theorise or quantify the destruction in the way that my colleagues found possible. They wrote with a sense of certainty and scientific distance in which I could not share, and with an authority in which I could not participate. Instead, I watched in horror as the people of my country were killed, as our landscape and history were destroyed, while others debated the merits of UNESCO and European safe havens for antiquities, though not for refugees. During that time, I carried on with my fieldwork in Kurdistan and south-eastern Turkey. And I was also in the midst of writing a textbook for teaching ancient Mesopotamian art and architecture.[4] With a sense of despair, I struggled to continue writing the chapters about Nimrud and Nineveh while simultaneously seeing on my screen the incessant news and images of their systematic demolition. I experienced this horror as an ungraspable thing, beyond the explanatory models of academic thought. But – in contradiction to my own visceral response, and as a way of coping – I also tried to untangle it and to historicise it, to pin it down in some way.

Throughout history, the destruction of monuments and, conversely, their preservation become aspects of warfare and violent conflict, and also of legal discourse. Built environments are deliberately targeted, just as trees and orchards are purposefully set on fire and water sources attacked, as strategies of war. The destruction of architecture, of built and natural environments, has often been validated by the idea of 'just war', and in recent decades, also justified by the military term 'collateral damage'. It is a type of warfare that is territorial. It seeks to erase and transform the urban spaces and landscapes of the region under attack. It is an attack not only on structures themselves as symbols but on the lives lived within and around them, the lives lived in relationship to them.[5] We can observe, then, that the destruction of environments, especially where there are shared spaces and shared histories of coexistence, is a specific type of warfare, directly tied to the aims of ethnic cleansing. Thoughtful reflection and theoretical analyses by scholars regarding such practices have been pursued for other areas of the world, and other wars.[6] The same scholarly reflection has not been brought to bear on the case of Iraq, however. Rather, the events of this period were generally explained through the lens of the ISIS fighters themselves, as a religious iconoclasm rooted in traditional forms of Islam.

While both direct iconoclasm and collateral destruction, no matter how one splits the difference, are understood as acts of warfare, at academic meetings I also stressed the ways in which preservation initiatives had now become an integral aspect of war and of conflict archaeology.

Preservation projects were becoming political pawns, and preservation technologies were emerging as visual props in cities like London, New York and Rome. Celebrating the triumph of technology, a replica of Palmyra's Arch of Triumph was presented to the public by Boris Johnson in Trafalgar Square in April of 2016,[7] and in the Roman Colosseum, 3D printed copies of things that ISIS had destroyed were exhibited in December of the same year.[8] The displays of these copies are interesting to consider as exhibitionary acts in themselves. The copies described everywhere as replicas of antiquities that were blown up by ISIS were not, in fact, replicas. The arch was much smaller in size and had erroneous architectural and decorative details, unlike the destroyed structure. The lamassu in the Colosseum was copied from one at the British Museum in London, leading the viewer to assume that Assyrian lamassu – each of which was in fact sculpted uniquely as a work of magnificent monumental sculpture – were as interchangeable as mass-produced images. Somehow following in the logic of ISIS, some proponents of this preservation technology felt that Iraqis who insisted on restoration of the shattered fragments of the ancient works were simply fetishising the original stone sculptures.

A great deal of attention and funding was channelled to these purported replicas. Watching all of this unfold, I was taken back to my earlier work on the ontology of the image and theoretical writings around mimesis. As if following the text by Jean Baudrillard as a set of instructions, the relationship between the real and representation was blurred.[9] Three-dimensional digital images were publicised as restorations of the original, and as objects of defiance against terrorism.[10] They were to be the new solution to heritage destruction. In all these displays, the companies providing the 3D printed technology may well have been interested in aiding matters of cultural heritage, but they also benefited from the commercial promotion of their own products. In the wake of ISIS, heritage appeared to become both a lucrative and strategic new direction for public-relations campaigns. I delivered lectures at Indiana University in Bloomington, at the Freie Universität in Berlin, and at the Graduate School of Architecture, Planning and Preservation at Columbia, all of them about destruction and preservation as aspects of war.[11] I then published an essay on this topic in the heritage preservation journal *Future Anterior*. That article appears as the second piece in this part. In it, I sought to highlight the ways that heritage preservation had now become a pawn in war and the cultural hegemony of soft-power politics.

In the midst of the increasing violence and atrocity of the ISIS years, much of the work that I did was outside the usual parameters of academic discourse. The first paper in this section, titled 'The absent past', was part of the second initiative I began at the time: The Future of the Past project, which was funded by a grant that I received from Columbia University's president, Lee Bollinger, as part of the university's support for global and publicly engaged scholarship.[12] With this multi-year funding in hand, and the backing of my university, I organised a series of workshops and closed-door meetings at the Columbia Global Centers in Istanbul and Amman. I also asked Joan Aruz, curator of ancient Near Eastern art at the Metropolitan Museum of Art – a close colleague whom I had known for many years – to collaborate on these projects. She was able to raise additional funding, and together we worked towards organising workshops, providing cameras and equipment, and training in documentation methods for Iraqi and Syrian museum photographers who could come to Istanbul and Amman, but not to New York. They were unable to acquire visas for meetings in the United States, especially after the election of Donald Trump and the instating of a new law at the start of his administration, which in jest, but half seriously also, came to be known in America as 'the Muslim ban'.

The regional workshops project was a joint Columbia University–Metropolitan Museum of Art initiative headed by myself and Aruz. All the meetings in Istanbul and Amman took place while Mosul and other cities were under ISIS occupation. 'The Absent Past' was delivered as the keynote speech for the Istanbul meeting in October of 2015. Because of the very real danger in which some of our colleagues were living, in Syria and Iraq, we had decided that these were to be closed-door meetings, without any publicity or accompanying publication.

Those who had travelled to Istanbul from Iraq and Syria included archaeologists and museum curators from the cities of Mosul and Aleppo, Baghdad, Kirkuk and Basra, as well as Slemani, Erbil and Dohuk in Iraqi Kurdistan. The participants contributed ideas for what would be useful in the following meetings, set to take place in Amman. In an effort to counter erasure, forms of documentation were requested by many of the participants. The ISIS destruction, which had seemed to gain momentum in the year 2015, destroying more heritage and religious sites, prompted us to have a difficult discussion and a vote. All those present preferred to keep the next meetings closed and unpublicised. In another group vote, Iraqi and Syrian colleagues requested that the website of the MMM project remain password protected for the time being. Organising these projects and workshops with colleagues from Iraq and Syria was a way to have a sustained relationship with them during a time of upheaval, when beneath our feet, whatever was left of our world seemed to be in the process of being pulled away. But I also had a feeling of personal discomfiture and withdrawal, of not wanting to participate in conferences or archaeological meetings at all. Total war always requires force beyond the military. It relies on disinformation and dissemination of images. It relies on dehumanising the other, and, as Trump's 'Muslim ban' demonstrated, this dehumanisation had spilled over to all of us from this region, regardless of our religion or ethnicity.

Victory on the battle field is supported by the battle for representation. This was also the case in antiquity, as I had written in my book *Rituals of War*.[13] In the years of ISIS occupation, the depravities and destructions of this group were widely disseminated in the press and news media. Remarkably, these reports relied on the propaganda materials created by the group itself. The Western press inadvertently became one of the widest disseminators of ISIS propaganda, presenting visual materials directly taken from ISIS's own websites. The ISIS videos, images and reports that the world was shown repeatedly through the main media outlets were choreographed and framed by their own production studios. Refracted through the ISIS lens, the images of the smashing of sculptures and blowing-up of heritage sites that are seared into our memories are ISIS productions, aided in their distribution by the Western press and news media. Slick, high-tech media representations were at the same time an advertisement for recruiting transnational religious militants and mercenaries, as thousands of them joined this multinational army. The media campaign was remarkable in its technologically advanced presentations and its choreography.[14] The violence against antiquities received a great deal of attention in blogs and social-media postings, but also in academic publications. Much of what was said, and the explanations that were given, was based on ideas of civilisation and barbarism that readers eagerly took in. The ISIS fighters themselves, as many Iraqis noted, appeared like villainous characters out of Hollywood cinema, with their cartoonish, Orientalising self-presentation. They appeared to have internalised Western cinematic stereotypes of what it meant to be an Oriental. Who, then, was the intended viewer of these scenes?

I continued to conduct fieldwork in Iraqi Kurdistan and south-eastern Anatolia, documenting monuments, architecture and rock reliefs.

This project occupied much of my time, and it became a refuge of sorts, as the work involved the intimacy of being there – the tangible and the experiential that this kind of archaeological work offers. At its initiation, I had envisioned MMM as a project that studies monuments, historical architecture and landscapes of memory. It would encompass the approaches of sensory and landscape archaeology, in that the processes of walking, climbing and viewing are incorporated into the study of the monuments and sites. The question of visibility and hiddenness in the terrain, the ways in which each location changes with times of day and with the seasons, so that light and shadows cast onto the sides of mountains, were part of the phenomenological and experiential interactions of this work. Some of these ideas were being explored by other theoretical archaeologists working elsewhere across Britain, Greece, Turkey and Central and South America in productive ways.[15] The disciplinary field of archaeology, and its colonial frames of knowledge and practice, was now also being questioned from within by a number of scholars, especially those working in fields related to the ancient Americas and Africa.[16]

Coloniality is also the framework through which we can understand collecting histories and the rise of the institution of the public museum. After 2017, I turned again to questions of looting, to histories of empire and to the collecting of antiquities, which I saw as an aspect of imperial wars. The relationship between imperialism and archaeology, which had long been a focus of my work on nineteenth-century archaeology, became a topic of contemporary relevance. I went back to speaking publicly about the impact of the Iraq War and its aftermath on the antiquities trade, on curating decisions in the foremost museums of Western Europe and North America. I also wanted to more directly address the continuing problem of the militarisation of archaeology and its practices. The papers included here, 'Destruction and preservation as aspects of just war', 'Blood antiquities', 'Decolonising the museum', and 'Technologies of power in archaeology' cover these topics. They also point to the long-term relationship between the field of archaeology, collecting practices and the long history of war in Iraq, a topic that reappears in 'Historical destruction in a forgotten war' and in the concluding chapter. These were historiographic issues about disciplinary practices and histories. They were also about the ways in which the Mesopotamian material was presented to the public in museums and public media.

At the same time, in the academic lectures I gave and the papers I published during this period, I wanted to take the reader to the past, to the ancient Mesopotamian historical consciousness. I described the way in which it was entwined with the standing monuments and historical architecture that was part of the urban fabric in antiquity, and part of the landscape that carries the traces of the past on its cliffs and mountain paths. And as ancient tells that, scattered throughout, punctuate the flatness of the south, stand as the constant signs of history, the perception of deep time was tied to these ancient sites. Thus, several of these essays move from the ancient past to the present and back again. I used this atemporal outline as a means to underscore the close entanglement of the past and the present in this land. I began to consider chance encounters in the afterlives of antiquity, in things that one finds in the landscape, in the crevices of mountains, and in the depth of the earth.[17] I am once again reminded of Gilgamesh, as one 'who saw the deep, the foundations of the land'. In the essay 'Mosul and Nineveh', included here, I also wrote about this sense of time and the return of images from the ancient earth beneath us. Following the depredations of ISIS, I found solace in the surprise discovery below a destroyed shrine in Mosul: a lamassu, an Assyrian winged bull, and relief sculptures of goddesses bearing flowers, below a destroyed shrine, all erupting out of the ground below the rubble.

The final piece in this part is derived from a chapter that I wrote upon being asked to address heritage destruction for a handbook on that theme. By way of conclusion, an expanded version of that chapter is presented as the final text of this volume. It revisits each of the themes covered in this volume and also introduces other episodes and aspects that have been left aside in this accounting. As I consider the history of heritage destruction, I connect the themes and issues through the period of the last twenty years, but I also return to the past, to the nineteenth century, when Iraq was part of the Ottoman Empire, and the discipline of ancient Near Eastern archaeology had not yet been formulated as such. That was the era in which the earliest European imperialist excavations started (soon followed by the American ones), and in which looting for the Western market became commonplace; it was when the discourse of antiquity came to be narrated from the perspective of those who retained imperial power. Imperial administrators, officers and spies established the field of Near Eastern archaeology, and their discourse remains entrenched. The relationship between Western power and the production of knowledge regarding the Orient, which Edward Said made clear, relied in no small part on antiquity and ideas of heritage.[18] Several of the themes covered in this volume can be traced back to that early tie of archaeology with imperialism. What followed afterwards was a long and interconnected series of events that I trace through the British Mandate, the Gulf Wars and their aftermath. This history of war and violence both led to and relied upon heritage destruction and looting. In this way, the essay presented here by way of a conclusion reflects upon all this destruction from the perspective of the *longue durée*.

Notes

1 They had already entered Ramadi from Syria in January of that year. See the first-hand account by the journalist James Verini, *They Will Have to Die Now: Mosul and the fall of the Caliphate* (New York: Norton, 2019).

2 https://mcid.mcah.columbia.edu/art-atlas/mapping-mesopotamian-monuments.

3 According to a report by John Spencer and Jayson Geroux of the Modern War Institute at West Point (15 September 2021): https://mwi.westpoint.edu/urban-warfare-project-case-study-2-battle-of-mosul/.

4 Zainab Bahrani, *Art of Mesopotamia* (New York: Thames & Hudson, 2017).

5 These aims have already been pointed out in the case of the Bosnian war by Martin Coward, 'Against anthropocentrism: The destruction of the built environment as a distinct form of political violence', *Review of International Studies* 32 (2006): 419–37.

6 For example, at the break-up of the former Yugoslavia in the 1990s, and in Israel-Palestine. For a discussion and references regarding the case of Bosnia, see Martin Coward, 'Against anthropocentrism: The destruction of the built environment as a distinct form of political violence', *Review of International Studies* 32 (2006): 419–37; Robert Bevan, *The Destruction of Memory* (London: Reaktion Books, 2006). For the case of Palestine, see Eyal Weizmann, *Hollow Land* (London: Verso, 2017); *Forensic Architecture* (New York: Zone Books, 2017); see also the work of the *Forensic Architecture* group: https://forensic-architecture.org.

7 See Lauren Turner, 'The ethics of 3D-printing Syria's cultural heritage', *Forbes*, 22 September 2016, https://www.bbc.com/news/uk-36070721.

8 A publication accompanied the exhibition: Francesco Rutelli, ed., *Rinascere dalle distruzioni: Ebla, Nimrud, Palmira* (Rome: Associazione incontro di civilita, 2016).

9 See, in particular, Jean Baudrillard, *Simulacres et Simulation* (Paris: Éditions Galilée, 1981).

10 See, for example, Raya Jalabi, 'Replica of Syrian arch destroyed by Isis unveiled in New York City', *The Guardian*, September 20 2016. https://www.theguardian.com/us-news/2016/sep/20/palmyra-arch-syria-new-york.

11 The Indiana University lecture, *Preservation in War: Mapping Mesopotamian monuments* (26 March 2018), is available online at https://www.youtube.com/watch?v=fXpc1lXntps.

12 See https://mcid.mcah.columbia.edu/art-atlas/mapping-mesopotamian-monuments/future-past-project.

13 Zainab Bahrani, *Rituals of War: The body and violence in Mesopotamia* (New York: Zone Books, 2008).

14 The most thoughtful accounts and analyses were written by Ömür Harmansah and Barry Flood. See Harmansah, 'Isis, heritage, and the spectacles of destruction in the global media', *Near Eastern Archaeology* 78 (2015): 170–7; Finbarr Barry Flood, 'Idol breaking as image making in the "Islamic State"', *Religion and Society* 7 (2016): 116–38.

15 Barbara Bender et al., *Stone Worlds: Narrative and reflexivity in landscape archaeology* (London: Routledge, 2016); Jo Lee Vergunst and Tim Ingold, *Ways of Walking* (London: Routledge, 2008); Christopher Tilley and Kate Cameron Daum, *An Anthropology of Landscape* (London: UCL Press, 2017); Felipe Rojas, *The Pasts of Roman Anatolia: Interpreters, traces, horizons* (Cambridge: Cambridge University Press, 2019).

16 See especially Alejandro Haber and Nick Shepherd, *After Ethics: Ancestral voices and post-disciplinary worlds in archaeology* (New York: Springer, 2015); Zainab Bahrani, Zeynep Çelik and Edhem Eldem, *Scramble for the Past: A story of archaeology in the Ottoman Empire, 1753–1914* (Istanbul: Salt, 2011).

17 'The Mesopotamian sublime', a lecture presented at the Ashmolean Museum, Oxford, in May 2017, and then published as 'The phenomenal sublime: Time, matter, image in Mesopotamia', in *Time in the History of Art: Temporality, chronology, and anachrony*, edited by Dan Karlholm

and Keith Moxey (London: Routledge, 2018), 171–84; 'The Return of Images: Chance encounters in the afterlives of antiquity', lecture presented at the Warburg Institute in London, May 2017, followed by a publication: 'Aby Warburg's Babylonian paradigm: Towards an epistemology of the irrational in the Bilderatlas', *RES: Anthropology and Aesthetics* 75/76 (2021): 250–65.

18 See Edward Said's seminal work, *Orientalism* (New York: Vintage, 1978).

17

The absent past: heritage destruction and historical erasure today

Istanbul conference: *The Future of the Past*, keynote lecture, 16 October 2015

’غِياب الماضي: تدمير التراث ومَحو التاريخ في الوَقت الحاضِر‘ مؤتمر إسطنبول: مُستقبَل الماضي، المحاضرة الافتِتاحيَّة، 16 تشرين الأول،2015.

Synopsis

This unpublished keynote speech was delivered in Istanbul in October 2015, at the height of the ISIS occupation of Iraq and Syria. The paper opens with a discussion of a Babylonian scholar called Nabu-zer-lishir, who lived in the sixth century BC, during the reign of the king Nabonidus, and whose scribal and archaeological activities were preserved in the archaeological record. The essay stresses the ways in which the ancient Mesopotamians were aware of their own past, and how they understood the archaeological remains that surrounded them as traces of that past. It goes on to discuss some of the medieval Islamic historians and geographers who wrote about ancient sites in Arabic and in Persian without any sense of condemnation and often with great admiration. It concludes by examining ISIS's destruction and the group's ideologies surrounding the deliberate erasure of that past.

المستخلص

تمَّ تقديم المُحاضرة الافتِتاحية غير المنشورة هذه في إسطنبول في تشرين الأول عام 2015، في خِضَّم احتلال داعش للأراضي العراقية والسورية. استُهِلَّت المَقالة بمناقشة لباحِثٍ بابلي يُدعى نابو-زير-إيشير كان قد عاشَ في القَرن السادس قبل الميلاد إبان

فترة حُكم الملك نابونايد، وقد حفظَ لنا السِجِّل الآثاري نشاطاته في التَّدوين والآثار. تؤَكِّد المقالة على الأساليب التي اعتَمَدها سُكّان وادي الرافِدَين القُدماء لإدراك ماضيهم، وكيف أنَّهم فَهموا البَقايا الأثَريّة التي تُحيطُ بهم على أنَّها آثارٌ يستدلّون بها على ذلك الماضي. كما تتناول المحاضرة مناقَشة بعض المؤرِّخين والجُغرافيين المُسلمين الَّذين عاشوا في القرون الوسطى والَّذين كَتَبوا عن المواقع القديمة باللُّغَتَين العربيَّة والفارسيَّة دون أن تُعبِّر كتاباتهم عن أي إدانة، بل إنَّها غالباً ما كانت تَنِمُّ عن إعجابٍ شَديد. تُختَتَم المقالة بدراسة للتدمير الذي مارسته داعش وأيديولوجية الجماعة حول هذا المَحو المُتعَمَّد للماضي.

In ancient Babylon there once lived a man called Nabu-zer-lishir. He was a scholar who was expert in ancient languages and scripts. He also directed excavations and recorded the architectural remains and artefacts that were found under his supervision. He lived in the sixth century BC, during the reign of the Babylonian king Nabonidus, but we know that he discovered remains of the mid-second millennium BC, from the time of the Kassite ruler Kurigalzu I, who lived 800 years earlier. He understood what these were and recorded them accurately. And even these artefacts themselves already contained a record of the earlier Kassite archaeological activity and interest in the past. Among those artefacts excavated by our scholar, Nabu-zer-lishir, was a text that recorded how Kurigalzu had restored the Emegalamma temple, 'the house of skilfully contrived MEs'[1] in the city of Agade, as a way of preparing for the Akitu new-year festival at the beginning of the springtime.

Nabu-zer-lishir was a scholar and an archaeologist, not unlike all of us who are gathered here for this meeting. He studied the traces of the past in artefacts and architecture. He knew the ancient languages and scripts, which he could read and translate, and which he recorded carefully. Among the texts that he reproduced – creating a copy by pressing the tablet on wet clay – was one that was even older than the Kassite-period document mentioned above. It was from the era of the Akkadian king Sharkalisharri, who ruled 2217–2193 BC. In fact, on the back of the impression, Nabu-zer-lishir carefully recorded where he had found this ancient text (which was already 1700 years old when he discovered it) and what was the material of the object on which it was written. Nabu-zer-lishir's story is not the only one we have from the Mesopotamian past. Indeed, there are many ancient documents that reveal to us the great antiquity of historical consciousness in this region. The ancient Mesopotamians were very aware of the extensive history of their land; they understood that it was extremely old, and they took pride in it. They felt it was their sacred duty to preserve it. They saw it as their ancestral past.

Today we echo these concerns. Thus, I would like to open this meeting by stating what may be the obvious: preservation of the past *is* important for the people of this part of the world. It is not just to pass the time of well-to-do people in Western nations. This is one of the main reasons for this meeting we are calling The Future of the Past. Unlike many of the conferences about the cultural heritage of the Middle East, taking place at this time, most of the speakers and panellists whose views we will hear in the next two days are from the region itself. The meeting has been called with a specific focus on Iraq and Syria, both of which are countries with very urgent concerns. Together with my co-organizers, Dr Joan Aruz and Dr Sheila Canby of the Metropolitan Museum of Art in New York, and Professor Christopher Roosevelt of Koç University, Istanbul, we have gathered together here in Istanbul so that scholars from Syria, Iraq and Turkey can attend, and so that their voices can be heard clearly. Although it is important to state that this region's past is global cultural heritage of interest to all, for those of us who are from here, it is also our specifically local heritage and a significant part of the characteristics of our lands.

Let me return to the ancient Mesopotamians. They understood archaeological artefacts as traces of the past, but when they put artefacts into the ground or erected them as architecture and monuments, the important thing we should understand is this: they saw them not simply as a way of looking back to their ancestors but of reaching out to the future – as an infinite form of presence through monuments and images, and through written historical accounts.[2] Their horizons of time were vast and distant, pushing forward into the future. Why was this the case? It was because of the manifest traces of the past, which also evidenced the historical antiquity of the land. They saw the future through the lens of the traces of the past.

This meeting's main concern is the preserving and safeguarding of our cultural heritage, especially the cultural patrimony of Iraq and Syria. This is primarily the area archaeologists call the land of the two rivers: Mesopotamia. Significantly for our conference and for our current concerns, the first historical evidence for preserving and conserving antiquities comes from this part of the world. We always say that writing was invented here, along with cities, the law, and so on, but we should add to this list of the beginnings of civilization the practices of archaeology and conservation. The first clearly attested acts of preservation, conservation and a form of archaeological research emerged in Mesopotamia. The Uruk vase, which became emblematic for the looting and destruction of the Iraq Museum in 2003, dates to 3300 BC (see Figures 8 and 9). When it was buried in the fourth millennium BC, it had already been repaired carefully, with a metal pin attaching a piece that had broken off at the top. This is a conscious act of conservation.

Some claim that concerns for the distant past are modern Western imports into the East; they are not. This is a point that I have demonstrated in some detail in my own research and books. These claims are made by those who try to convince us that, in our lands, we did not understand the past until Europeans taught us to do so. But these mistaken claims are now also being used by some in the region itself for their own goals. Some have come to believe we should reject the past; that caring for it is an imported Western concern. In a recent lecture I gave, there were present some scholars of the modern era in the audience who challenged me on this point. I was told 'you cannot speak about preservation, as that is a modern Western concept'. But this assertion is, of course, completely erroneous and not based on any research into ancient texts and practices. Engagement with the past is neither a uniquely Western concern nor a modern invention. It has existed since the earliest recorded history, when kings restored and renovated architecture and protected historical and sacred places that archaeologists would now call 'heritage sites'.

The rise of scientific archaeology in Europe in the nineteenth century brought about a new and different engagement with the past that defined itself as a science. This was an important moment in the history of scholarship and museology, a turning point that formed the basis for the way that we conduct our work today. However, it was certainly not the first historical moment in which there was an interest in the ruins of this part of the world. In the early Arabic and Persian traditions of Islamic scholarship, writers such as Ibn Hawqal (AD ca. 920–978) already went to see Babylon and wrote about it in the tenth century AD.[3] Benjamin of Tudela (a rabbi from Spain) referred to the ruins of the palace of Nebuchadnezzar in Babylon, where he visited.[4] Ibn Jubayr (AD 1145–1217) and Abu al-Fida (AD 1273–1331), al-Mas'udi (AD 896–957) and al-Muqqadasi (AD 945–1000), and several other scholars had regularly described the exact locations of Nineveh and Babylon.[5] In the Ottoman Empire, Mehmet Zilli, known as Evliya Celebi, described ancient buildings during travels in his *Seyahatname*, written in the mid-seventeenth century.[6] In Iran, the Qajar dynasty likened its authority to that of ancient kings and borrowed iconography directly from ancient sculptures.[7]

These sites and monuments, these remains of history have formed and defined the landscape of the region for many centuries. Without them, we cannot understand what this region is, nor what it has been.

When we ignore them, the region becomes something else. It becomes a place with no tangible past, a place whose history is wiped out and rewritten. Why is this the case? History is always a narrative, but the phenomenon of the solid material remains have stood there nevertheless, and they had to be explained or subsumed into the stories. The standing monuments and traces of the past were long understood as part of the ancient and mythical history of the land and its peoples.

For the first time in thousands of years, these remains are now being systematically wiped out. We are now faced with confronting not a solid and tangible presence of the past, but a conspicuous glaring absence. Entirely new definitions and stories are being told, stories that fit better with the current goals of conquest and genocide. This ancient land is being erased and transformed into what can be described as a terra nullius, an empty land, devoid of people and history, ready to be colonised and occupied as a vast and empty frontier for whoever wishes to take it. These aims and strategies of violence are enabled by, and erected upon, the absence of the past. I would stress, therefore, that the evidence of the past and history is not just the collateral damage of war. Its destruction is a strategy of erasure, reconfiguration and conquest of land.

There is now an existential threat to the Middle East by the erasure of the history of its multiple cultures and peoples, of its distant past and its recent past. Not only in Iraq, Syria, and southeastern Anatolia – the areas that we are discussing in our meeting – but also in Yemen, in Tunisia and Libya, in Egypt, in Lebanon and Palestine, everywhere our heritage, our pluralistic historical roots, and our rich cultures are endangered. The past of the Middle East is not a simple, homogeneous thing. The beauty of this past is its diversity. Heritage preservation is not just a luxury for the tourist industry. It is essential for the history of the region. These remains of antiquity and historical buildings have existed for thousands of years. People have lived with them in peace, but not only that; they have seen them as part of their natural landscape and its identity. Now, this landscape is threatened with erasure.

What is worrying is not just the deliberate destruction and iconoclasm of historical buildings or images but a total erasure of what does not fit in the new narrative of ethnic or religious purity. Thus, ancient sites, historical Islamic architecture and twentieth-century secular buildings are all attacked for similar reasons. This destruction has several causes. We have seen the devastating destruction of sites by terrorism and warfare, whether by state powers and militaries or by terrorist groups, but that is not all. The creation of exclusionary narratives is beginning to take hold across communities. We are seeing the rewriting and re-identification of heritage sites of all eras, ancient to modern, along ethnocentric lines in ways that are erroneous and unacceptable because they perform historical erasure in their own way. We notice some poorly thought-out archaeological projects emerging. We see the mass looting of archaeological sites, museums and libraries for a global free market in our heritage. And we are witnessing the terrible damage done by unrestrained and unsupervised development projects that do not always follow the rule of law when it comes to the legal imperative of conducting archaeological surveys before bulldozing, drilling or tearing down old architecture and restructuring traditional urban centres. Here, the burden and responsibility is not only on local people and governments but on the international, European and US firms that come in to conduct the work. All of these forms of destruction are areas that we will address in the next days.

Another main problem that has arisen, and that first became clear in 2003, at the start of the Iraq War, is the spread of both information and misinformation. With the war, we saw the increase of websites and not-for-profit organisations that set themselves up in the West as representatives of the Iraq Museum and Iraqi archaeology. Unfortunately, many of these were self-appointed experts whose aim was to acquire donations or to influence public discussion in some way. Today, with the widespread use of the internet, there is even more misinformation being disseminated. Some questionable websites have even been relied upon by the press as sources of authority. At times, sensitive information about the locations of monuments, or even of our colleagues who are working in dangerous zones, are posted online, thus exposing them to danger.

We are gathered here in Turkey, in the region being directly affected, alongside Iraq and Syria. Most of the scholars present at our conference are from this area, and we asked them here specifically so we can hear their views. We have gathered together a group that includes specialists in pre-Islamic antiquity, Islamic art and archaeology, and the modern architecture and art of the region. In many meetings and discussions about the threat to cultural heritage in the Middle East, the voices of local scholars are too often excluded or not listened to seriously as the voices of colleagues who are also stakeholders. Here, we want to change that working method. The future of the past in Iraq and Syria may be a question of global cultural heritage as defined by UNESCO and other international organisations, but it is far more urgent and devastating for the people of these lands. On the other hand, local institutions have a responsibility as well, a responsibility to protect this heritage and to educate children about it, and to do this without falling into the trap of ethnocentricity and exclusionary, sectarian politics.

To end, I hope you'll allow me to turn briefly to my own work at Columbia University, a project that hopes (in a small way, at least) to fight the process of cultural erasure I just described. As a means of countering all this destruction, three years ago I established a fieldwork project that I direct, called Mapping Mesopotamian Monuments.[8] With my team (some of them are here today: Helen Malko, Turkan Pilavci and Serdar Yalcin), we have conducted work recording monuments and architecture across northern Iraqi Kurdistan in Dohuk, Erbil and Sulaymaniyah, and in southeastern Anatolia. Our aim is to continue this work in the rest of Iraq to the south, and eventually also in Syria. We are not mapping tells, or conducting the standard archaeological surveys, but focussing specifically on monuments and architecture. We have no historical or religious boundaries for our project; we document inclusively. Our work has already documented many ancient Mesopotamian monuments and rock reliefs, Early Islamic and Early Christian works of architecture, mosques and madrasas, churches and monasteries, bridges and aqueducts, and Ottoman-era and early twentieth-century buildings. We use a range of technologies including photogrammetry, orthorectified and perspectival stills, and high-resolution 360-degree immersive panoramic records, while mapping things geospatially. For each work we have assessed the condition and written detailed descriptions. The archive of thousands of images we have made in the field is curated in a closed website (see Figure 25).

We abhor and lament the horrendous events that have overtaken our lands, killed our people and destroyed our history. However, in this meeting, The Future of the Past, our goals are rather practical. The aim of those of us who organised the conference, with the full support of our home institutions (Columbia University, Koç University and the Metropolitan Museum of Art) is to make real plans for moving forward. In the next few months, we hope to create a network of cooperation for work across East and West. As we are not emperors and kings, but scholars and archaeologists, like our great ancestor Nabuzer-lishir, it is only by research and documentation, by the taking on of students and post-doctoral researchers from Iraq, Syria and Turkey into our home institutions, by adopting archaeological and preservation projects together with our colleagues here, and by having open lines of communication, that we can counter this existential threat to our shared history.

Notes

1 Early Sumerian list of concepts and things associated with the arts of civilization.
2 See Z. Bahrani, *The Infinite Image: Art, time, and the aesthetic dimension in antiquity* (London: Reaktion, 2014).
3 *Kitab Surat al-ard* (Beirut: Daar Maktabat al-Hayah, 1992).
4 *Sefer ha-Masa'ot;, The Itinerary of Benjamin of Tudela: Critical text, translation and commentary*, edited and translated by Nathan M. Adler (New York: Philipp Feldheim, 1907).
5 Ibn Jabayr, *Rihlat Ibn Jubayr: The travels of Ibn Jubair*, edited and translated by William Wright (Leiden: Brill, 1852). Abu al-Feda, *Taqwim al-Buldan*; *Taqwim al-Buldan*, edited and translated by W. M. Slane and J. T. Reinaud (Paris: L'imprimerie Royale, 1840). Al-Mas'udi, *Muruj adh-dhahab*; *Les prairies d'or*, edited and translated by C. Barbier de Meynard and A. Pavet de Courteille, revised by C. Pellat (Paris: Société asiatique, 1962–71). Al-Muqqadasi, *Ahsan al-taqasim fi ma'rifat al-aqalim: The best divisions for knowledge of the regions*, edited and translated by Basil A. Collins (Reading: Garnet, 1994).
6 *An Ottoman Traveller: Selections from the book of travels of Evliya Çelebi*, edited and translated by Robert Dankoff and Sooyong Kim (London: Eland, 2010).
7 See, for example, the Tekye Moaven al-Molk in Kermanshah, Iran.
8 https://mcid.mcah.columbia.edu/art-atlas/mapping-mesopotamian-monuments.

18

Destruction and preservation as aspects of just war

Future Anterior: Journal of Historic Preservation 14 (2017): 107–26

’الدَمار والحِفاظ كمظاهِر للحَرب العادِلة‘ *المستقبل لِلأمام: مجلة الحفاظ التاريخي* 14 (2017): 107–126.

Synopsis

This article argues that the concern with monument destruction in warfare is as old as the world’s earliest historical texts and monuments, upon which were inscriptions warning of their potential destruction and removal as acts of war. Here, I point out that this remarkable historical evidence, known from the monuments and texts that survive from antiquity, is from the lands currently known as Iraq and Syria. When this paper was written and first delivered at the Fitch Colloquium for historic preservation in 2016, that history was in the process of being systematically obliterated by ISIS. In some cases, such as that of Palmyra, the wisdom of UNESCO’s hasty declaration that it would immediately restore the site upon ousting ISIS was questioned by many. For this reason, the article focuses on both destruction and preservation as aspects of warfare, the aims of such destruction as well as the role and politics of preservation in these wars.

المستخلص

تُجادِل هذه المقالة بأنَّ الاهتمام في تدمير الآثار في الحرب قَديمٌ بقِدَم نصوص العالم التاريخية وآثاره، وعَلَيه كانت هناك كتابات منقوشة تُحَذِّر من تدميرِها المُحتَمَل أو إزالتها كأعمال حرب. هُنا، أُشير بأنَّ هذا الدَليل التاريخي اللافِت للانتباه والذي عُرِفَ

من الآثار والنُصوص التي نَجَت من العُصور القديمة هو من الأرض التي تُعرَف حالياً بالعراق وسوريا. عندما كُتِبَت هذه الورقة البحثية وأُلقِيَت لأول مرة في ندوة فيتش عن الحِفاظ التاريخي عام 2016، كان هذا التاريخ يتَعرَّض لعملية إلغاء مُنَظَّم من قِبَل داعش. في بعض الحالات، كما هو الأمر مع تَدمُر، شَكَّك الكثير في حكمة الإعلان المُتَسرِّع لليونسكو بأنَّها ستُباشِر بترميم الموقع فَورَ طَرد داعش. لهذا السبب، تُركِّز المقالة على التدمير والحفاظ كَونَهما من مظاهر الحَرب، وعلى أهداف هكذا تدمير فضلاً عن دور سياسات الحِفاظ في هذه الحروب.

Two thousand five hundred years before the beginning of the Christian era, a Sumerian monument was erected in the south of modern-day Iraq (Figure 26). The monument takes the form of a large stele, carved on both sides with relief images and inscribed with a lengthy text about border disputes and warfare. Although much attention has been given to various features of the stele, one small aspect of the ancient text that has not been given due attention or recognition is rather noteworthy. Among the oaths that were sworn to the gods at the end of the war and recorded on this stele are promises that the warring parties would neither destroy nor dislocate the monument.[1] To date, this stele is the earliest known historical monument, and it tells us that already at that time, the deliberate destruction or removal of a monument from its site was to be taken as an act of war.

In contemporary scholarship, we often hear or read that cultural preservation is a modern and Western concern, and that laws of war concerning what is now referred to as heritage are aspects of Western modernity alone, not recognized in earlier eras. This is not the case. Although I want to address the current genocidal violence in Iraq and Syria and the strategies of historical erasure that are part and parcel of it, I would first like to go back in time to ancient Mesopotamia. I present the evidence from antiquity not simply as a lesson in history but to make the case that human beings and monuments are entangled in their histories. Mesopotamia stands as an example of at least one well-recorded ancient culture where monuments were understood as having a vital agency of their own. This agency was not ascribed to them but inherent within their logic as monuments, and their destruction was seen as having direct effects on the people, the land, the king, and his reign.[2]

The attempt to eradicate the past of Syria and Iraq is aimed at the obliteration of this earliest Mesopotamian history, a history that the local populations consider to be their own heritage and a basis of their collective past, something that transcends religion and ethnicity.[3] It is for this reason that historical monuments are now deliberately targeted; it is a strategy that aims to create a *terra nullius,* meaning a land that belongs to no one and has no prior historical claims, rendering it a no-man's land available for conquest. Thus the strategy of obliteration aims to create a land ready for the rewriting of history with a new vision, cleansed of its pre-Islamic past and cleansed also of any evidence of the thousands of years of existence of peoples and religions that do not suit the worldview of the ideology of Wahabism.[4] To counter that obliteration of history and to demonstrate how people and edifices were closely linked, I will recount the earliest writings on the place of monuments found in discourses of just war and war crimes, and the significant textual and archaeological evidence for the ancient Mesopotamian concerns with architectural preservation and restoration.

The ancient Mesopotamians who lived in what is now Iraq, Northeastern Syria, and Southeastern Turkey were probably the first people in the world to create inscribed historical monuments whose purpose was to endure into the distant future.[5] We read in the ancient texts that their monuments were conceived of as site-specific works meant to be present for all time. Their inscriptions often address viewers who were to see the monument in the distant future.[6] These works were made of various materials and in many forms, including free-standing steles or slabs of sculpted and inscribed stones, and relief sculptures carved into the cliffs of the mountainsides and set in magnificent works of architecture. Their materials, stone or brick, were considered to have inherent supernatural qualities. The monumental buildings were both religious and secular in nature. The ancient Mesopotamians also had a literature that praised these works as remarkable and astonishing things that future generations should admire, the first poetical descriptions of architecture we have. In these ancient texts, future generations were asked specifically to preserve these works. When monuments and architectural edifices were destroyed, when cities were ravaged by war, laments and requiems were written and sung on behalf of the destroyed built structures, just as they were for the people who had been killed, enslaved, and devastated. They were all considered aspects of the same destruction.[7] These acts of war and discourses of war and its aftermath, were also defined as part of the ME, the early Sumerian list of concepts and things that are associated with civilization. The ME include the arts, music, sculpture, and all kinds of positive and creative things and activities. But they also include aspects of life that are negative, such as warfare. For the Mesopotamians, seeing war as part of the ME was a way of acknowledging that warfare is an inevitable aspect of civilization, and therefore rules of war were established.[8]

The Sumerians already practiced what we later call in Latin *jus ad bellum,* or 'just war'. The act of war against another city-state was not acceptable unless it was defensive. The stele with which I began this article was erected by Eannatum of Lagash (modern Telloh in southern Iraq) and is the earliest known public, historical monument. It is a monument to victory, but at the same time it is also a contractual agreement, a peace treaty set up after the end of the battle between the city-states of Lagash and its neighbor Umma. Before the battle with Umma, Eannatum received the divine message in a dream oracle that sanctioned the war, and he justified his battle as a defense of the territory of Lagash. Already in the mid-third millennium BC the Sumerians practiced diplomacy. Before a war, envoys were sent to try to find a diplomatic solution for border conflicts. It was only when these failed that a messenger would be sent with a declaration of war, in advance of the actual attack. The taking of lives, even for the king and his military, was a source of great anxiety and required justification and sanction from the gods. Among the oaths that were made repeatedly were ones related to the protection of monuments themselves. Kings had to swear that they would not transgress borders, and also that they would not destroy monuments, so the destruction of monuments was already defined as an act of war in the third millennium BC. The destruction of a monument was considered legitimate reason to launch a just war, a war that was sanctioned by the gods. Throughout Mesopotamian history, monument destruction, or the theft and dislocation of monuments and statues, was often declared as the ostensible reason for launching a just war. As the stele of Eannatum makes clear, the destruction of a monument was seen as a criminal act, and it was tantamount to the breaking of a peace treaty.

The opposite side of this anxiety over the destruction of monuments is the ancient concern with preservation and conservation of architecture and monuments. Extensive information about restoration and preservation of works of historical architecture also exists, especially in ritual texts. About two thousand years after the Sumerian stele of Eannatum was erected, texts still reveal that these concerns remained in full force. During the reconstruction of a building, the brick god required prayers. Instructions for architectural restoration dating to the Seleucid era (fourth through third centuries BC) say:

> When the wall of a temple falls into ruin, in order to demolish and re-found that temple, the diviner shall investigate the site [for ancient remains]. The builder of the temple shall put on clean clothes and put a tin bracelet on his arm; he shall take an axe of lead, remove the first brick, and put it in restricted place. You set up

an offering table in front of that brick god of the foundations, and you offer sacrifices.[9]

These instructions for a restoration ritual show that architectural rituals and preservation rites that had begun in Sumer in the early third millennium BC still existed in some form thousands of years later in the fourth century BC. The text orders the *kalu* priest[10] to remove the first brick and place it on an altar. The *kalu* priest was then to sing the lamentations according to an age-old Mesopotamian tradition of laments and dirges sung for the destruction of cities and their architecture. These laments had been sung for the destruction of cities and for the terrible loss of temples and their magnificent sculptures during warfare as early as the late third millennium BC.[11]

In the Seleucid ritual quoted above, there was some sense that the original brick set upon the altar had to be appeased; it was the representative of the brick god, *Kulla.* Its removal from the original context of the building was played out as a temporary dislocation, while the repairs were being made as carefully as possible, following the original ground plans of the temple. When an ancient wall had to be pulled down and rebuilt, a process of mourning thus had to take place in order to bridge the gap between the existence of the old wall and the rebuilding of the new one. In another passage, the text also makes clear that the building site had to be surveyed by the *baru* (the seer priest), so that nothing would be inadvertently missed or damaged in the process of reconstruction.

The ancient Mesopotamians were constantly concerned with the reverence and respect for the remains of the past, and Mesopotamia is the first place where we can study these acts of preservation from both textual and archaeological evidence. We can even say that the reverence for the past and the concern with preservation of their ancient cities was distinctive of Mesopotamia, and these concerns are at times similar to those of our own time.

A lengthy compendium of omens known as *Šumma alu* (If a city), after its opening line, shows the concern with preservation well. The text provides a long list of omens that have to do with conservation and preservation practices and makes clear that they are intended not only for the king and those in power but also for common people:

> If a man repairs a sanctuary: he will have good luck
> If a man tears down a sanctuary: the river will swallow him
> If someone relocates a chapel: that man will go to ruin
> If a man repairs something old: that man's god will come to him[12]

These are but a few lines from a long list of forms of restoration and preservation of things, from images of gods and heroes to entire buildings and more limited architectural repairs. The text even has a section of concerns for surveyors who are planning to build at a particular location, so that if a man plans to build a house, and, while digging the foundations, finds something in the ground, he must follow particular procedures for preservation. All ancient objects found in the ground or that remained standing in temples or public places were considered to belong to the terrain and its history; their preservation was propitious for the people of the land and their future.

Demolition and preservation

Despite repeated cycles of war and devastation throughout the millennia of ancient history, the antiquities of the land nevertheless survived in some form or another. When in the second century BC the governor of Lagash, Adad-nadin-ahhe (and his builders) found the statues of King Gudea who had set them up two thousand years earlier, the later ruler had them placed in his newly constructed palace. Not only did he collect them and set them up carefully for display, but he ordered his scholars and scribes (who were able to read ancient languages and scripts) to imitate the Sumerian methods of building and of writing inscriptions that he used in his own palace. They made inscriptions written in Aramaic and Greek in such a way that they looked like the bricks inscribed with Gudea's name written in ancient Sumerian.[13] This was one of the earliest extant forms of antiquarian collecting and study of the past, and it prefigures the interests and activities that we see, for example, in the Italian Renaissance. These were ancient forms of preserving the past as a way to form ideological links to the antiquity of the land, but were also as pious acts, and in the pursuit and preservation of historical knowledge.

I have covered this ancient historical information in some detail for several reasons. First, to point out that people and monuments are intertwined, and that this entanglement was recognized in the literature and rituals of antiquity. Second, preservation and conservation are not modern Western ideas – a claim that is often made today and is also now used to justify the demolition of historical sites. The historical evidence is to the contrary, and it is exactly this evidence that is being wiped out today. Along with the murder and displacement of the population, the aim of this violent erasure is the rewriting of history and the restructuring of the landscape for geopolitical goals.

Rather than following cultural preservation policies that highlight heritage primarily in relation to tourist sites or concepts of global cultural heritage, as well-meaning as these are, we must consider the aims of this current erasure that targets the local population and the local landscape. Groups such as ISIS claim that their destruction of pre-Islamic monuments and archaeological sites, Shiite and Yazidi shrines, as well as Christian churches and monasteries, are all justified acts of religious war, but their larger goals have clearly been territorial, including the murderous ethnic cleansing of the population in regions that they wish to rule.

While it is clear today – as United Nations resolutions and international laws have acknowledged – that cultural destruction is an act of war, and even a war crime, which in August 2016 the International Criminal Court prosecuted in relation to the demolition of tombs in Timbuktu, this kind of prosecution has been somewhat selective. Many acts of direct targeting of heritage sites by UN member states that have taken place in recent years pass without much comment from the international community.

Furthermore, much of the work on preservation in war today is closely linked with government policies. Heritage is destroyed in war, ancient sites are occupied or deliberately attacked, but restoration is now also used as a declaration of victory, and it is also a means of profit for organizations that are awarded lucrative restoration and development contracts on political grounds. Governments and organizations compete for the control of the restoration of sites, as we saw was the case after the removal of ISIS from Palmyra in Syria.[14] At the same time, many funding agencies in the United States and Western Europe appear to be more concerned with showcasing new digital technologies than with tangible material or historical monuments. Some of these initiatives appropriate the heritage of Syria and Iraq for their own marketing purposes and profit in disturbing ways. While one may expect some companies to prefer the production of polyurethane replicas to restoring antiquities because of their own interests and potential profits, there is now also an effort to impose these replicas upon the ancient sites themselves without regard for local views. This push for replicas has been aptly referred to as a new digital colonialism by some archaeologists.[15] Interestingly, the policy of replicas placed on heritage sites is one that was traditionally rejected by UNESCO and by archaeological practices in general. One of the requirements for the inscription of a site as a UNESCO World Heritage site is its 'authenticity'. A decade ago UNESCO rejected Iraq's bid to place Babylon on the World Heritage list because the reconstructions of some of the walls on site were inauthentic. Ironically, replication on site, using modern synthetic materials and 3D printing techniques, is now being promoted by preservationists in the United States and Western Europe as the best course of action for the future of the sites in Iraq and Syria that have been destroyed in war (for example Figures 27 and 28).[16]

Since 2003, war has devastated Iraq and Syria. As I write this essay, our people are being killed and displaced, they are enslaved and tortured, cities are demolished and much more. In many cases, it is clear that the attacks on monuments are part of the strategy to erase the local populations and their histories and to use culture as a means to divide and wipe out history and people alike. This aspect of the cultural destruction has had little attention in comparison to the idea that sites such as Palmyra in Syria or Nimrud in Iraq are World Heritage Sites that need to be rescued because they are the origins of Western history or Global Heritage. In this way, cultural heritage policy today dissociates the historical sites from both landscape and people.

In September 2016, the president of France, François Hollande, announced a $100 million dollar fund to protect cultural heritage, especially in Syria and Iraq.[17] These funds (once they are raised) are to be allocated to postwar restoration, while part of Hollande's plan is to offer asylum in Europe to artifacts that are in danger. While this is no doubt an admirable pledge to protect culture, the reluctance to take in human refugees stands in marked contrast to the concern for heritage. The disconnection of Mesopotamian history from the landscape and the people of the Middle East is exactly what earlier scholarship of Orientalist and postcolonial criticism attempted to point out. In the nineteenth century, collections of antiquities in museums such as the Louvre and the British Museum often presented their acquisitions as a form of rescue and preservation from the ignorant populations unable to either understand or value the past.[18] This renewed dissociation in much preservation policy is all the more surprising given that the reason for the ISIS attacks on heritage sites such as Nimrud, Nineveh, Palmyra, as well as religious shrines and sanctuaries of any undesirable religious group – from Christians to Sufis, Shi'ites and Yazidis – is the erasure of the presence and histories of the diversity of peoples in Iraq and Syria, and the rewriting of the local history in their own vision, cleansed of the lives and histories of others.

At Columbia University's Art History and Archaeology Department, we had already been immersed in a field project before the ISIS takeover of Mosul and the declaration of the caliphate there. The Mapping Mesopotamian Monuments topographical survey that I direct was not in fact formulated as a reaction to the ISIS attacks on historical monuments. I first envisaged this project in 2004 when I was working in Iraq, and the project was originally a response to the destruction of heritage that had resulted from the US and coalition invasion of Iraq in the 2003 war and the occupation that followed. After waiting for US troops officially to withdraw from Iraq, thus ending the US occupation of Iraq in 2011, I launched the field project in 2012, just after the occupation forces had left. Therefore, the project was not initiated with the current conflict in mind but as a response to the earlier US-led war. We began the Mapping Mesopotamian Monuments field survey in the north of Iraq, in Iraqi Kurdistan, and have to date covered the monuments, historical architecture, and rock reliefs in the provinces of Dohuk, Erbil, and Sulaymaniyah/Slemani, as well as south-eastern Turkey. As ISIS took over Mosul after our work began, we postponed the documentation of the region of Mosul and the Nineveh province until a later date.

The project is a topographical survey of standing historical architecture and monuments from South Eastern Anatolia and Iraqi Kurdistan to southern Iraq. It covers all historical periods from ancient to modern, including Mesopotamian rock reliefs in the cliffs, early Christian monasteries and churches, early Islamic, Ottoman, and twentieth-century architecture. The Columbia survey covers all historical eras and types of monuments. The wide range of places, architectural structures, and standing monuments that we cover aims to record the rich diversity of this land and its history, a diversity that is being deliberately targeted and erased. The team I direct is formed of archaeologists from Columbia University as well as colleagues based in Iraq at the State Board of Antiquities and Heritage, both from Baghdad and from Iraqi Kurdistan. We work together onsite to map and document monuments and to assess their conditions. This information may be taken up for future preservation work. All of us on the team feel that our work is to create a historical record to counter deliberate erasure of our history. This kind of documentation can also be a source of evidence for future legal trials for war crimes and for any future demands for reparations for destruction.

Some part of this work that we are conducting can now be seen on the Columbia University Art History Department website (see Figure 25). The largest amount of catalogued information, however, is password protected and is now available only if one contacts our content curator directly. Decisions about open access have been difficult in the past two years since ISIS launched their campaign of monument destruction and the deliberate targeting of sites in Iraq and Syria. While the aim of the project is to have open access to all, we have had to face the reality of dangers for our team members in Iraq as well as the possibility that our website might provide locations and information that could be used to target sites.

An additional obstacle for this fieldwork has been the limitations on funding agencies, here in the West, who cannot permit teams like ours to spend their funds in payment to local archaeologists or other workers. As a result, much of the funding that has been allocated for cultural heritage preservation projects in Syria and Iraq has little to do with these lands and is more likely to be allocated to institutions in the United States or Western Europe. In the meantime, many pledges that were made more than a decade ago to provide even the simplest equipment, such as storage cases for museums, have never come through. These announcements appear in press releases and are usually given a great deal of coverage in the news media. However, often the promised aid never arrives.

The problems of preservation in war we are facing today also include the fact that state actors and occupying powers often have hasty restoration or preservation initiatives as a way to claim victory. This was clearly the case with a statement by Russia and UNESCO that they planned to restore Palmyra, soon after it was retaken from ISIS. In response to this declaration, a group of archaeologists (I was among them) wrote a letter to UNESCO asking that no restoration take place until the site could be surveyed.[19] Lest one thinks that the Palmyra restoration plan was unique, such work at ancient sites had already taken place in Iraq during the US military occupation.[20] While preservation and destruction have long been linked to war and political policy, we now have the added interests of private technology companies setting agendas for preservation work and its methods. In the midst of all these international plans for the future of the historical architecture, monuments, and sites of Iraq and Syria, what we have not heard are the voices of local scholars or local people. This exclusion is perhaps the direct result of the continuing claims – made by some influential cultural heritage preservationists and museum specialists in the West – that the local Iraqis and Syrians have no relationship with, or interest in, the ancient sites. These claims echo the ideology of ISIS, a deliberate dissociation of people from their historical landscape. With the Mapping Mesopotamian Monuments project, our aim is to work in an independent way to document historical architecture and sites that are the history of the great diversity of the land. It is this diversity that is now under attack, in part through the destruction of monuments.

Notes

1 J. S. Cooper, *Sumerian and Akkadian Royal Inscriptions*, vol. 1, inscription La.3.1 (New Haven, CT: The American Oriental Society, 1986), 33–9.

2 The power and agency of images and monuments in Mesopotamia has been the main core of my academic work throughout my career. Beginning with the 1995 article 'Assault and abduction: The fate of the royal image in the Ancient Near East', *Art History* 18 (3) (1995): 363–82; followed by *The Graven Image: Representation in Babylonia and Assyria* (Philadelphia: University of Pennsylvania Press, 2003), and more recently *The Infinite Image: Art, time, and the aesthetic dimension in antiquity* (London: Reaktion Books, 2014). As I have made these arguments through numerous books and articles over 20 years, I direct the reader to these publications rather than repeating them here.

3 I have made this claim in many of my publications, beginning in the 1990s. See my 'Conjuring Mesopotamia: Imaginative geography and a world past', in *Archaeology Under Fire*, edited by Lynn Meskell, 159–74 (London: Routledge, 1998). For recent news regarding the local sense of identity tied to the ancient remains see: https://www.theguardian.com/world/2016/nov/24/piecing-back-together-iraqi-archeological-gem-blown-sky-high-by-isis. There are also several reports in the Arabic-language press that record similar sentiments expressed by Iraqi soldiers and militia troops who first arrived at the site of Nimrud in November 2016. It is therefore remarkable that the stereotypes of the local ignorance of history continue to dominate both academic writing and accounts in the popular press, where arguments are usually made that this heritage is global and ought not to be considered the property of the nation-states where it now stands. Rather, it should be taken to locations in Europe for safekeeping, as suggested, for example, by the politician François Hollande and by the museum director James Cuno. These calls, for protecting the antiquities from the natives, echo the nineteenth-century discussions regarding the taking of antiquities from the region to museums in Paris and London.

4 Wahabism is a sect of Islam that was formed in the eighteenth century AD in what is now Saudi Arabia. It follows the teachings of Muhammed bin Abd al Wahab (1703–1792). It is the dominant sect of Saudi Arabia and Qatar. See 'Wahhabiyah' in *The Oxford Encyclopedia of the Islamic World* (Oxford: Oxford University Press, 2009).

5 See Zainab Bahrani, *Rituals of War* (New York: Zone Books, 2008), 125ff.

6 Zainab Bahrani, *The Infinite Image*.

7 Bahrani, *Rituals of War*. These laments with their descriptions of civilian deaths and destruction of historical architecture are particularly poignant and moving in the context of today's violence.

8 Bahrani, *Rituals of War*, 9–21.

9 Richard S. Ellis, *Foundation Deposits in Ancient Mesopotamia* (New Haven, CT: Yale University Press, 1968), 184.

10 The Kalu priest was a lamentation priest in ancient Mesopotamia.

11 Bahrani, *The Infinite Image*, 108–9.

12 Bahrani, *Rituals of War*, 216–17.

13 Bahrani, *The Infinite Image*, 217–38.

14 This rush to restore Palmyra was opposed by many archaeologists who have spent decades working there before the war, especially Andreas Schmidt-Colinet; see: https://www.eurozine.com/we-should-do-nothing-on-the-history-destruction-and rebuilding-of-palmyra/.

15 See Sarah Bond, 'The ethics of 3D-printing Syria's cultural heritage', *Forbes*, 22 September 2016.

16 See Daniel Zalewski, 'The factory of fakes', *The New Yorker*, 28 November 2016.

17 David D'Arcy, *The Art Newspaper*, 21 September 2016: https://theartnewspaper.com/news/fran-ois-hollande-announces-100m-fund-to-protect-cultural-heritage-in-the-middle-east/.

18 See Zainab Bahrani et al., *Scramble for the Past: A story of archaeology in the Ottoman Empire, 1753–1914* (Istanbul: SALT, 2011) and Bahrani, 'Conjuring Mesopotamia'.

19 Shirin International, a group of archaeologists who had previously worked in Syria until 2011, signed the petition that was sent to UNESCO, 19 April 2016: http://shirin-international.org/?page_id=2731.

20 See Zainab Bahrani, 'Archaeology and the strategies of war', in *The Cultural Cleansing of Iraq*, edited by Raymond W. Baker, Shereen T. Ismael and Tareq Y. Ismael, 67–81 (London: Pluto Books, 2010).

19

Blood antiquities and the global art market

Asian Art Museum, San Francisco, 3 April 2021

’آثار الدَم وسوق الفَن العالمي‘ مَتحَف الفَن الآسيوي، سان فرانسيسكو، 3 نيسان، 2021.

Synopsis

This is the text of a talk that was delivered at the Asian Art Museum in San Francisco, California, in 2021. The talk discussed the global market in antiquities, and the role of public museums in this trade. It addresses the illegal collecting of antiquities from places such as Iraq and Egypt, for museums such as the Museum of the Bible in Washington, DC, and the selling of antiquities held in older collections.

المستخلص

إن هذا هو نَصُّ الكَلِمة التي تمَّ إلقاؤها في مَتحَف الفَن الآسيوي في سان فرانسيسكو في كاليفورنيا عام 2021. لقد ناقَشَت الكلمة السوق العالمية المختصة بالآثار، ودَور المتاحف العامة في هذه التجارة. لقد تناولت الكلمة الجَّمع غير المَشروع للآثار من أماكن كالعراق ومصر، للمتاحف كمتحف الكتاب المُقَدَّس في العاصمة واشنطُن، وبَيع الآثار الموجودة في المجموعات القديمة.

Thank you for inviting me here today, and for the opportunity to speak about the global marketing of antiquities. I will focus on the issue as it affects West Asia (the area usually referred to as the Middle East), where there has been a great deal of looting and cultural-heritage destruction in recent years.

Since the earliest days of the new science of archaeology and the establishment of public museums in the nineteenth century, first in Europe and then in the United States, there have been three main arguments made against the removal and marketing of antiquities, architectural elements and monuments.

The first is the scholarly argument. Archaeologists have long pointed out that looted artefacts result in the destruction of historical and archaeological contexts and information, and that while a work of art, an artefact or a text may be a source of knowledge or aesthetic value in itself, its larger archaeological, scientific context and complex history is destroyed and lost. Through looting holes and destructive pits and tunnels across archaeological sites, or through hacking out parts of reliefs or friezes from larger architectural structures, the extraction of antiquities for the market means the comprehensive destruction of history. Examples of this kind of activity are widespread today, as demonstrated by the pitted landscape of the site of Umma, destroyed by looter holes (Figure 29). Hundreds of sites in the south of Iraq now have this appearance, all as a result of the antiquities trade.

But early archaeologists also participated in such destruction for the purposes of museum collecting, most notably for the newly established British Museum and the Louvre. During the nineteenth century and continuing into most of the twentieth, museums saw themselves as salvaging things from (in their words) the barbaric East, 'the Orient', where people were seen as incapable of both understanding antiquities and caring for them. Museums in economically and politically dominant imperial centres, so it went, could better care for discoveries made in the global periphery and regions of colonial occupation.

In today's world of new museology, with its calls for decolonization and social and restorative justice in museums, these earlier histories of collecting have begun to be confronted. At the same time, we are now also addressing the ways in which museum displays in so-called encyclopaedic art museums are not neutral spaces but zones in which cultural and racial hierarchies are performed and perpetuated, and in which interpretations of material culture are tied to the geopolitical claims of the collecting centres. Questions of provenance and acquisition histories are therefore not limited to our present moment; they are intertwined with earlier histories of collecting and formations of such collections, which takes us beyond legal claims. I have gone over these points because one of the main justifications for collecting antiquities today is still the claim that, by doing so, the antiquities are being rescued and salvaged from others who are less capable.

The second argument against the antiquities market is the legal one. The international legal frameworks that were put in place against the trafficking of antiquities are well known. In addition to these, antiquities laws were in place in many of the countries of West Asia (those under the Ottoman Empire) beginning in the nineteenth century. Already at that time, it was illegal to dig or to remove antiquities from Ottoman lands without permission from the Sublime Porte (the imperial centre) in Istanbul. And the parameters of international law today are powerful arguments against the trading of heritage and antiquities. UNESCO is currently celebrating the 50th anniversary of the 1970 UNESCO convention, which bans the import, export or transportation of antiquities and cultural heritage.[1] The legal constrictions are nevertheless either ignored or circumvented in many cases, and unfortunately this has not been limited to trade or dealing; it has been practiced by some public museums as well.

The most recent example is the Museum of the Bible in Washington, DC, established by the Green family, owners of the Hobby Lobby, in 2017. As several scholars and journalists have pointed out, their acquisition practices – including falsifying information about cuneiform tablets looted from sites in Iraq in order to transport them across borders labelled as house decor, and their bizarre practice of purchasing ancient mummy masks in order to dissolve them, in search for papyrus manuscripts – are a breach of the ethics of both conservation and museum stewardship. The collecting practices of this new museum have broken the law (they were required by law to repatriate antiquities to Iraq and elsewhere in the Middle East), but they also raise other questions.

This brings me to the third argument: the ethical one. What does restorative justice in the museum mean? Some objects or some collections were clearly acquired in ways that are outside the international legal framework, as I have noted. Artworks and artefacts are now at the centre of restitution and repatriation discussions, and in some cases there seems to be no question that they must be repatriated on legal grounds. But what can we say about situations where the legal restrictions are not at issue but the museum might have ethical responsibilities? A good example of such a grey zone is the case of the Virginia Theological Seminary (VTS). In their art collection was an Assyrian relief from Nimrud, acquired for $75 in 1859 from the British excavator Austen Henry Layard, who was digging at Nimrud, by an American man called Henri Haskell, who legally transported it into the US, according to the laws of the time. In 2018, the seminary decided to sell the relief. This was in the immediate aftermath of ISIS/Daesh, which had just taken over vast swathes of Syria and Iraq, enslaving hundreds of women and girls and killing thousands of people. Hundreds of thousands of people also became displaced and continue to live in camps today. As ISIS destroyed and blew up major Assyrian sites such as Nimrud and Nineveh (as well as religious shrines, churches, mosques and minarets), the market price for Assyrian antiquities shot up. VTS, a religious and – one would assume – ethically grounded institution, apparently decided that this disastrous moment would fetch the best price for the Assyrian relief in their care. They auctioned the relief to the highest bidder, and it sold for $31 million to an anonymous private collector.[2] The sale was completely legal. Critics of the sale complained that it was wrong because it went to a private collector and could no longer be seen by the public. Some tweeted that the relief had been illegally acquired in the first place. However, in my view, what is a more important issue is the larger ethical question – when the legality of the sale is not in itself a good enough justification for selling the relief. The fact that VTS chose this moment to benefit from the disaster that befell the people of Iraq is not a legal matter. The callous indifference of the seminary is perfectly legal. But it is reprehensible, nevertheless.

The sale of the VTS relief drives up the prices and escalates looting and plunder. The network of trade of antiquities and heritage involves the arms trade and violent warfare. In the past few years, it has become clear that it is implicated in slavery and the killing of people. The market in antiquities results in site destruction and loss of history, as scholars have made clear, but more importantly, this seemingly elegant and humanist pastime supports a network of violence.

Museums today are looking at a sea change before them, partly as a result of growing public awareness around provenance and collecting. The idea that encyclopaedic art museums are neutral spaces for scholarly knowledge has never been an entirely convincing one, even in the earliest days of its formation. Yet this idea continues to be used to justify collecting. Some argue that museums must continue to collect for the purposes of scholarship and the pursuit of knowledge. But it is unclear why this would be the case when major museums hold thousands of objects and texts that remain unpublished. The museum is meant to be a public trust, and the public now demands stories of provenance that have more transparency, along with historical displays that don't perpetuate colonial narratives. These are challenging times for museums, but they have the potential for real change.

Notes

1 https://en.unesco.org/fighttrafficking/1970.
2 See the Christie's sale record at https://www.christies.com/en/lot/lot-6164182.

20

Decolonising the museum

Cambridge University, 4 May 2021

’ديكولنيالية المتحف‘ جامعة كامبرج، 4 آيار، 2021.

Synopsis

In 2021 I was asked to speak at the Museum of Archaeology and Anthropology at Cambridge University in the UK on the subject of decolonising the museum. This short paper is the text of that talk. It briefly covers the imperial histories of collecting and museum displays of antiquities in the so-called encyclopaedic museums, and it concludes by highlighting how the curatorial and exhibitionary practices that still dominate major museums continue the imperial narratives set in place during the nineteenth and early twentieth centuries. The talk was followed by a lively discussion with students and colleagues at Cambridge regarding the question of museums as colonial sites.

المستخلص

في عام 2021 طُلِبَ مني أن أتحدَّث في متحف الاثار والانثروبولوجيا التابع لجامعة كامبرج في المملكة المتحدة عن موضوع جعل المتحف ديكولونيالياً (بمعنى إزالة الطابع الامبريالي عنه). إنَّ هذه الورقة البحثية القصيرة هي نَصٌّ تلك الكلمة التي ألقَيتُها هناك. فهي تتناول بإيجاز التاريخ الامبريالي لجمع الآثار والعروض المتحفية لها داخل ما يُعرَف بالمتاحف الموسوعية، وتُختَتَم المقالة بتسليط الضَّوء على الكيفيَة التي تستمر بها المُمارسات التنظيمية والاستعراضية التي تُهَيمن على المتاحف الكُبرى في الروايات الامبريالية التي تَمَّ اعتمادها منذ القرن 19 ومطلع القرن 20. لقد أعْقَبَت هذه الكلمة مناقَشة حَيَوية مع الطَلَبة والزُّملاء في جامعة كامبرج فيما يخُص مسألة المتاحف كمواقع كولونيالية.

What does it mean to decolonise the museum? In terms of museum critiques and practices, the current African-led movement for the restitution of the Benin bronzes is powerful and encouraging, and it is bringing about real changes.[1] Restitution decisions most clearly point to the shared histories of modern European museums and colonialism. Yet these efforts can't stop at restitution alone. A decolonisation of the museum, which is what this panel calls for, should not simply be about the return of particular works that were looted during periods of colonialism. In addition, it means that there is a need to acknowledge the histories of museums and their collections, that is, when, how and why they were formed and acquired. It means scrutinising the politics and ideologies of institutions and forms of display, and the scholarship that underpins them – with what Foucault points out as the power–knowledge nexus.[2]

As we are speaking in an archaeology/anthropology museum today, we can stress how a hierarchy of classification of cultures was set in place during eras of colonialism and imperialism, a hierarchy of European ascendency that still dominates so many displays both in archaeological museums and in the so-called encyclopaedic art museums. The modern museum system is closely tied to imperialism and colonialism, and while certain aspects have been modified over time, the outlines and effects of that system remain in place. Since the 1970s, the field of museology has studied the ways in which museums have been tied to empire, and how race and racism were at the centre of the exhibitionary order. But at the curatorial level, this is certainly an area that needs to be given a great deal more attention than it has. It is clear that today, traditional, colonial forms of display, and the notion of the encyclopaedic art museum itself, still dominate the interpretation of artworks, cultures and histories, and this alienates people of colour, minorities and people from former colonies.

It seems to me that there are three main issues that need to be considered when we speak of decolonising the museum, even while I stress that the museum is by definition an institution that is difficult to disentangle from its historical links to colonialism and empire. Decolonising the museum cannot be about the erasure or concealment of that close tie. I will mention the three issues briefly so that we can interrogate them further on. The first one is the exclusionary nature of curatorial staffing, where people of colour, from former colonised lands or from the Global South are rarely hired for such positions, and when they are, they are often marginalised within the institution. This lack of representation in staffing does in turn have a direct impact on curatorial decisions in general and on choices made in display narratives, which creates spaces that might seem welcoming (or not) to particular groups of people in the community or to museum visitors in general. Thus, the lack of diversity in the museum is not just about who gets the jobs and financial benefits. It has to do with the kinds of narratives that are told within the museum context – narratives that become the officially sanctioned ones, because of the institutional authority of the museum.

The second issue I want to mention is the nature or content of archaeological and ancient art exhibitions themselves. These exhibitions mostly present histories of colonised peoples and colonised lands, and/or exotic objects that were acquired at the height of imperialist expansion in distant places, yet the host museums don't usually address issues of provenance and geopolitics. At times, as we have seen recently at the British Museum's exhibition about the Assyrian king Ashurbanipal, they are funded by corporations that have been invested in extraction and colonial damage in the same places from which the antiquities displayed were removed.[3] This is not a matter of arguing that the removal of the Assyrian antiquities shown at the British Museum was legal or illegal. It is more an observation about the utter lack of sensitivity in the institution's decision-making surrounding the display of an ancient culture from Iraq, a country still reeling from the aftermath of a war and occupation that the UK spearheaded with the US in 2003. As a result, the exhibition, emblazoned with a large BP logo, came off like an imperial triumphal statement. While the branding was called out by activists and protestors at the time of the exhibition,[4] the curatorial aspects were also problematic: the exhibition and its publicity relied heavily on sensationalising Orientalist tropes – stereotypes of Oriental despotism and decadence – many of which would have fit well within the nineteenth-century literature of imperialist archaeologies.

This brings me to the third aspect of decolonisation that I would like to stress, which is scholarship. I work in two different but overlapping fields. One is the history of art, and the other is the field that is still known as ancient Near Eastern archaeology (West Asian archaeology). While art history and museum studies have confronted some of these issues, Near Eastern archaeology has been rather resistant to change. There is a disconnect between the practices of Near Eastern archaeology and museum displays and the idea that there are any living people or societies in that part of the world.

This disconnection was so distressing to me early in my career that it led me to write an article in the 1990s, called 'Conjuring Mesopotamia: Imaginative geography and a world past', in which I argued that the field was entrenched in the aims and ideologies of colonial-imperialism, aims which – among other things – sought to classify populations in racial terms.[5] That text later became a staple in archaeology classes, reprinted in archaeological theory textbooks and widely read in adjacent fields of research; even so, the discipline of ancient Near Eastern archaeology has yet to bridge the divide that allocated antiquity to Western notions of history and collecting while disregarding living communities in places like Iraq, Syria, Turkey and elsewhere in the region where I work. Worse yet, local populations are at times considered to be unfortunate obstacles to the pursuit of a pure knowledge about the past.

In another case, in my 2003 book, *The Graven Image*, I made an argument about the concept of the non-mimetic image in Mesopotamian antiquity in one of the chapters.[6] That chapter was quoted and cited widely in the past twenty years. However, my mimesis argument was decontextualised from the main point of the book. The first three chapters and the concluding chapter of that same book presented a post-colonial polemic about archaeology and imperialism, about racial theory and museum displays. The larger arguments the book made – about cultural translation and subject positions, or the links between scientific archaeology, the collecting of antiquities and colonialism – were less welcome at the time, although now, twenty years later, these critiques appear to be re-emerging and seem to be of interest to a new generation of scholars in the field. Yet I do think there is cause to be optimistic, as a panel such as this one, focused on decolonising the museum, is part of a movement that unifies and brings together alliances of people and scholars working in different fields, from different countries, and from different walks of life, but sharing in a common goal as we stand together to make our voices heard.

Notes

1 See, for example, Felwine Sarr and Bénédicte Savoy, *The Restitution of African Cultural Heritage: Toward a new relational ethics*, trans. Drew S. Burk (Paris: Philippe Rey, 2018).

2 See especially Michel Foucault, *Power/Knowledge: Selected interviews and other writings, 1972–1977* (New York: Pantheon Books, 1980).

3 See https://www.britishmuseum.org/exhibitions/i-am-ashurbanipal-king-world-king-assyria. Note the prominent 'supported by BP' signage and text on the landing page.

4 See Mattha Busby, 'Campaigners protest against BP support of British Museum', *The Guardian*, 16 February 2019, https://www.theguardian.com/culture/2019/feb/16/campaigners-protest-against-bp-sponsorship-of-british-museum.

5 Zainab Bahrani, 'Conjuring Mesopotamia: Imaginative geography and a world past', in *Archaeology Under Fire: Nationalism, politics and heritage in the Eastern Mediterranean and Middle East*, edited by Lynn Meskell (London: Routledge, 1998), 159–74.

6 Zainab Bahrani, *The Graven Image* (Philadelphia: University of Pennsylvania Press, 2003). In particular, see Chapter 5, '*Salmu*: representation in the real'. For the theoretical arguments about race, archaeology and imperialism, see Chapter 1 in the same book.

21 Technologies of power in archaeology

Columbia University, 25 February 2022

’تكنولوجيا القوَّة في علم الآثار‘ جامعة كولومبيا، 25 شباط، 2022.

Synopsis

This talk was part of the conference Technologies of Power, which took place at Columbia University in 2021–2 and was presented as an online series of ‘virtual conversations’.[1] The main theme of the conference was concerned with how the development of technologies of power and warfare have influenced the study and teaching of the humanities and social sciences. While other colleagues covered a range of topics in the social sciences, I addressed the role of technologies of war in archaeological practices. In particular, I pointed out archaeology’s extensive use of technological equipment that was first developed for military use and first tested out in the US wars in Iraq, beginning with the 1991 war.

المستخلص

جاءَت هذه الكلمة كمُشاركة ضمن فعاليات مؤتمر *تكنولوجيا القوَّة*، والذي عُقِد في جامعة كولومبيا في عامَي 2021–2022 والذي تم تقديمه على شكل سلسلة من’ المُحادَثات الافتراضيّة‘ عبر الانترنَت. يهتم الموضوع الأساس للمؤتمر بالكيفية التي أثَّرَ بها تطوُّر تكنولوجيا القوة والحرب في دراسة وتدريس العلوم الإنسانية والاجتماعية. قام زُملاء آخرون بتغطية مجموعة من المواضيع في العلوم الاجتماعية، بينَما تناولتُ أنا دور تكنولوجيا (تقنيات) الحرب في المُمارسات الآثارية. لقد أشَرتُ بالتحديد إلى الاستعمال الواسع للمُعدّات التكنولوجية التي تمَّ تطويرها في الأساس لأغراضٍ عسكرية وكان الاختبار الأول لها في حروب الولايات المتَّحدة في العراق، بِدءاً بحرًب عام 1991.

In a meeting at the UN Security Council in February 2003, the US Secretary of State, Colin Powell, presented intelligence from satellite images as proof that Iraq had weapons of mass destruction.[2] Though we now know that the information gathered from those images was wrong, the following month, the war and long-term occupation of Iraq began. And as my colleague Laura Kurgan has observed, it was partly based on the idea of the infallibility of such an image and the technology that produced it.

My research in the history of art and archaeology explores the history of the image, the practices of mimesis, and philosophies of representation. From the other side of history, in the distant past, the ancient Babylonians and Assyrians understood that reality and representation were interdependent, and also that technologies of the image were among the technologies of war. Images and maps were also central to the success of the nineteenth-century imperial/colonial mission in the Middle East, in which archaeology participated. The topics I want to discuss in the context of this series of humanities talks and methodologies have to do with the ways in which archaeology is at once implicated in – and can be read against and challenge – the new technologies of power.

I will begin with mapping. Some now speak of the militarization of archaeology as a discipline, its embeddedness within the aims of war and occupation. Its new dependence on forms of remote sensing and geospatial mapping (as with aspects of warfare today) also involves experts who work remotely from distanced computer screens. But since its earliest days, mapping has been one of the main activities of archaeologists and Orientalists in Iraq (ancient Mesopotamia). Though the militarization of archaeological practice is perhaps clearer now, as drones and digital technologies that were developed for the military – and some of them first used for reconnaissance and smart bombing in Iraq, during the First Gulf War in 1991 – are now commonly used by archaeologists. Like colonial-era cartography, these new techniques can provide great accuracy, but they also raise a number of questions about scopic regimes and formations of viewership.

How are we to read this new scientific archaeological view from nowhere, claiming neutrality? What is the position of the viewer as subject? How does the image express its authority? And how does the aspect of temporality come into play within such images, which are tagged geospatially and temporally? Art historians and historians of science have asked these kinds of questions in relation to earlier eras of imperialism. My work addresses how today, with archaeology's increasing reliance on declassified spy images, such as from CIA Corona satellites, remote sensing and so on (see Figure 30), we seem to be returning to the idea of the possibility of an unmediated representation.

I am interested in ontologies of archaeological scientific images, and the epistemological claims that they make – and also in how the subject position of the archaeologist to some extent comes to be constructed by these images and is implicated in their forms of viewing, as well as in the gazes that they generate. How does this new form of visual information and imaging developed for warfare, this exacting digital measurability of place or monument, erase its own representational apparatus? In the nineteenth century, Orientalist paintings such as Gérôme's *Snake Charmer* (Figure 31) were produced as a way of 'knowing' what was purported to be the reality of the exotic and decadent Orient, the 'paintedness' of them was denied by means of the very processes of their painting, as the art historian Linda Nochlin pointed out so brilliantly in 1983.[3] The forms of exactitude without interpretation that military technologies have given archaeology, also produce their own effects.

The second, related topic is collecting. Collecting antiquities involves the dislocation and disruption of object relations in assemblages, and repositioning in forms of display. As such, colonial collecting practices are inscribed in techniques of power. This was not just a taking of symbolic capital of the antique, that could be amassed in one place, like the movement of the statues of the gods in antiquity; it was directly related to landscapes and people. The removal of monuments and forced movements of populations have long gone hand in hand, so that the Persian king Cyrus's decree, which permitted displaced populations to return home in the sixth century BC, also included the restitution of statues.[4] Looting of archaeological sites for the global antiquities market can now be tracked with satellite images, so that we can see and document the devastation of the land for the illicit trade in heritage commodities. The techniques of power into which collecting is inscribed, and participates in, have to do with environments and landscapes, but they are also implicated in the writing of histories, and the narratives that are told in museum displays and in texts. While coloniality was the condition that permitted both early archaeology and the nineteenth-century collecting practices which allowed the encyclopaedic art museum to come into existence, a similar situation and condition is the context that permits both looting and the new archaeological technologies in Iraq.

This brings me to the third aspect: narrating. All of these technologies – GIS mapping, remotely sensed data, and declassified military satellite images – are a means of representing and managing data, and so of narrating and display, that involves the archaeological sciences. The writing out of the subject position of the observer in the archaeological work, then, also impacts the writing of the historical account. Aerial imaging elevates the eye of the archaeologist, so that archaeology is reconceptualized as a distanced view that is in some ways the direct opposite of traditional fieldwork (though it also involves the older methods of digging in areas that are pinpointed by that view). The view from above, remote sensing, and so on, are also mediated by the technological military lens itself. Archaeologists have not given much thought to these aspects of their military technologies – technologies that were developed (in some cases) for targeting and smart bombing Iraq. On the other hand, several artists have been critically engaging with these new relations of spy satellites, drone imaging, warfare and archaeology, using technologies in reversed ways. And in our Columbia project, Mapping Mesopotamian Monuments, we also turn away from standard methods (see Figure 25).[5] We are using the new technologies to map a different kind of archaeological encounter, one that is phenomenologically tied to the landscape, and that maps the multi-temporal historical relationship of the living population to monuments and ancient sites – sites and antiquities that have been in many cases forcibly removed and appropriated for lucrative global markets in cultural heritage and encyclopaedic museums. We work in a transdisciplinary way. In addition, I have now started a new collaborative project with the Iraqi artist Hanaa Malallah, tracing the links between colonialism and archaeology and repurposing technologies of power in a way that works more like bricolage, turning them to the service of exposing the destruction of war and colonial violence.[6]

To conclude, I would like to direct your view to a work of art. In a fascinating multimedia work by Malallah (2016–17), we see an encounter between a drone and a Sumerian ziggurat/temple tower (Figure 32).[7] Here, you see that the all-encompassing and masterful view of the drone is countered by the enduring and monumental force of the ancient ziggurat.

Notes

1 https://technologiesofpower.com.
2 See the UN press release (5 February 2003) at https://press.un.org/en/2003/sc7658.doc.htm.
3 Linda Nochlin, 'The imaginary Orient', *Art in America* 71 (5) (May 1983): 118–31.

4 For the text and translation of the Cyrus cylinder, see Amelie Kuhrt, *The Persian Empire: Sources and documents* (London: Routledge, 2007), 70–4.

5 https://mcid.mcah.columbia.edu/art-atlas/mapping-mesopotamian-monuments.

6 See our jointly written essays presented online at https://www.hanaa-malallah.com/blog-1.

7 The video component of the work can be viewed at https://www.hanaa-malallah.com/copy-of-biohazard-al-karada.

22
Historical destruction in a forgotten war

in *Theater of Operations: The Gulf Wars, 1991–2011*, edited by P. Eleey and R. Katrib, 233–47. New York: Museum of Modern Art, 2020

’التَدمير التاريخي في حَربٍ مَنسيَّة‘ في مَسرح *العَمليّات: حروب الخَليج، 1991–2011*، تحرير ب. إيلي و ر. كاترب، 233–247، نيويورك: متحف الفن الحديث (2020).

Synopsis

This essay addresses the destruction of history and heritage in Iraq, covering the First Gulf War in 1991 and the period of the international embargo on Iraq. It describes some of the damage to monuments and sites, and the impact that the war and embargo had on the population. Written within the context of an exhibition and a book that linked the two Gulf Wars, the essay also demonstrates that the impact of the destruction of the 1990s is still visible today.

المستخلص

تتناوَل هذه المقالة تدمير التاريخ والتراث في العراق، وقد شملَت بتغطيتِها حربَ الخليج الأولى عام 1991 وفترة الحصار الدوَلي الذي تمَّ فَرضُه على العراق. لقد وَصَفَت المقالة بعض الأضرار التي لَحِقَت بالآثار والمواقع، فضلاً عن الأثَر الذي خَلَّفَه كُلٌّ من الحَرب والحصار على الشَّعب. لقد كُتِبَت هذه المقالة في سِياق معرضٍ وكتابٍ تناوَلا العلاقة بين حَربَي الخليج الأولى والثانية، لقد بَيَّنَت المقالة كذلك بأنَّ الأَثَر الذي أسفَر عنه الدَّمار في تسعينيات القرن المنصرم ما زالَ مَلحوظاً حتى يومِنا هذا.

We have already buried them, they can no longer be counted.

General Norman Schwarzkopf[1]

The non-will to know is part of the non-war.

Jean Baudrillard [2]

In April 2003, as the Iraqi state capitulated to the invading US and coalition forces, one of the first decisions made by the US Central Command was to base their forces in government locations. These included many cultural and archaeological sites as well as major monuments. Among the heritage sites and historical monuments occupied by US troops in the aftermath of the ground war was the Shaheed Monument, a war memorial in Baghdad designed by the Iraqi artist Ismail Fattah (Figures 20 and 21). The 40-meter-high design, a fractured turquoise dome divided into two halves to be read as part of an original whole, appears as if riven by the ruthlessness of war.

Ismail Fattah's monument was conceived as a memorial for those who had died in the long and brutal Iran–Iraq War (1980–8), with the fallen comprised of soldiers conscripted from an unwilling population by the Baathist regime. However, in time, the monument came to stand in memoriam to the dead soldiers of the 1991 Gulf War also. In 2003, US tanks and troops took over the Shaheed Memorial, stationing their military base within the architectural structure and surrounding complex, while desecrating the site. Inside the cenotaph, the names of the fallen and missing Iraqi soldiers had been inscribed individually, as many found in war memorials worldwide, such as the Vietnam Veteran's memorial in Washington, DC, designed by Maya Lin. US soldiers covered and defaced the names of the Iraqi war dead with markers of their victory. The memorial museum and circular platform of the monument that extends into the Tigris river were damaged when the US military converted the site to a motor pool for their 68-tonne Abrams tanks. The Iraqi draftees of the 1991 Gulf War, whose deaths or body counts were neither tracked by the US forces nor fully recorded in Iraq, had also been remembered there at the Shaheed Monument as a memorial for their families to remember them by in local and unofficial practices of mourning and remembrance. As with the 2003 war, no official count was made of those Iraqis who died in the 1991 Gulf War, whether civilian or military. The US commander in 1991, General Schwarzkopf said: 'We have already buried them, they can no longer be counted'.

While the First Gulf War did not see ancient sites or historical monuments deliberately targeted in aerial bombardment, several historical monuments were nevertheless damaged. The ancient Ziggurat of Ur (the Temple Tower of the Moon God, dating to 2100 BC) and the adjacent ancient sanctuary were hit by US missiles, which left large craters up to ten meters in diameter and four meters deep, damaging the sacred precinct. Shrapnel blasted the ziggurat during the explosions, creating approximately four hundred holes in the side of the structure.[3] To the southeast of Ur, the archaeological site of Tell al-Lahm was also occupied by the US military. To accommodate the troops, the military conducted large-scale machinery excavations, destroying the ancient Sumerian and Babylonian archaeological layers.[4] The irreparable damage of historical sites prefigured what was to come in 2003–4: the occupation of major heritage sites such as Babylon, Ur, and Kish, among others, as US and coalition military bases.[5] With notable exceptions, this damage has not been studied or even duly acknowledged, having been overshadowed by the cultural destruction of the 2003 war, and the 2013–18 demolition and looting by ISIS that followed soon after the end of the US occupation of Iraq.[6] While historical sites were damaged in 1991, no inventory was taken in the aftermath. Although both the Directorate of Antiquities and Heritage of Iraq and UNESCO requested an inventory, because of the terms of the international embargo set by the UN Security Council, the request was denied.

Some locations suffered structural damage due to the scale of the sorties and the power of the bombing campaign. The aerial bombardment of January and February 1991 was massive: The amount of explosives dropped on Iraq in the monthlong assault surpassed that of the entire allied offensive of the Second World War.[7] Continuing economic sanctions established by UN Resolution 661 of August 1990, followed the assault, sanctions that came to be called 'The Siege' in Iraq.[8] The medieval university complex in Baghdad, the Mustansiriyeh, was damaged during the air campaign. The Great Arch of Ctesiphon (Figure 1), known as Taq Kesra or Ayvan-i Kesra (the iwan of Khusraw, the Sasanian king), was also damaged by the aerial bombardment and by the lack of conservation materials and expertise during the years of sanctions. The colossal arch, standing at twenty-six meters high, is the last remaining vaulted iwan of the grand Parthian-Sasanian era palaces at al Mada'in, near Seleucia on the Tigris. It is the largest single-span, parabolic barrel vault in the world. The structure is a remarkable feat in ancient Mesopotamian brickwork and construction techniques and had, prior to the US bombing campaign in 1991 that resulted in a large crack in the vault, withstood the tests of time. It is still in danger of collapse.[9] Not only is Ctesiphon known for its historical significance in Iraq and the region as a landmark structure from late antiquity, but it was also the source of inspiration for the Iraqi Modernist Pioneers Movement during the mid-twentieth century. Architects such as Rifat al Chadirji turned to the arch in their development of mid-twentieth century forms.[10] When such monuments and sites are endangered or destroyed, the damage affects far more than the historical structure itself. It affects the people's sense of context and belonging in this ancient land.

In 1991, a missile hit the Bughday Khatoun memorial shrine (*marqad* in Arabic), an architectural complex that has arcades of pointed arches surrounding a large open court and a building surmounted by a turquoise dome. Its foundation dates to 1361 AD. An Iraqi regime missile hit the side of the courtyard, where the rubble still remains at the exact location today (Figure 33).[11] Kirkuk, one of the oldest continuously inhabited cities remaining from antiquity, has at its center a citadel sitting upon an archaeological mound, similar to that found in the historical city center of Erbil. During Kirkuk's anti-government uprisings following the 1991 war, the city's population was punished by the regime with indiscriminate attacks. By the end of the decade, the regime also demolished much of the historical architecture on the citadel and its surroundings. Due to the UN sanctions prohibiting the importation of materials and outside expertise, no systematic documentation, preservation, and conservation work in the ancient citadel has yet been possible.

After the 1991 war, seeing a weakened state, people in both north and south of Iraq made a concerted effort to overthrow the Baathist regime of Saddam Hussein. The Baathist response to this effort was brutal, and in the chaos that took place, nine of the thirteen regional museums were looted and damaged. Their contents were destined for an international black market in antiquities that was to increase exponentially during the years of the embargo, an illicit process that would only grow following the 2003 war and occupation. Thousands of Islamic-era manuscripts, Mesopotamian artifacts, and cuneiform tablets were looted during the First Gulf War.[12] In the following years of the sanctions, the looting of heritage sites increased to previously unknown scales.

Meanwhile, the archaeological sites in Iraq also saw a massive increase in looting for the internationally lucrative illicit trade in antiquities. In countries such as the US, UK, Switzerland, Israel, and Japan, illicitly acquired antiquities were purchased by museums and authenticated by some leading Western Assyriologists, with some in the upper echelons of the Baathist regime participating in the black market trafficking of their country's heritage.[13] The Iraqi Directorate of Antiquities, in vain, lodged complaints to colleagues in the international community of scholars, but there was little interest at the time in countering this flow of antiquities into the global market. Artifacts and manuscripts have been acquired by those who, in the name of academic and urbane humanist activities, benefit from the destruction of history and the spoils of wars that have occurred in Iraq.

At the same time, almost all research stopped. The thirteen-year-long embargo meant that no archaeologists, preservationists, conservators, or other scholars based outside of the country could work in Iraq. The simplest items of scholarship and teaching were banned from importation as part of the UN-managed blockade. Iraq could no longer receive scientific journals or books. Pencils and paper for school children were banned, as the lead in pencils was deemed a 'dual use' item – meaning that they could support WMD (weapons of mass destruction) programs. The Iraqi author Haifa Zangana remembers sending a gift to her nieces and nephews in Mosul in 1995. The gift box contained, 'one pencil case, three erasers, three sharpeners, six fountain pens, two markers, one glue stick, and two ball point pens'. The envelope was returned stamped: 'Due to international sanctions against Iraq, we are not able to forward your packet'.[14]

The sanctions decimated the population rather than the regime. Artists, scholars, and museum professionals, cut off from the world, nevertheless came up with creative forms and used locally sourced materials for their production. While much of the rest of the world was becoming linked through visual media and electronic communication at greater and greater speed, the stranglehold of the embargo only brought Iraq increasing isolation. Artists began to make their own paper, often looking to the traditions of medieval illuminated manuscripts, which they creatively turned to for developing new contemporary forms and projects. They also began to reference the destruction of the ancient Near Eastern past, a theme that was to become central once again following the destruction of heritage sites and museums in 2003.[15] Many artists and intellectuals were forced into exile.

The impact of the war and the international embargo not only destroyed heritage sites and museums, but more importantly, it destroyed life, education, and knowledge. It destroyed childhoods and lives, cutting Iraqis off from the world. All universities suffered from the sanctions, as teaching materials and equipment were also subject to the terms of the UN embargo. Similarly, hospitals and clinics were severely crippled; medicines, medical equipment, and necessities such as radioisotopes used for cancer treatments were banned. Hundreds of thousands of people died from illness and hunger as a result of these sanctions. UNICEF estimated that half-a-million children died as a result of the first five years of the ruthless sanctions. In May 1996, the US Ambassador to the United Nations, Madeleine Albright, was asked by the journalist Lesley Stahl to comment on the deaths during an interview on *60 Minutes*. Stahl asked, 'We have heard that half-a-million children have died. I mean, that is more children than died in Hiroshima. And, you know, is the price worth it?' Albright responded, 'I think that is a very hard choice, but the price, we think, the price is worth it'.[16]

Notes

1 Norman Schwartzkopf, quoted in Jean Baudrillard, *The Gulf War Did Not Take Place* (Bloomington: Indiana University Press, 1995), 74.

2 Baudrillard, *The Gulf War Did Not Take Place*, 74.

3 McGuire Gibson, 'The loss of archaeological context and the illegal trade in Mesopotamian antiquities', *Culture Without Context* 1 (1997): 6.

4 Gibson, 'The loss of archaeological context'.

5 See Zainab Bahrani, 'Archaeology and the strategies of war', in *Cultural Cleansing in Iraq*, edited by Raymond W. Baker, Shereen T. Ismael and Tareq Y. Ismael (London: Pluto Press, 2010), 67–81.

6 For the extensive destruction of culture during the 2003 war and first years of the US occupation of Iraq, see the collected papers in Baker, Ismael and Ismael, *Cultural Cleansing*, 67–81.

7 For the political context, see the collected essays in Tareq Y. Ismael and Jacqueline S. Ismael, *The Gulf War and the New World Order* (Gainesville: University Press of Florida, 1994). The comparison with World War II does not include the nuclear bombs that the United States dropped on Japan, however.

8 Paul Patton, 'Introduction', in Baudrillard, *The Gulf War*, 1; George Gerbner, 'Persian Gulf War, the movie', in *Triumph of the Image: The media's war in the Persian Gulf: A global perspective*, edited by Hamid Mowlana, George Gerbner and Herbert l. Schiller (Boulder, CO: Westview Press, 1992), 252; Haifa Zangana, *City of Widows: An lraqi woman's account of war and resistance* (New York: Seven Stories Press, 2007).

9 The crack caused by the US bombing is acknowledged by the US Department of Defense. See '054. Salman Pak, Tak Kisra (ancient: *Ctesiphon*)', Significant Sites, The Center for Environmental Management of Military Lands (CEMML), Colorado State University, https://www.cemml.colostate.edu/cultural/09476/iraq05-054.html (accessed 28 August 2019).

10 See for example Rifat Chadirji's 1959 monument to the Unknown Soldier as well as other works that make use of the iwan form by the same architect. See Rifat Chadirji, *Concepts and Influences: Towards a regionalized international architecture* (London: KPI, 1986).

11 The author was in Kirkuk a week before submitting this essay for publication and saw the damage and rubble still in place.

12 There was a concerted effort to create inventories of the looted works and to call for their return to Iraq. Nevertheless, some of these works began to appear in the international market for antiquities. See McGuire Gibson and Augusta McMahon, *Lost Heritage: Antiquities Stolen from Iraq's Regional Museums*, fasc. 2 (London: British School of Archaeology in Iraq, 1993); fasc. 1 (Chicago: American Association for Research in Baghdad, 1992); Heather D. Baker, Roger J. Matthews, and J. Nicholas Postgate, *Lost Heritage: Antiquities Stolen from Iraq's Regional Museums*, fasc. 2 (London: British School of Archaeology in Iraq, 1993); Hideo Fujii and Kazumi Oguchi, *Lost Heritage: Antiquities Stolen from Iraq's Regional Museums*, fasc. 3 (Tokyo: Institute for Cultural Studies of Ancient Iraq, Kokushian University, 1996); including list of stolen historical manuscripts.

13 Gibson, *Culture*. See also R. C. Longworth, 'Iraq artifacts stolen during war', *Chicago Tribune*, 5 March 1992.
14 Zangana, *City of Widows*, 75.
15 Zainab Bahrani and Nada Shabout, *Modernism and Iraq* (New York: Columbia University Press, 2009).
16 John Manslagt, 'Madeline Albright – 60 Minutes', YouTube video, 0:22, 28 June 2008. https://www.youtube.com/watch?v=Fb1X1CP9qr4.

23

Mosul and Nineveh

As *Mossoul et Ninive*, published in *Cités millénaires: Voyage virtuel de Palmyre à Mossoul*, edited by Audrey Azoulay, 22–7. Paris: Hazan, 2018

'الموصل ونينوى' في *مُدُن الألفيَّة: رحلة افتراضية من تَدمُر إلى الموصل*، تحرير أودري آزولَي، 22–27، باريس: هازان (2018).

Synopsis

This chapter was originally written for an exhibition at the Institut du monde arabe, Paris, in 2018.[1] It focuses on the history of the city of Mosul in the north of Iraq, a place that was severely damaged by the ISIS war and occupation. While Mosul is best known as an Islamic city with its medieval mosques and famed leaning minaret, the mounds of the ancient city of Nineveh stand just across the Tigris River. Nineveh was one of the Assyrian cities excavated in the mid-nineteenth century by European archaeologists. Nearby is also the Assyrian city of Kalhu/Nimrud, whose standing remains – which included the famed Assyrian gates of winged bulls – were blown up by ISIS. This essay was also written in response to the ISIS destruction, but it ends with some signs of hope for the future – signalled by the accidental discovery of more winged bulls, hidden below the historical architecture, during the restoration project that followed.

المستخلص

كُتِبَ هذا الفصل بادئ الأمر لمعرضٍ أُقيمَ في معهد العالم العربي في باريس عام 2018. ركَّز الفَصل على تاريخ مدينةً الموصل في شمال العراق، فهي ذلك المكان

الذي تضرَّر بشِدّة خلال الحرب مع داعش واحتلالها له. بينما ذاع سيطُ الموصل كمدينةٍ إسلامية بمساجدِها القَروسطية ومنارَتِها الحَدباء الشَّهيرة، فإنَّ مدينة نينوى القديمة بتلالِها تطلُّ عليها عبرَ نهرِ دجلة. لقد كانت نينوى إحدى المُدُن الآشوريّة التي تمَّ التنقيب فيها في أواسط القرن 19 من قِبَل آثاريين أوروبيين. على مَقربةٍ منها تَقفُ أطلال مدينة كالخو/النمرود الآشوريّة – بضمنها البوّابات الآشوريّة ذات الثيران المُجنَّحة – التي فجَّرَتها داعش. إنَّ هذه المقالة قد كُتِبَت كذلك رَدّاً على التدمير الذي مارسته داعش، لكنَّ المقالة خُتِمَت ببوادر الأمل في المستقبل – في إشارة إلى الاكتشاف العَرَضي للمَزيد من الثيران المُجنَّحة، المُختَفية تحت العمارة التاريخية، أثناء العمل في مشروع الترميم الذي أعقب التدمير.

In his topographical encyclopaedia, written in Arabic between 1224 and 1228 AD and titled *Mu'jam al Buldan*, Yaqut al-Rumi al-Baghdadi (al Hamawi) devoted several pages to the city of Mosul. He described it as a magnificent city on the Tigris and referred to it as the gate of Iraq. He then went on to say that Mosul was a very ancient city with Nineveh on its eastern side. During the days of the ancient Persian empire, Yaqut tells us, it was called Naw Ardashir or Baw Ardashir (he is careful to explain that he is not quite certain about the first letter). Earlier, the ancient Greek writer Xenophon referred to the city of Mosul in the fifth century BC, when he passed by it with a mercenary army. He wrote that it was called Mespila, a name that is the root of the modern Arabic name we use today. Early Islamic scholarship treated the knowledge of the city's antiquity as a matter of scientific fact and repeatedly stated that Mosul was adjacent to the major pre-Islamic city of Nineveh. Unlike some other ancient Near Eastern sites, Nineveh was therefore not discovered by Western archaeologists in the nineteenth century with the rise of what we now call 'scientific archaeology'. It was always known to the local communities of Mosul, who called the area of the east side of the Tigris river 'Naynawah' (Nineveh). And it is clear from Yaqut's historical essay about this city that the people of the thirteenth century called the east side of the Tigris across from Mosul 'Nineveh'. Yaqut was not the only author who wrote this down. Ibn Hawqal (943–969 AD), al-Mas'udi (d. 957 AD), and Ibn Jubayr (1145–1217), who all knew the location of Nineveh, did so as well. And when the German physician Leonhart Rauwolff reached the city, sometime between 1573 and 1576, and when the Italian adventurer Pietro della Valle did so, in 1616 or 1617, they were shown the location of Nineveh and learned from the local population that Mosul was earlier called 'Nineveh'. These remains of ancient Nineveh are archaeological mounds of ruins or, in Arabic, 'tells'. In the Ottoman period they distinguished between two archaeological mounds: Nabi Yunis and Koyunjik.

Nineveh was the famed ancient capital of the Assyrian empire in the seventh century BC, but it existed long before that. Prehistoric finds reveal that the site was occupied in the Neolithic period, about 7000 BC. While most of the Assyrian remains are on the east side of the river, settlement on the west side of the Tigris goes back to at least the Middle Assyrian era in the second millennium BC. The heyday of the city was in the first millennium BC, when Assyrian kings built several palaces at Nineveh and had their walls covered with magnificent sculpted reliefs. It was the king Sennacherib, who made Nineveh the administrative capital of the Assyrian Empire in 704 BC. One can still see visible remains of the ancient Assyrian city walls he had constructed, as well as of an extensive canal system he had built in the region to bring water to the city and the surrounding lands. The inner wall of the city was called 'The Wall whose Splendour Overwhelms the Enemy'; it was constructed between 702 and 690 BC. With a thickness of forty bricks, it had a height of up to two hundred courses of bricks. Inside the city Sennacherib had many new buildings constructed, and he renovated older architecture. In the inscriptions where he describes these works, he states that Nineveh is the city loved by Ishtar, a city whose plans had been drawn from eternity in the constellations.

Ishtar was one of the main deities of the Mesopotamian pantheon. She was a goddess associated with the planet Venus, and she was also the protector of the king. We know that she had a very ancient temple at Nineveh, in the Koyunjik mound, because the Assyrian king Shamshi-Adad I (1796–1775 BC) said that he renovated the temple that had been built by the Akkadian king Manishtushu (2270–2255 BC). Nearby to Ishtar's home was another temple dedicated to Nabu, the god of writing and scholarship, and many more temples to the gods of Mesopotamia are known from the ancient texts and archaeological remains of Nineveh.

After Sennacherib, other Assyrian kings, in particular, Esarhaddon (680–669 BC) and Ashurbanipal (668–627 BC) built and renovated the architecture of this imperial centre and added to its gardens and orchards. In their royal annals, the kings were always careful to stress the protection and restoration of ancient buildings alongside the building of the new. The relief sculptures of the Assyrian palaces they constructed are among the most impressive works of ancient art known today, where large-scale, complex visual narratives are used to depict courtly life, wars and royal lion hunts. These pictorial reliefs are usually accompanied by inscriptions in Akkadian cuneiform script. And at Nineveh, numerous texts written on clay tablets, from archives and libraries, both private and public, have also been found. One of the most spectacular discoveries made at Nineveh was by the archaeologist Hormuzd Rassam, a man from Mosul itself, who worked for the British Museum in London. In the 1850s Rassam excavated a vast royal library that dates to the reign of King Ashurbanipal. It is the oldest royal library known in world history. It housed thousands of texts of various forms of scholarship and literature, and included works such as the Epic of Gilgamesh, the world's oldest epic story. Some of the works in the library were contemporary, and other works were writings that were already centuries old and had been carefully copied out and studied. The scribes wrote at the end of the tablets that they belonged to 'the palace of Ashurbanipal'. There were scientific texts and medical texts as well as religious and literary works, all written in Sumerian and Akkadian, the two main scholarly languages of Mesopotamia. The scribes and scholars of the Assyrian royal court studied, analysed, copied and catalogued this collection of manuscripts. Today it is one of the most important sources of information for the scholarship of the ancient Near East, as the library aimed to gather together all the works of literature and scholarship from ancient Mesopotamia.

The city of Nineveh was the largest city in the world in 700 BC, a metropolis with people from across the empire living in it. There were Phoenicians, Judeans, Greeks and Egyptians, as well as people from the Mesopotamian population itself. The fall of Nineveh in 612 BC to a Babylonian-Median military coalition was the end of the Assyrian empire's power. But Nineveh continued to be settled in the Parthian and the Sasanian eras, although at a smaller scale, until the arrival of Islam in 637 AD.

Nineveh became the site of the mausoleum of the prophet Yunis, where a mosque with a minaret was eventually built; this was carefully maintained and renovated through the centuries. The shrine of Nabi Yunis (Arabic for 'Prophet Jonah') was revered by Muslims, Christians and Jews alike, so that throughout its years of existence, it was a place of worship not limited to one religion or ethnic group. We know this coexistence and multiculturalism was true for the entire city of Mosul and Nineveh, where there were already Christian monasteries and churches built during the time of Khusraw II, the Sasanian king, and Christianity flourished in Mosul until 2013. The city of Mosul, as Nineveh before it, was multicultural and multilinguistic during its long history. In the late nineteenth century the city of Mosul had a population of around 40,000 people, including 7000 Christians and 1500 Jews, as well as large numbers of Yazidis, Mandeans and other minority religions.

We know from ancient texts that the archaeological mound on which the shrine of Nabi Yunis was built was once the site of an Assyrian palace and arsenal. Because the mausoleum was built on an archaeological tell that is one of the mounds forming the ruins of Nineveh, every once in a while, throughout its history, things have emerged from the ground beneath. The entire mound of Nabi Yunis consists of ancient remains. Large-scale sculptures – the colossal bulls with wings and anthropomorphic heads wearing divine horned crowns, known in cuneiform texts as 'lamassu' – were found there in the nineteenth and the twentieth centuries. The lamassu statues stood in pairs at the gates of Assyrian palaces, guarding the entrances. The texts say that they were magical beasts who came down from the mountains to protect the palace and the land. They were considered to be powerful creatures with a will and an agency of their own.

In June 2014 ISIS took Mosul and eventually destroyed 25 shrines, 37 churches and monasteries, and more than 70 mosques in the area. In 2017 it dynamited the beautiful Nuri mosque, built by Imad al-Din Zengi in 1170 AD. Ironically, ISIS destroyed most of the Islamic heritage of the city, thus erasing some of the most important Islamic heritage in the world. The pre-Islamic evidence, which ISIS also aimed to destroy, however, remains strong. When ISIS destroyed the Nabi Yunis shrine in 2014, it was a hideous act of hatred against a multicultural shrine revered by all people. It was meant as an annihilation of a shared identity and coexistence. But rather than being a victory for intolerance, from out of the ruins arose new Assyrian sculptures, like a phoenix from the ashes. Limestone reliefs with female goddesses standing in a row, holding sacred plants and sprinkling the area with holy water, emerged from the ground, and with them, a lamassu statue, the winged bulls and protecting magical guardians of Assyria (see Figure 34). Elsewhere ISIS had destroyed lamassu statues, Assyrian and other Mesopotamian antiquities and recorded their hateful acts in videos shown all over the world, but the lamassu reappeared here in full force, as if to say: 'You cannot defeat us or erase us from history. We will continue to rise again'.

Note

1 First published in French.

24

Conclusion

Warfare, creative destruction and the politics of preservation

الخاتمة. ’الحَرب، والتَدمير الخَلّاق، وسياسات الحِفاظ‘

Synopsis

This concluding chapter expands on an essay called 'Iraq: Creative destruction and cultural heritage in the warscape', which I wrote for the *Routledge Handbook of Art and Heritage Destruction* (2023). It presents an overview across the *longue durée* of Mesopotamian archaeology, tracing the destruction and erasure of history in modern Iraq and Iraqi Kurdistan through the era of colonialism, the British Mandate, the Gulf Wars, the US occupation and its aftermath, arguing that the recent destruction can be better understood in this long-term view of a history of violence related to geopolitical aims and access to resources, where unconstrained development and aspects of the postwar heritage industry itself have now become additional instruments of historical and archaeological destruction.

المستخلص

يَعتَمِد الفصل الختامي مقالةً بعنوان ’ العراق: التَدمير الخَلّاق و التراث الحَضاري في ظِلِّ الحَرب‘، والتي كتبتُها لكُتَيِّب *من إصدار روتلدج عن الفن وتدمير التراث* (2023). تُقدِّم المقالة نبذةً عن الأمد الطويل لعلم آثار وادي الرافدين، مقتفيةً آثار التدمير ومَحو التاريخ في العراق الحديث وإقليم كردستان العراق عبر عصر الكولونيالية، والانتداب البريطاني، وحروب الخليج، والاحتلال الأمريكي، وتَبِعاتِه، مُحاجِجَةً بأَنَّ الدمار الذي حدث مؤخَّراً يمكن فهمه بشكلٍ أفضل من خلال رؤية بعيدة المدى لتاريخ العُنف المُرتبط بأهداف جيوسياسية والوصول الى الموارد، حيث يصبح

التطوير غير المُقيَّد وجوانب صناعة تراث ما بعد الحرب أصبَحَت الآن بحد ذاتَها أدَوات إضافيّة للتّدمير التاريخي والآثاري.

An accounting of historical destruction in Iraq might begin in the present moment and move back to the past as in an archaeological process of uncovering layers in the ground. These strata bear the traces of activities that are left behind, with each ensuing generation appearing upon, and taking up as its own, the ravaged landscape of the earlier ones. An ancient land of wide vistas punctuated with ruins and vestiges of the past gradually rises to the craggy mountains to the east and north; a land with centuries of tells, historical architecture, monuments and antiquities, Iraq has seen considerable destruction through decades of warfare in the twentieth century, and increasingly also by development and resource extraction. There is little doubt that the latter is directly tied to the former in several ways, and more recently has taken the form of what David Harvey calls neoliberal creative destruction.[1] The episodes of Daesh (Islamic State) destruction of heritage sites and museums are perhaps best known to readers. They were documented and disseminated globally by the perpetrators in the advanced forms of visual media productions that have been carefully analysed by several scholars and widely commented upon in the press.[2] Here, rather than chronicling or analysing this Daesh destruction, which was so clearly abhorrent in its violence aimed at both the erasure of history and lives of human beings, I will shift the focus slightly and begin earlier in the story. By way of a conclusion, this chapter will thus explore the larger landscape of destruction from the rise of imperialist-colonial archaeology until today, arguing that episodes such as those of Daesh are better understood within the genealogy of violence in modern Iraq. The geographical transformation of this area by means of a long war involved the tangled web of the geopolitical, the biopolitical and the geoeconomic.[3] This entanglement, I argue, includes the landscape of what has come to be defined as 'cultural heritage'. This process continued uninterrupted when the modern nation-state of Iraq became a staging ground for wars, and for strategies of occupation that depended upon the reconfiguration of landscapes and neighbourhoods, and the dislocation (most often forced) of peoples and communities, both of which involved, to a greater or lesser extent, the instrumentalisation of ideas of heritage and the built environment, as well as the introduction of new cultural definitions and historical representations. After a brief overview of the rise of the discipline of scientific archaeology in the Ottoman provinces – a process that ushered in a new age of destructive appropriation and collecting – I present here a broadly sketched account of the period of the Gulf wars and their aftermath, spanning the decades from 1990 to 2023. This period is characterised by war, terrorism and military occupation, by looting for an international market of heritage commodities, and by development, all of which have resulted in a large-scale destruction and recasting of historical environments, ecologies and landscapes, secular and religious monuments, as well as traditional neighbourhoods within urban centres.

The 2003 US-led war and occupation of Iraq ended in late 2011, yet there has been no archaeological survey of war damage that resulted from the 2003–11 occupation, just as there has been no accountability for environmental damage or for civilian deaths; the exact numbers of Iraqi deaths are still unknown, with estimates varying widely, depending on the source. It may seem that an academic essay on cultural heritage and archaeology ought not to raise issues such as the laws of war and death counts; however, the entangled forms of destruction I am referring to here can also be understood along the lines of biopolitics. One cannot address the recent Daesh attacks on monuments and architectural structures without any mention of slavery and of death. As with the 2003–11 US occupation of Iraq, the injury and destruction resulting from the 1991 Gulf War and the decade of embargo that followed has yet to be recognised, either in terms of death counts and human suffering, such as the direct bombing of civilians in the Amiriyah air raid shelter in 1991,[4] or in an accounting of historical damage and cultural loss.

After 2014, Daesh turned both the destruction of monuments and the killing of human beings into an international spectacle.[5] These horrendous acts captured the attention of the world, reviving debates around both Islamic aniconism and Islamophobic and racist stereotypes. However, considering the entanglement of people, monuments and landscapes here means that the destruction of the built environment and archaeological terrain was not iconoclastic (in the historical sense of the term) so much as biopolitical. It fits within a framework of division and allocation, of the association of what came to be defined as pure ethnic or sectarian groupings with buildings, shrines and heritage sites. Heritage, after all, is a construction; it is not a neutral category to set apart from others. The definition and categorisation of heritage sites in ethnocentric and sectarian terms, which Saddam Hussein promoted especially in the last decade of his rule, has only increased in Iraq since 2003. At first encouraged by the Coalition Provisional Authority of occupied Iraq, and then by the new sectarian government apparatuses and their related distribution of finances and heritage administration positions along sectarian lines in what is known as the *muhasasa* system.

Cultural heritage, a term used in policy papers and academic publications, is inadequately theorised. It is often presented either as a clear-cut and universal term, or conversely, as a purely Western idea imposed on people who are otherwise unaware of their historical surroundings. Yet apart from the epiphenomenal world of NGOs and ivory-tower archaeology, there is nevertheless the lived experience of people in relation to historical and natural environments. The destruction of these environments results in the loss of people's ways of life and livelihoods, such as farming and sheep-herding, and in their abilities to participate in religious ceremonies at sacred sites that have stood for centuries, or at revered locations like springs, rivers and sacred trees, where unorthodox spirituality and rituals have been practised through the ages. The loss and erasure is also that of the related tangible and intangible heritage and ways of life associated with such places. Beyond these forms of destruction, in the past decade, international preservation efforts have also emerged as an aspect of the larger problems with development and restructuring that result in long-term damage, dislocation and redefinitions of historical monuments along ethno-sectarian lines.[6] These projects are often initiated and supported by funding organisations outside Iraq and accepted by the Baghdad and Erbil governments for purposes of economic development. Lost between these powers are communities and people whose daily lives are in and around the sites – sites whose labelling and classification as cultural heritage usually leads to the exclusion or dislocation of these same communities.

As I have stated above, among all the episodes of cultural heritage destruction in Iraq (also in Syria and parts of Turkey), the last period of terror-instigated violence has received by far the greatest amount of attention in scholarship and in the media alike. The iconoclastic justifications presented in the Daesh propaganda videos have often been taken at face value, as Ömür Harmansah has pointed out,[7] even on the occasions when their acts seem not to be (strictly speaking) iconoclastic – for example, in the destruction of a structural element such as a wall, or an Islamic religious building such as a mosque without any images. Because of preconceptions about 'the Orient', or Islam, these acts are most often simply described as an aspect of Islamic iconoclasm.

In this long-term account, I keep primarily to the Gulf Wars, although taking into consideration forms of destruction that are not at first glance the obvious results of military activity. My aim here is not to provide a comprehensive survey of all forms of cultural heritage destruction but to describe the links between war, development and biopolitics: conjoining the creative destruction of neoliberalism with the domain of life, its social management and regulation through strategies of knowledge-production about cultural heritage on the one hand, and the death and displacement of people and the devastation of environments on the other.

Colonial archaeology: collecting for the Empire

In the nineteenth century, digging at ruins, including the extraction and transportation of antiquities, increased both in terms of proportion and scale, in comparison to earlier centuries. Although travellers had always come to the east, and many of them had picked up antiquities to take back to Europe, the magnitude of acquisition in the nineteenth century was unprecedented. These forms of appropriation increasingly relied upon more complex technologies of removal and shipment in order – for example – to take large-scale architectural sculptures to the newly established museums in London and Paris.[8] This turn of events in which diplomats, spies and East India Company officials in the Ottoman Vilayat (provinces) of Basra, Baghdad and Mosul, turned to digging, is marked by a growing employment of such new technologies and developments in industrial engineering, and in the growth of popular print media that supported the efforts of removing antiquities. It also conscripted the acquiescence of people at home in Europe, by presenting these efforts in such a way as to allow the public to feel invested as subjects and citizens at the centre of a civilising empire.[9] It was an effort that allowed the new museum collections to anchor the positionality of the imperial subject at the centre of an imperial range of acquisition, so that from London or Paris the far reaches of a vast and exotic geographical stretch could be substantiated materially, and defined historically at the same time. Thus, the activities of early archaeology and collecting came to mark an era of territorial claim to a landscape which was soon reconfigured and renamed partly by means of the discursive, and increasingly relied on new archaeological definitions and labels to conjure Mesopotamia. They purported to delineate with the scientific accuracy of the mapmaker's craft and the archaeologist's eye, a land that could be classified and chronologised, packed and shipped, known by the intrepid Orientalists but not by the primitive Orientals who misapprehended their own past.[10] As in the biopolitical strategies already noted, colonial archaeology sought not only to acquire material objects and monuments for economic value or as cultural capital, but also to shape relations to the past – by means of both dislocation and the exercise of particular forms of knowledge and expertise, for example, in museums and scholarship.[11]

Gulf wars: the new category of collateral damage

This was the background of the discipline of Near Eastern archaeology when, in 1990, the First Gulf War was declared. In 1991, the United States did not target ancient sites or historical monuments with aerial bombardment; scholars in the US had made the case that they were 'global cultural heritage', and as such should be avoided. Yet several monuments and sites were nevertheless hit in what became the new category of 'collateral damage'. This military category was first applied in the Vietnam War, and it is now a commonly used expression in warfare and in popular culture alike, but at the time of the First Gulf War it was a newly deployed term that sanitised the violence of warfare and civilian deaths – as the deaths of human beings also came to be described as collateral damage. The stepped ziggurat and sacred precinct of the moon god at Ur, dating to 2100 BC, were hit by US missiles that left large craters, each ten metres in diameter and four metres deep. The sides of the ziggurat were blasted with about 400 holes.[12] To the southeast of Ur, the archaeological site of Tell al-Lahm was used as a US military position, where large-scale machinery excavations took place to accommodate the troops, thus destroying the ancient Sumerian and Babylonian layers.[13] The latter case was like an ancient Mesopotamian portent that prefigured what was to come in 2003–4, when several major heritage sites, among them Babylon, Ur and Kish, were occupied by the military.[14] These military occupations of heritage sites have neither been studied by those whose focus is archaeological or cultural heritage theory and history, nor even duly acknowledged. They were overshadowed by other aspects of strategic destruction in Iraq, and later, by the 2014–17 demolition and looting by Daesh that was to follow. In sum, while several historical sites were damaged in 1991, no survey or inventory took place in the aftermath of war. Although such an inventory was requested, both by the Directorate of Antiquities and Heritage in Baghdad and by UNESCO, the request was denied by the UN Security Council because of the international embargo on Iraq.[15] As the embargo was followed by the 2003 war and occupation, no survey of damage to heritage was ever undertaken. Upon the traces of that war, yet another war and occupation deposited further layers of violent destruction.

In addition to the use of sites for military purposes, some places suffered structural damage because of the scale of the sorties and the power of the bombing campaign of January–February 1991. According to accounts at the time, the quantity of explosives dropped on Iraq in that month-long air assault surpassed that of the entire allied offensive of the Second World War. The Iraqi dead were never counted.[16] Among the historical buildings damaged indirectly in the air campaign was the medieval university complex in Baghdad, the Mustansiriyeh. Another such place affected by the aerial bombardment, and further by the lack of conservation materials during the years of sanctions, was the Arch of Ctesiphon, known as Taq Kesra or Ayvan-i Kesra (the arch of Khusraw, the Sasanian king; see Figure 1). This colossal arch, 84 feet (26 m) high, is the last remaining vaulted iwan of the Parthian/Sasanian-era palace at al-Mada'in. It is the largest single-span parabolic barrel vault in the world. The structure is a remarkable feat in ancient brickwork and construction techniques, and it had long withstood the tests of time. As a result of the US bombing campaign in 1991, however, a new crack appeared in the vault, which is still in danger of collapse. Yet a report on the recent stabilisation effort evades any mention of that war, stating that the damage is due to neglect and climate change.[17] Such evasions of war damage bring Mike Davis's observations regarding the social construction of natural disaster to a new level of obfuscation.[18] The Arch of Ctesiphon is a good example of how the historical architectural monuments of Iraq, now classified as cultural heritage, had been significant in Iraq long before the invention of that classification. The monument was known in Iraq and the wider region as a landmark structure from Late Antiquity; it was highly valued by local populations throughout the Ottoman era as it was (and is still today) considered to be the site of a divine miracle in the Muslim traditions of Iraq and Iran. It also became a source of inspiration for the Iraqi Modernist Pioneers movement of the mid-twentieth century.[19] Thus, when such monuments and sites are endangered or destroyed, the damage is not limited to the historical structure alone; rather, it affects one's sense of context and belonging in a landscape where ancient sites are the places of age-old stories about our past.

The 1991 war was immediately followed by the uprisings of the population in both the north and the south in a concerted effort to overthrow the Saddam Hussein Baathist government. These were soon quashed by the regime. At Kirkuk – one of the oldest continuously inhabited cities in Iraq, with a citadel upon a tell – the city's population was punished with bombing attacks and the demolition of historical architecture and its surroundings. An Iraqi regime missile aimed at the citadel hit the Bughday Khatoun shrine. Known as Gök Kümbet (Sky Cupola) or Qubba al-Khadhra (the Green Dome), it dates to AD 1361. The missile hit the side of the courtyard colonnade, where the rubble still remained at the exact location when I saw it in 2019 (see Figure 33).[20]

The economic sanctions established by UN Resolution 661 of August 1990, sanctions that in Iraq came to be called 'the Siege', meant that no preservation and conservation efforts could take place, and that materials necessary for such work could not be brought into Iraq.[21] These severe international sanctions remained in place until the 2003 war. The destruction and loss that resulted from the embargo included an estimated half a million children dead; they were also seen as collateral damage.

The Baathist regime's response to the 1991 uprisings was brutal, and in the chaos that took place, nine of the thirteen regional museums were looted and damaged. Their contents were destined for an international market in antiquities that was to grow exponentially during the years of the embargo, and even more so during the 2003 war and occupation. Thousands of Islamic era manuscripts, ancient artefacts and cuneiform tablets were looted in 1991.[22] During the 13 years of the international sanctions, the looting of heritage sites increased to previously unknown scales.

Because of the embargo, scholars from outside could no longer work in Iraq. More importantly, the simplest items of scholarship and teaching were banned. Iraq could no longer receive journals or books. Pencils and paper for schoolchildren were prohibited, being characterised as 'dual usage', that is, potential weapons and thus dangerous items.[23] The sanctions decimated the population rather than the regime. Iraqi artists and writers responded to this devastation by adopting and transforming heritage traditions into their contemporary art. They took up the theme of the destruction of antiquity and history, an antiwar theme that was to become central once again, following the 2003 war.[24]

Due to both the international sanctions and the internal political oppression, many artists and intellectuals were forced into exile. Meanwhile, in addition to the plundered museums, archaeological sites suffered a massive increase in looting for the lucrative international trade in antiquities. In the countries such as the US, UK, Switzerland, Israel and Japan, illicitly acquired antiquities were purchased by museums and authenticated by leading Western Assyriologists eager to publish any newly unearthed cuneiform text, regardless of the destruction, while officials high up in the Baathist regime also participated in this selling off of the country's heritage for their own profit.[25] The staff of the Iraqi Directorate of Antiquities lodged complaints to colleagues in the international community of scholars, to no avail. There was little interest in countering this flow of antiquities into this growing consumer market, a market that was now also supported by the claims of the term 'global cultural heritage' – a notion of heritage posited as an opposition to national claims, seen as retentionist by those who argued for the benefit of the removal of antiquities from what came to be termed 'source countries'. There was also little interest among Western scholars in discontinuing the publication of these stolen objects. Artefacts and manuscripts have now been fully appropriated into collections, in the name of learned and urbane humanist concerns, aided by institutions and scholars who, while presented as the caretakers of global cultural heritage, benefit from the destruction of history and the spoils of wars.

Occupation: spectacles and strategies of war

During the 2003 war and immediate period of occupation that followed, museums and archaeological sites were looted, and historical monuments and architecture again suffered extensive damage. These disasters were accompanied by the large-scale destruction and looting of archives and libraries. The material and tangible losses were exacerbated by a decision of the Coalition Provisional Authority which resulted in long-term historical erasure. Under the rule of Paul Bremer, a de-Baathification process was decreed that removed museum staff, archaeologists and academics from their posts, gutting museums and institutions of higher learning and pushing many academics, professionals and intellectuals to leave the country. At the same time, and continuing for the following five years, Iraq saw a massive wave of targeted assassinations of leading scholars and scientists. Issam al-Rawi, a professor of geology at Baghdad University and head of the Iraqi Union of University Professors, recorded hundreds of names along with their areas of expertise before he, too, was murdered in 2006.[26] Those responsible for the assassinations have not been identified. What is clear, however, is that at the State Board of Antiquities and Heritage, at museums and universities, the de-Baathification process brought about long-term institutional damage well beyond the initial days of looting and burning. The Bremer plan resulted in a large-scale destruction and evisceration of apparatuses of knowledge and memory. The physical damage and losses that occurred as a consequence of the looting of museums and the burning of the National Library and State Archives – all of which took place during the ground war in the spring of 2003 – were thus accompanied by the demolition of forms and institutions of historical and archival knowledge, and the killing or displacement of hundreds of academics and intellectuals of Iraq.

At official 'heritage sites' – that is, sites listed or categorised as 'heritage' by organisations such as UNESCO or classified as significant monuments by disciplinary fields such as art history and archaeology – another type of destruction took place.[27] In the spring of 2003, US and coalition forces took over the ancient city of Babylon and transformed it into a military base, known by the names Camp Alpha, Camp Babylon, or sometimes simply 'The Ruins'.[28] It was the largest base outside Baghdad, housing thousands of US and coalition troops, as well as large installations of the military contractor, KBR. The camp required extensive digging for sewers and water pipes for barracks. It also required large-scale bulldozing and flattening of the ground next to the palace of Nebuchadnezzar and the Hellenistic theatre, for the expansion of a helicopter landing zone. The military and KBR dug trenches across Babylon and covered it with tanks and heavy vehicles.[29] They used the Hellenistic theatre and the Babylonian processional way for military parades and ceremonies to celebrate their victory.[30] Walls were damaged by soldiers, some of whom casually removed ancient bricks and objects as souvenirs of a tour of duty. The damage to the structures and to the archaeological layers was extensive and irreversible. After months of negotiation and discussion with Iraqi archaeologists and representatives of the Iraqi Ministry of Culture, the military agreed to shut the camp and remove the installations. When a UNESCO report was drawn up some years later, the document was flawed by the fact that it was produced as a result of an internal investigation by official representatives of the same occupying powers responsible for the damage that they were tasked to investigate. A lead author was John Curtis, a curator at the British Museum, whose galleries display many antiquities from Iraq acquired with the nineteenth-century practices described above. Wall texts, installed there for public outreach purposes, described the damage at Babylon; yet written in the passive voice, they avoided reference to the forces responsible, which included the British military. Large exhibitions on pre-Islamic eras of Iraq's history increased in popularity in the years immediately following the invasion, highlighting this ancient past as global cultural heritage in the leading museums of Europe and the US, while the violent realities of military occupation that existed at the same time in Iraq were hidden from view.[31]

As a result of the military occupation of Babylon, the walls of the Ishtar Gate that remained in place, including the large stretches of bricks bearing bulls and dragons (as well other architectural structures across Babylon), were also badly damaged. Troops stationed there were under the impression that these walls were not ancient material but had been built by the previous dictator Saddam Hussein. Indeed, in the 1980s Saddam Hussein had ordered reconstructions to be built along the processional way, with bricks bearing his own inscriptions in Arabic, no doubt to cast himself as a ruler with ties to the Babylonian kings, and criticisms of these badly made reconstructions on site were justified. Yet the soldiers were unable to see the difference between reconstructions and ancient walls and, assuming that they were all modern structures, thought little of defacing them. In part this was due to the careless conflation by archaeologists and heritage organisations of all of Babylon's ruins with the Baathist reconstructions.

A hundred years earlier, the German architect Robert Koldewey had excavated at Babylon. The German excavations were a turning point in archaeology, in that Koldewey abandoned the techniques used by the British adventurer and politician, Austen Henry Layard, at Assyrian sites in the north. Layard's techniques had involved the digging of tunnels through palaces in order to remove the stone relief sculptures and large-scale lamassus that can be seen in the illustrations to his bestseller books, where they are shown pulled with ropes by an army of Arab workmen while Layard stands above on a baulk, supervising the labour force from the upper level, as if to indicate Britain's control of both monuments and people. A parallel process occurred with the French excavations near Mosul, led by Paul-Émile Botta, a French diplomat. As contemporaneous letters and documents in the archives of both the British Museum and the Louvre reveal, this destructive process had, as its primary goal, the removal of objects in order to stock the museum. In comparison, the German team's excavations at Babylon were conducted with more care for the architectural remains and a better system of recording. Nevertheless, the glazed brickwork of the Ishtar Gate and the processional way reliefs which Koldewey's team had uncovered were later transported to Berlin. The site was stripped of most of its surfaces, although the impressive unglazed brick walls that bear bulls and dragons, the paved path of the processional way, foundations and walls of a number of temples, and parts of the palaces remained in place. The 1980s reconstructions were thus a misguided effort to rebuild at a site bereft of structures and brickwork taken to Berlin in the early twentieth century. Their removal resulted in long-term, multiple layers of destruction at Babylon. Now listed as a UNESCO World Heritage Site, Babylon has thus been subjected to large-scale damage since the earliest excavations. During the 2003 war and occupation, several official heritage sites were used as military bases in a similar way, although Babylon was the largest of these encampments.[32] Postwar surveys of all the military damage caused by the occupation of heritage sites have yet to be conducted.

During the 2003 war and its aftermath, looting and the illicit trade in antiquities have been especially destructive. The illicit trade continues unabated, with recent purchases of stolen works, most notably by the Museum of the Bible in Washington, DC. After investigations by US law enforcement agencies, as well as legal battles, the museum is now in the process of repatriating stolen objects to Iraq. Another aspect of the loss of historical or heritage material from Iraq that ought to be considered under acts of erasure and control of the narrative is the burning and removal of archives.[33] Archives taken from the country in the early days of the occupation have been the subject of heated debates about the right to historical documents.[34] In 2003, approximately 100 million pages of documents were seized and taken to a warehouse in Qatar to be searched for evidence of weapons of mass destruction.[35] Other archives were removed for purposes of conservation. The latter include archives of the former Baath regime, files kept from the surveillance of the Iraqi people, as well as the Iraqi Jewish Archive of documents and religious texts of the Iraqi Jews who were forced out of Iraq in the mid-twentieth century. The Baath archive was finally returned to Iraq in August of 2020, but its seizure and relocation to the US for 17 years meant that knowledge was inaccessible to Iraqis. That the removal and control of archives influences control over the writing of history is self-evident, as several scholars have pointed out.[36]

Terrorism: the erasure of a history of diversity

Alongside the killing and enslavement of the population, a vast and extensive destruction of historical cities and monuments took place under the regime of Daesh, which took over large swathes of Iraq and Syria beginning in 2013. As Daesh had taken the city of Mosul in northern Iraq as their centre in 2014, the greatest amount of destruction occurred there. The Mosul Museum, the Assyrian capitals of Nimrud/Kalhu and Nineveh, and numerous other historical and religious monuments were attacked. The Nergal Gate at Nineveh became emblematic of this destruction, due to the repeated use and circulation of the 2015 video in which a member of Daesh uses a jackhammer to drill the face of a lamassu of the eighth century BC. These attacks resulted in extensive damage in Mosul, but also notably in Sinjar and elsewhere across Iraq, including Kirkuk and the regions of Diyala, Salahaddin and Anbar.

As this period has been well studied by others, both statistically and from a sociohistorical interpretive view,[37] I will focus here only on one monument: the shrine of Nabi Yunis (the prophet Jonah) at Mosul. The destruction of this historical-religious site, and shrines similar to it, demonstrates that the attacks were not limited to a single religion or community alone (although there is no question that the Yazidi community was a foremost target of annihilation, and that a large part of the Christian population was either attacked or displaced); rather, Nabi Yunis was a place for joint worship. It did not represent tolerance of the other but, more accurately, was by definition a site of interfaith practices and traditions, where people of different faiths held many of the same shrines to be sacred. Nabi Yunis stood for this possibility of peaceful coexistence. Its destruction (and that of many other sites destroyed by Daesh) also indicates a desire to eliminate the material evidence of this history of interfaith practices. Interfaith shrines are (or were) widespread in Iraq. In fact, numerous shrines throughout the country had been multireligious, as can be seen in an example recently described by Jane Arraf: Baghdad's Tomb of Joshua.[38] It was also not uncommon in the traditions of Iraq for a Christian to make a vow (*nithir*) in a mosque or for a Muslim to make a vow in a church, and historically, at least some Yazidi and Shiite shrines were one and the same.[39] One of Daesh's aims was to erase this interwoven history. Alongside the genocidal killing of people was the aim to obliterate the material evidence of their existence. The current ethno-sectarian ideologies of the state of Iraq, including in Iraqi Kurdistan, have also rewritten these histories of interfaith diversity for their own political goals – at times erasing traditional toponyms in use for centuries, another strategy of erasure well known to colonialism and ethno-nationalism. It is unfortunate that some Western scholars have participated in this ethnic cleansing of history for personal gain and access. In parallel with these internal state efforts, and the complicity of some scholars, international funding agencies for preservation projects have often chosen to delineate sites and shrines along clear-cut and delimited sectarian or ethnic lines. Thus, both local and international decisions separate and redefine religious sites and histories that in the past were far more fluid and indefinite, and might even be described as erratic and haphazard, growing out of the unstructured (and uncategorisable) lived experience of people in a diverse multilingual and multireligious society.

In many ways, the crisis mode of reaction to Daesh has inadvertently perpetuated their ideology through narratives of destruction and funding support often defined along ethnocentric, religious and sectarian lines. An industry of 'cultural heritage crisis response' has now emerged as a result of Daesh, and that industry has propelled NGOs, academic appointments and publications. To be sure, many working in this area are making important contributions, but the situation is nevertheless problematic. A new class of archaeologists and heritage professionals, many of whom have never been to Iraq and know none of its languages or traditions, present themselves as spokespeople for us, and for what constitutes our cultural heritage, thus reviving the most basic tenets of Orientalism. Remarkably, this is not a situation that Western scholarship would find acceptable for other groups of subjugated peoples in colonial or postcolonial contexts. The new sector of heritage professionals is increasingly tied to the political and economic investment aimed at the neoliberal restructuring of Iraq that was initiated in 2003. Postwar heritage preservation and postwar aid for development are thus also an aspect of warfare and occupation, and not simply a separate area of concern.[40]

Development, cultural heritage and the politics of the past

The Daesh episode was not the first time that religious fanatics had targeted Iraq's famed historical shrines. In the spring of 1802, an army of Wahhabi marauders from Arabia, about 12,000 men, entered the country, attacking and plundering the Shiite pilgrimage sites at Kerbala.[41] Thousands of people were killed in the process. These shrines were restored and refurbished soon after, but today they are once again endangered, this time by development plans. Indeed, unsustainable development is now one of the biggest threats. Near the ancient city of Assur, listed as a UNESCO world heritage site, a dam is now planned (the Makhoul dam), which will flood a large area around the city and destroy numerous smaller ancient sites nearby, including the Middle Assyrian capital, Kar Tukulti-Ninurta. Everywhere across the country, development is set to destroy sites that are classified as cultural heritage, but equally important is that traditional neighbourhoods are quickly vanishing.

Sultan Murad IV had renovated the walls and gates of the city of Baghdad in the seventeenth century, but the Ottoman governor and reformist Midhat Pasha ordered extensive demolition for the sake of urban development and expansion of the city between 1869–72, such that much of the historical city was demolished in the nineteenth-century push for modernisation.[42] Another massive restructuring of neighbourhoods took place in 2003–4, under the rule of the Coalition Provisional Authority headed by Paul Bremer. This time the changes were not simply a loss of historical architectural fabric, but included population displacement and relocation into purified ethno-sectarian zones.[43] At Erbil in Iraqi Kurdistan, the ancient citadel with its Ottoman houses has had extensive renovations supported by international heritage organisations, which involved removing the occupants. The lower town below, its streets filled with equally significant Ottoman-era houses and streets, however, is being left to collapse, no doubt to permit profitable development in that prime location at the centre of the city. The sprawling traditional neighbourhood of courtyard-style brickwork houses and khans (inns) also had its population removed, ostensibly for the purposes of renovation, and it is now a ghost town of Ottoman-era ruins.

The historical destruction of Iraq in what was formerly the Ottoman vilayets of Basra, Baghdad and Mosul began with imperial-colonial archaeology. As the newly emerging discipline of archaeology arose in the nineteenth century, the land designated Mesopotamia and associated with a biblical past was claimed by the West as its own, first in mytho-historical terms and, after the fall of the Ottoman Empire, as part of the mandates under British and French colonial occupations. The influx of archaeologists set to explore the legendary ruins of Nineveh and Babylon in the nineteenth century, and to collect antiquities for their imperial museums, led to the removal of entire walls and structures to the West, leaving behind devastated contexts. In many ways, this was a process that depended upon redefinitions of antiquity, which the discipline of archaeology itself dissociated from the living people and the land, both physically and discursively.[44] Later, the ways in which people and historical environments were entwined were then also disrupted and directly targeted by the Gulf Wars and by Daesh. This targeting of lives and contexts of living, of the material evidence of diversity, alongside the removal of archives and the direction of expertise, enabled the restructuring of knowledge and the biopolitical management of populations. The destruction of historical monuments and sites, of archives and material traces of the past, cannot be understood as epiphenomena unrelated to colonial-imperialist interests. A decolonisation of archaeology and cultural heritage practices must address this fraught history, in which layers of destruction continue to spur on ever-new forms of destruction for development and tourism, and an ever-increasing insistence on ethno-sectarianism through the category of heritage, pushed both by the state and by the international funding agencies. Cultural heritage management is now entrenched within a neoliberal apparatus of transformation in Iraq. Heritage practices, whether internal state initiatives or international preservation efforts, are now often outlined in sectarianising and divisive ways. In a decolonising effort, the fields of archaeology and cultural heritage studies might begin to rectify this history of violence by reflecting on their own contributions to this ongoing destruction, silencing and erasure of the varied and diverse peoples and landscapes of this ancient land.

Notes

1 David Harvey, 'Neoliberalism as creative destruction', *Annals of the American Academy of Political and Social Sciences* 610 (2007): 22–44.
2 Ömür Harmansah, 'ISIS, heritage, and the spectacles of destruction in the global media', *Near Eastern Archaeology* 78 (2015): 170–7; Finbarr Barry Flood, 'Idol breaking as image making in the Islamic State', *Religion and Society* 7 (2016): 116–38; Emma Cunliffe and Luigi Curini, 'Isis and heritage destruction: A sentiment analysis', *Antiquity* 92 (364) (2018): 1094–111; Benjamin Isakhan and José Antonio Gonzáles Zarandona, 'Layers of religious iconoclasm under the Islamic State symbolic sectarianism and pre-monotheistic iconoclasm', *International Journal of Heritage Studies* 24 (2018): 1–16.
3 Derek Gregory, 'The everywhere war', *The Geographical Journal* 177 (2011): 238–50.
4 Nora Boustany, 'Bombs kill victims as they slept', *Washington Post*, 14 February 1991, https://www.washingtonpost.com/wp-srv/inatl/longterm/fogofwar/archive/post021391_2.htm.
5 Harmansah, 'ISIS, heritage, and the spectacles of destruction'; Flood, 'Idol breaking as image making in the Islamic State'.
6 Zainab Bahrani, 'Destruction and preservation as aspects of just war', *Future Anterior: Journal of historic preservation* 14 (2017): 107–26.
7 Harmansah, 'ISIS, heritage, and the spectacles of destruction'.
8 Zainab Bahrani, Zeynep Çelik and Edhem Eldem, eds, *Scramble for the Past: A story of archaeology in the Ottoman Empire, 1753–1914* (Istanbul: SALT, 2011); Zeynep Çelik, *About Antiquities: Politics of archaeology in the Ottoman Empire* (Austin: University of Texas Press, 2016).
9 Tony Bennett, *Pasts Beyond Memory: Evolution, museums, colonialism* (London: Routledge, 2004); Shawn Malley, *From Archaeology to Spectacle in Victorian Britain* (Farnham: Ashgate, 2012).
10 Edward W. Said, *Orientalism* (New York: Pantheon Books, 1978); Zainab Bahrani, 'Conjuring Mesopotamia: Imaginative geography and a world past', in *Archaeology Under Fire*, edited by Lynn M. Meskell, 159–74 (London: Routledge, 1998); *The Graven Image: Representation in Babylonia and Assyria* (Philadelphia: University of Pennsylvania Press, 2003).
11 Said, *Orientalism*; Michel Foucault, *The Archaeology of Knowledge* (New York: Pantheon Books, 1982 [1969]; Bennett, *Pasts Beyond Memory.*
12 McGuire Gibson, 'The loss of archaeological context and the illegal trade in Mesopotamian antiquities', *Culture without Context* 1 (1997): 6–8 (on this point, see p. 6).
13 Gibson, 'The loss of archaeological context'.
14 Zainab Bahrani, 'Archaeology and the strategies of war', in *The Cultural Cleansing in Iraq*, edited by Raymond W. Baker, Sheeren T. Ismael and Tareq Y. Ismael, 67–81 (London: Pluto Press, 2010).
15 Gibson, 'The loss of archaeological context'.
16 Jean Baudrillard, *La Guerre du Golfe n'a pas eu lieu* (Paris: Galilée, 1991); Tareq Y. Ismael and Jacqueline S. Ismael, *The Gulf War and the New World Order* (Gainesville: University Press of Florida, 1994); Zainab Bahrani, 'Historical destruction in a forgotten war', in *Theater of Operations: The Gulf Wars, 1991–2011*, edited by P. Eleey and R. Katrib, 233–47 (New York: Museum of Modern Art, 2020).

17 Melissa Gronlund, 'Arch of Ctesiphon: Clock is ticking to preserve 1,700-year-old ancient arch in Iraq', *The National News*, 14 February 2021. https://www.thenationalnews.com/arts-culture/art/arch-of-ctesiphon-clock-is-ticking-to-preserve-1-700-year-old-ancient-arch-in-iraq-1.1165341.

18 Mike Davis, *Ecology of Fear: Los Angeles and the imagination of disaster* (New York: Metropolitan Books, 1998), 9.

19 Zainab Bahrani, 'Historical destruction in a forgotten war', in *Theater of Operations: The Gulf Wars 1991–2011*, edited by Peter Eleey and Ruba Katrib, 233–47 (New York: Museum of Modern Art, 2020).

20 Bahrani, 'Historical destruction in a forgotten war'.

21 George Gerbner, 'Persian Gulf War, the movie', in *Triumph of the Image: The media's war in the Persian Gulf: A global perspective*, edited by Hamid Mowlana, George Gerbner and Herbert I. Schiller (Boulder: Westview Press, 1992), 252; Haifa Zangana, *City of Widows* (New York: Seven Stories Press, 2007).

22 McGuire Gibson and Augusta McMahon, *Lost Heritage: Antiquities stolen from Iraq's regional museums,* fasc. 1 (Chicago: Oriental Institute Publications, 1992); Heather D. Baker, Roger J. Matthews and J. Nicholas Postgate, *Lost Heritage: Antiquities stolen from Iraq's regional museums,* fasc. 2 (London: British School of Archaeology in Iraq, 1993); Hideo Fujii and Kazumi Oguchi. *Lost Heritage: Antiquities stolen from Iraq's regional museums,* fasc. 3 (Tokyo: Institute for Cultural Studies of Ancient Iraq, 1996).

23 Gerbner, 'Persian Gulf War, the movie', 252; Zangana, *City of Widows*.

24 Peter Eleey and Ruba Katrib, eds, *Theater of Operations: The Gulf Wars 1991–2011* (New York: MOMA, 2020).

25 Gibson, 'The loss of archaeological context'; R. C. Longworth, 'Iraqi artifacts stolen during war', *Chicago Tribune*, 5 March 1992. https://www.chicagotribune.com/news/ct-xpm-1992-03-05-9201210178-story.html.

26 Raymond W. Baker, Sheeren T. Ismael and Tareq Y. Ismael, eds, *The Cultural Cleansing of Iraq* (London: Pluto Press, 2010).

27 Bahrani, 'Archaeology and the strategies of war'.

28 The remarks on the military occupation at Babylon are based on my own observations while working there in the spring and summer of 2004.

29 Zainab Bahrani, 'Babylon: A case study in the military occupation of an archaeological site', in *Of the Past for the Future: Integrating archaeology and conservation. Congress proceedings from World Archaeological Congress 5*, edited by Neville Agnew and Janet Bridgeland, 240–7 (Los Angeles: Getty Conservation Institute, 2005); 'The battle for Babylon', in *The Destruction of Cultural Heritage in Iraq*, edited by Peter Stone and Joanne Farchakh Bajjaly, 165–71 (Woodbridge: Boydell Press, 2008); 'Archaeology and the strategies of war'; Mehiyar Kathem and Dhiaa Kareem Ali, 'Decolonising Babylon', *International Journal of Heritage Studies* 26 (2020): 163–77.

30 Nicholas Mirzoeff, *Watching Babylon: The war in Iraq and global visual culture* (London: Routledge, 2004).

31 Alexander Nagel, review of *The World Between Empires: Art and identity in the ancient Middle East*, CAA reviews, June 2020. http://caareviews.org/reviews/3593.

32 Bahrani, 'The battle for Babylon'; 'Archaeology and the strategies of war'.

33 Nabil al-Tikriti, '"Stuff happens": A brief overview of the 2003 destruction of Iraqi manuscript collections, archives, and libraries', *Library Trends* 55 (2007): 730–55.

34 Saad Eskander, 'Minerva research initiative: Searching for the truth or denying Iraqis the right to know the truth?' *Social Science Research Council*, October 2008. https://web.archive.org/web/20100630170753/http://essays.ssrc.org/minerva/2008/10/29/eskander/; 'Wars, uprisings, invasions, and terrorism: the looting and recovery of Iraq's cultural property', in *3rd International Conference of Experts on the Return of Cultural Property*, edited by Suzana Chulia-Kapelōnē (Athens: Hellenic Ministry of Culture and Sports, 2014), 175–82; Wisam H. Alshaibi, 'Weaponizing Iraq's archives', *Middle East Report* 291 (2019): 3–9; Rebecca A. Whiting, 'Destruction and displacement: the 2003 war and the struggle for Iraq's records', in *Archives: Power, truth, and fiction*, edited by Andrew Prescott and Alison Wiggins (Oxford: Oxford University Press, 2023), 455–70.

35 Whiting, 'Destruction and displacement'.

36 Eskander, 'Minerva research initiative'; Whiting, 'Destruction and displacement'.

37 Harmansah, 'ISIS, heritage, and the spectacles of destruction'; Flood, 'Idol breaking as image making in the Islamic State'; Cunliffe and Curini, 'Isis and heritage destruction'.

38 Jane Arraf, 'Tomb of Joshua, revered prophet, beckons believers in Baghdad', *New York Times*, 20 February 2021. https://www.nytimes.com/2021/02/20/world/middleeast/baghdad-iraq-joshua-tomb.html.

39 Lamia Gailani, 'What's happening to Iraq's heritage', lecture presented at the Metropolitan Museum of Art, New York, 10 December 2014.

40 Bahrani, 'Destruction and preservation'.

41 Ebubekir Çeylan, *The Ottoman Origins of Modern Iraq: Political reform, modernization and development in the nineteenth-century Middle East* (London: I.B. Taurus, 2011).

42 Çeylan, *The Ottoman Origins of Modern Iraq*, 183–6.

43 Mona Damluji, 'Securing democracy in Iraq: Sectarian politics and segregation in Baghdad, 2003–2007', *Traditional Dwellings and Settlements Review* 21 (2) (2010): 71–87.

44 Bahrani, 'Conjuring Mesopotamia'; *The Graven Image*.

Index

Figures are denoted by the use of italic page numbers and notes by 'n'.

www.ingramcontent.com/pod-product-compliance
Lightning Source LLC
LaVergne TN
LVHW051155260826
846302LV00011B/72